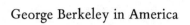

George Berkeley in America

John Smibert, *The Bermuda Group: Dean George Berkeley and His Family*. Yale University Art Gallery, Gift of Isaac Lothrop.

George Berkeley in America

Edwin S. Gaustad

New Haven and London   Yale University Press

Published with assistance from the
Kingsley Trust Association Publication Fund
established by the Scroll and Key Society of Yale College.

Designed by John O. C. McCrillis
and set in IBM Aldine type.
Printed in the United States of America by
The Murray Printing Co., Inc., Westford, Massachusetts.

Library of Congress Cataloging in Publication Data

Gaustad, Edwin Scott.
    George Berkeley in America.

    Includes bibliographical references and index.
    1. Berkeley, George, Bp. of Cloyne, 1685-1753—
Homes and haunts—Rhode Island—Newport.
2. Philosophers—England—Biography. 3. United
States—Civilization—To 1783. I. Title.
B1347.G38 1979   192[B]   79-64076
ISBN 0-300-02394-4

11   10   9   8   7   6   5   4   3   2

Yes, Santa Claus,

there is a

Virginia

$\mathcal{C}$ontents

Preface

When I had the privilege a few years ago of dining with the late A. A. Luce at Trinity College, Dublin, he politely inquired how a (mere) historian could possibly be interested in George Berkeley. For Canon Luce, it was clear that Berkeley was firmly and wholly rooted in the philosophers' turf. I suggested that Berkeley-as-philosopher was—at least to the historian of early America—only a modest fragment of the whole man whom some Americans came to know and many more came to honor. So early did George Berkeley enter into an unborn nation's cultural bloodstream that, centuries later, he has not been bled out. The story here recounted concerns the many-sidedness of that restless genius, particularly as it expressed itself in or left its mark on a portion of the New World.

Writing a book over a period of years does not necessarily enhance the final product; it does enhance and enlarge the gratitude, the indebtedness, to those who with such readiness and good will have assisted, guided, advised, located, and responded. At Trinity College, in addition to the kindnesses shown by Professor Luce, a visiting American scholar, Harry M. Bracken, helped to make the brief stay there both pleasant and profitable, as did the librarians of the college and of the nearby Marsh Library. Visiting the latter is like entering into the library Berkeley knew and used as a student, for it has changed so little since his own time. In Edinburgh, George E. Davie offered freely from his own fund of Berkeleiana even as he guided me to the most relevant repositories in Scotland. In London, the courtesies multiplied many times over. Mrs. Belle

Pridmore, at the Society for the Propagation of the Gospel
Library, did, through her unfailing hospitality, give to the
phrase "archival research" a far happier connotation than it
generally enjoys. At the archives of the Society for Promoting Christian Knowledge, Mr. Arthur E. Barker literally
turned over his office to me for days at a time. Generous
assistance as well from the librarians at Lambeth Palace,
Sion College, St. Paul's Cathedral, and above all the British
Museum, made the months in London a scholar's delight.

In this country Mrs. Gladys Bolhouse time and again
coaxed the vaults of the Newport Historical Society into
yielding up their secrets. And Canon Lockett F. Ballard of
Trinity Episcopal Church, himself fascinated by the Berkeley saga, went beyond the call of duty in encouraging my
investigations and sharing his own. The Colonial Dames of
Rhode Island, especially Mrs. Margery Wheeler and Mrs.
Emily Sherman, made it possible for me to live for a month
in Berkeley's own Rhode Island home, Whitehall. The staffs
of the Athenaeum Library (in Newport) and the Rhode
Island Historical Society (in Providence) also made their
resources available. The University of California has
assisted not only through its several libraries and their
staffs, but through intramural support and a sabbatical
leave as well. I am grateful to Wake Forest University, specifically to Emmett W. Hamrick and the Department of
Religion, for permission to use materials delivered in the
1979 Samuel Robinson Lectures, and to the editors of
Church History for permission to use in chapter 2 some
material first appearing in their pages. Grants from the
American Council of Learned Societies and the American
Philosophical Society also furthered this project in its
early stages.

Finally, as fellow investigator and so much more, my wife
has joined me in the pilgrimage to Kilkenny, Trinity, and

London; to Newport and Middletown; to Cloyne and Oxford, walking where George Berkeley walked and attempting to think his thoughts after him. This book is for her.

E. S. G.

A PLAN of
the
TOWN OF NEWPORT
in
RHODE ISLAND.
Surveyed by CHARLES BLASKOWITZ,
Engraved and Publish'd
BY
WILL.ᵐ FADEN, Charing Cross Sept.ʳ 1ˢᵗ 1777.

Scale of Feet.

GOAT
Fort

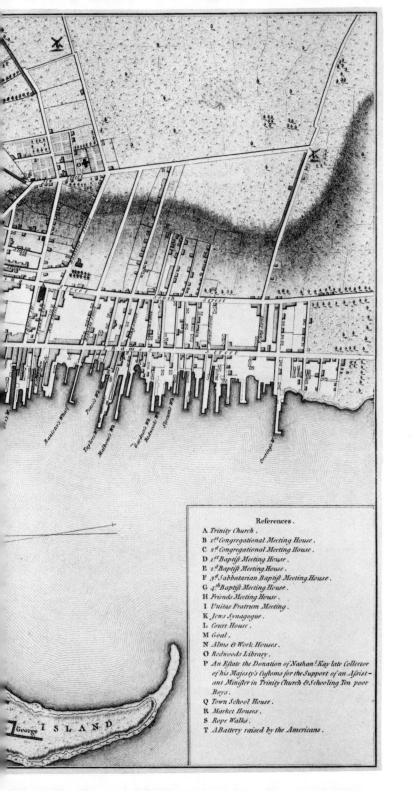

South Street

George ISLAND

References.

A Trinity Church.
B 1st Congregational Meeting House.
C 2d Congregational Meeting House.
D 1st Baptist Meeting House.
E 2d Baptist Meeting House.
F 3d Sabbatarian Baptist Meeting House.
G 4th Baptist Meeting House.
H Friends Meeting House.
I Unitas Fratrum Meeting.
K Jews Synagogue.
L Court House.
M Goal.
N Alms & Work Houses.
O Redwoods Library.
P An Estate the Donation of Nathanl Kay late Collector
   of his Majesty's Customs for the Support of an Assist-
   ant Minister in Trinity Church & Schooling Ten poor
   Boys.
Q Town School House.
R Market Houses.
S Rope Walks.
T A Battery raised by the Americans.

1 Newport: 1730

January. The best Physick in this Month, is warm
Cloaths, good Fires, and a merry honest Wife.
James Franklin, *The Rhode-Island
Almanack, For the Year, 1728,* Newport

"The only considerable place" in Rhode Island, Governor
Joseph Jenckes said of Newport in his 1731 report to England's Board of Trade.[1] Less than a century old, Newport,
on the Island of Aquidneck, had managed to become a real
town in a land where towns were few and cities nonexistent.
With a population approaching five thousand souls (an "exact census" for 1730 counted 3,843 whites, 649 blacks, and
148 Indians), Newport contained four-fifths of the island's
population and about one-fourth of the total population of
the Colony of Rhode Island and Providence Plantations.[2]
The deep natural harbor at the mouth of Narragansett Bay
gave Newport an early lead in commerce and trade, with her
sloops not only plying the coast to Boston but venturing
regularly to the West Indies, less frequently to Italy and
Holland. Newport's ships carried horses, livestock, and lum-
ber to the West Indies, returning with cargoes of sugar,
molasses, and cocoa. As early as 1700 slave ships sailed from
the town; a quarter-century later the trading of rum for

---

1. Calendar of State Papers, Colonial Series, *America and West Indies, 1731*
(London, 1938), p. 328.

2. Ibid., p. 329. Jenckes reported in 1731 that the entire colony had 15,302
whites, 1,668 blacks, and 985 Indians, "very peaceable." For the 1730 census of
Newport, see John Callender, *An Historical Discourse on the Civil and Religious
Affairs of the Colony of Rhode-Island and Providence Plantations* . . . (Boston,
1739; reprint of 3d ed. [1843], Freeport, N. Y., 1971), pp. 94-95.

1

slaves made "that unrighteous traffic" even more profitable.[3] Clockmakers (e.g., William Claggett), stone masons
(e.g., John Angel), tailors, carpenters, surveyors, bricklayers,
tanners, weavers, butchers, brewers, civil officers, and farmers added to Newport's wealth and to its urban complexity.[4]

Founded in 1639, Newport appeared on the Rhode Island
scene only three years after Roger Williams had bartered
with the Indians for that bit of land which became the settlement of Providence. Exiled from Massachusetts in 1635
for his determined and infuriating criticism of Puritan policies in that Bay Colony, Williams launched the tiny and
despised colony on its unsteady, ever turbulent course.
When still other dissenters aroused the ire of Massachusetts
officialdom, Williams persuaded the Narragansett Indians to
make Aquidneck Island available as a refuge from religious
persecution. To that island, therefore, came a remarkable
assortment of malcontents and eccentrics, of the ambitious
and the shiftless, of the visionary and the heroic, of those
indifferent to all religion and those indifferent to all else
but religion.

Anne Hutchinson, who in Boston had talked too much of
grace (God's unmerited gifts to man) and too little of works
(man's orderly, obedient response to God and His appointed
authorities), arrived on Aquidneck in 1638 but by 1642 had
moved on to Long Island where the following year she was
slain by Indians. Samuel Gorton, likewise among the early
settlers of Aquidneck's northern end (the even smaller town
of Portsmouth), believed in an especially unnerving form of
intimacy with God and in potential human perfection; he
also soon moved on, but only to the nearby mainland where in

3. See James B. Hedges, *The Browns of Providence Plantations* (Cambridge,
Mass., 1952), Vol. 1, chap. 4.

4. See Carl Bridenbaugh, *Cities in the Wilderness* (New York, 1938; rev. ed.,
London, 1970).

1642 he founded the town of Warwick. A former Massachusetts magistrate, William Coddington, played a leading role
both in the colony's political and religious life, the latter
as an early and influential Quaker. John Clarke, Puritan
become Baptist and a political opponent of Coddington's,
joined with over thirty others to bring Newport into existence; of even greater historical significance, Clarke spent
twelve years in England thereafter in order to secure Rhode
Island's permanent and liberal charter in 1663.[5]

In seventeenth-century Newport, Baptists and Quakers
dominated the religious scene. John Clarke and colleagues
watched over the settlement's first church (clearly Calvinist
and Baptist by 1644) from its beginning in 1638 to Clarke's
death in 1676. That church gave rise to others, not through
paternal sponsorship but through fractious dispute: a Six
Principle Baptist Church (Arminian in theology) in 1654,
and a Seventh-Day Baptist Church in 1671. Quakers arrived
as early as 1656, organizing a meeting that became the
principal center for Friends not only in Rhode Island but
in all of New England. New England's chief denominational
expression of Puritanism, Congregationalism, did not come
to Newport until near the end of the century, with a first
congregation formally instituted in 1720 and a second in
1728. Also in the final decade of the seventeenth century,
Anglicanism entered Newport through the ministrations of
John Lockyer (? -1704). But Lockyer was soon replaced
by James Honeyman (ca. 1675-1750) whose long tenure in
the colonial port gave direction to the development of

5. On the colonial history of Rhode Island, see the excellent survey by Sydney
V. James, *Colonial Rhode Island—A History* (New York, 1975), particularly
the reliable, usable bibliography, pp. 385-411. For brief sketches of Williams,
Hutchinson, Gorton, Coddington, and Clarke, see the *Dictionary of American
Biography*. Drawing upon her doctoral dissertation at the University of Iowa,
Sheila Skemp offers a brief synopsis of "George Berkeley's Newport Experience"
in *Rhode Island History* 37, no. 2 (May, 1978): 53-63.

Anglicanism for half a century. Honeyman, moreover, held the distinction of being the first Church of England missionary sent to New England by the Society for the Propagation of the Gospel in Foreign Parts (SPG).

This society, founded in London by Thomas Bray in 1701, constituted Anglicanism's formal response to the growth of dissent and irreligion (the two often seemed synonymous) in Britain's colonies abroad. No bishop of the Church of England resided in America, and no bishop residing in England had responsibility only for America. Almost casually, the bishop of London had his diocese somewhat enlarged to include the foreign plantations, but neither special funds nor additional personnel nor appropriate ecclesiastical machinery augmented his already heavy duties. A sprawling mission field ready for harvest, the colonies called out (or so it seemed to loyal churchmen in England) for more laborers to help bring that harvest in: to convert the Indian and the black, to reform the morals and fill the minds of the whites, to provide clergy and build churches, to distribute good books and inculcate sound doctrine—in short, to save England's colonies for England's Church.

Arriving in Newport in 1704, Honeyman as well as the Society and the Church of England all got off to a shaky start. Dissent was powerful, the Society feeble, and Honeyman suspect. Only recently arrived in America, Honeyman had initially been assigned to Jamaica on Long Island. There rumors reached the parishioners that Honeyman's character was not above reproach. His usefulness in that locale apparently damaged beyond repair, New York's governor, the imperious Edward Cornbury, decided that Honeyman should be transferred to Newport. The transfer duly accomplished, Honeyman found himself still subjected to a whispering campaign made the more unsettling by evidence that

Newporters were about to invite another missionary in his
place: Christopher Bridges, who then served as Samuel
Myles's assistant at King's Chapel in Boston. But Bridges
had problems, too; after much correspondence, madden-
ingly slow, and much deliberation, hopelessly remote, the
Society in 1709 (May 20) reaffirmed Honeyman as its
choice for Newport. By October of that year, a much tried
Honeyman could at last report that "all things are quiet and
easy in Church which flourishes beyond his expectation;
that they have a vestry chose; that he has settled himself in
a married state."[6] His salary—a point of continuing dis-
tress—set at £30 per year, the long and finally stable career
of Honeyman at last got underway.

Yet even after a full decade of devoted service, Honeyman
found the state of religion in and around Newport in 1714
to be "very melancholy." Writing to Francis Nicholson,
"Her Majesty's Commissioner for enquiring into the state of
ecclesiastical affairs in North America" (and former governor of Virginia and Maryland), Honeyman reported the
"fatal delusion of Quakerism" to be the "most prevailing
heresy" among Rhode Islanders, around one-fourth of the
population belonging to "this infection." Second in size
"are those under the Denomination of Anabaptists." Though
divided on such matters as observance of the sabbath day
and the laying on of hands, the Baptists were united at least
in this: their inflexibility and dogmatism. Led by "persons
of little knowledge and less learning," the Baptists "may
justly be reckoned a fifth of all the People." Third, the fol-
lowers of Samuel Gorton, embracing "the most wild & extravagant Scheme of Religion," dominate particular towns

6. Society for the Propagation of the Gospel (hereafter SPG) Archives,
Minutes, 2:12; also 1:117; and 2:31. And see J. K. Nelson, "Anglican Missions
in America, 1701-1725 . . ." (Ph.D. diss., Northwestern University, 1962),
pp. 476-78.

(e.g., Warwick), but thank God not Newport. After Quakers,
Baptists, and Gortonites, Honeyman next ranked those who
"do not think it for their ease and the enjoyment of their
Vices to trouble themselves with any Notions of Religion,
and so they deny the truth of all." Congregationalists, not
strong in Rhode Island generally, had made their presence
felt in Newport where "they have a large Meeting and a
Teacher, tho' without any discipline or administration of
the Sacraments by him."

"But blessed be God there is still a remnant . . . some good
members of the Church of England in Narragansett, and the
congregation in this town [Newport]." The sad effect of so
many divisions and "pernicious Errors" in religion, however,
was to bring all into disrepute. People openly showed contempt for religious ordinances, repeatedly profaned the
Sabbath, and engaged in such immorality "as would put a
modest Heathen to the Blush." If anyone should ask why
England's true church was so cast down in this, England's
colony, the answer was clear for those who would listen:
(1) no "Regular settled Ministry under the inspection of a
Bishop"; (2) no "good Education" (the natural enemy of
"Gross Corruptions in Religion"), there being "no Schools
of Learning upon a publick foundation in this Province";
and (3) no governmental support for true religion; the efforts
of ministers and schoolmasters come to nought "unless
Countenanced and Supported by the Secular Arm." But the
likelihood of any reform on that last point was slight,
Honeyman acknowledged, since in Rhode Island one gets
elected not by favoring the Church of England but by
"professing an Aversion to it."[7]

Because of his broadened responsibilities overseas, the
bishop of London also served as an ex officio member of
Board of Trade. That board, created in 1696, while only

7. SPG Archives, Letter Books, Series A, 9:386-91 (May 7, 1714).

advisory to the king and his Privy Council, did in fact exercise great power over the colonies since its advice was so regularly followed. By no means limiting its agenda to trade alone, the board for a time gave direction and clarity to Britian's imperial policies. Edmund Gibson, translated to the bishopric of London in 1723, tried to direct the affairs of a diocese that was without geographical limit, without resident bishops, and without a dependable secular arm. Like the board, Bishop Gibson thought it first appropriate that he inform himself as accurately as possible concerning the true state of affairs in the colonial plantations. And the affairs with which he chiefly concerned himself were ecclesiastical.

When Gibson issued his "Queries" in 1724, the Church of England had improved somewhat over the earlier "melancholy" period. New England generally and Newport specifically had shown encouraging vital signs. In 1722, to cite a famous example, three prominent young men suddenly converted from Congregationalism to Anglicanism, a dramatic turn of events that brought hope to the latter and trauma to the former. For it happened in the very citadel of Connecticut Puritanism: young Yale College. There Samuel Johnson (1696-1772), Timothy Cutler (1684-1765), and Daniel Brown (1698-1723) forsook the establishment in favor of the heretofore despised and rejected Church of England.[8] Following this "great apostacy," Johnson—formerly a tutor at Yale—became an Anglican priest in Stratford, Connecticut, and an Anglican leader far beyond the borders of that small town. Timothy Cutler, in 1722 serving as nothing less than Yale's rector, moved to a pulpit in Boston where he exercised vigorous and often arrogant influence. Daniel Brown, also a

---

8. Especially rejected in Connecticut, the only colony in America not to have by this time a single settled Anglican clergyman. Richard Warch, *School of the Prophets: Yale College 1701-1740* (New Haven, 1973), p. 102.

Yale tutor, joined Johnson and Cutler in sailing for England
late in 1722 to be ordained along with his fellows in March
of the following year; unfortunately, he died of smallpox
shortly thereafter.

While other New England converts followed in the train
of these three, the New Haven "Hurle-Burle" gave particular
comfort to a beleaguered Anglican minority even as it
brought suspicion to and the near collapse of the still struggling Puritan college.[9] From Yale's point of view, the serpent
had struck from within its very bosom. From James Honeyman's point of view, these three worthy gentlemen, acting
"upon pure Principle and Conviction," now cast themselves
onto another bosom: "the Bosom of the Church where, we
humbly hope, They will be kindly received and tenderly
cherished." Writing to the bishop of London in the fall of
1722, the Newport church pointedly observed that a kind
reception given to these three would encourage many others
to follow in their wake, thereby shaking "the Foundations
of Schism in these Countreys."[10]

The Newport church could also rejoice in the growth of
its own parish. Late in 1723, Honeyman reported to the SPG
that in a two-year period he had baptized eighty persons,
including three Negroes, two Indians, and two mulattoes.
Indeed, such had been their growth that the time had come
to build a church. "Our New Church will be a fine building
but vastly exceed the Sum we at first proposed to Expend
upon it: We trust Providence will carry us thro' our Difficulties."[11] Responding to Bishop Gibson's "Queries" in April,
1724, Honeyman indicated that construction was then underway. More than "fifty Communicants properly belonging
to this church" attended the administration of the Lord's

9. Ibid.; see all of chapter 4, "A Most Grevous Rout and Hurle-Burle."
10. Fulham Papers, 8: 133-34 (Oct. 29, 1722).
11. Ibid., pp. 145-46 (Nov. 19, 1723).

supper every first Sunday. Despite the many competing sects, despite the failure of Rhode Island's government to make any provisions for ministers ("I have no House or Glebe but what I rent"), Honeyman could report a progress that was real.[12] By the time Trinity's handsome wooden structure was completed in 1726, Newport logically served as nerve center and meeting ground for Anglican leaders from all of New England.[13]

In July of 1725, six clergymen gathered together for the first time in Newport to discuss their mutual problems and to promote "the Common good of the Church." They composed separate communications to the king who ruled them, to the Society which employed them, and to the bishop who watched over them. To George I they professed their "firmest Loyalty and Affection"; to the SPG they reported the progress they were making; and to Edmund Gibson, they complained about the absence of two of their number (Henry Harris of Boston and David Mossom of Marblehead). But in all three letters, one theme was common: the urgent, critical, and immediate need for a bishop to reside among them. To the king they respectfully made the case that the "infant & weak condition" of their churches would "be much raised whenever we shall be made happy with One whom Your Majesty shall think worthy of the Episcopal Character with us."[14] To the Society, the six missionaries spoke of the "multitudes" in New England who "long & pray for this great Blessing of a worthy Bishop with us." They pointed out what indeed the Society well knew: namely,

12. Ibid., pp. 188-89 (April 23, 1724).
13. This building of impressive dignity imitated some of Christopher Wren's more modest architectural achievements. Richard Munday, a Master Carpenter of Newport, was the builder. See A. F. Downing and V. J. Scully, Jr., *The Architectural Heritage of Newport, Rhode Island* (New York, rev. ed., 1967), pp. 53-59, plates 48-56.
14. Fulham Papers, 4: 161-62 (July 21, 1725).

that "the hazards of the Seas & Sickness [recalling Daniel
Brown] & the Charges of Travel discourage [many] from
the Service of the Church & tempt them to inlist themselves
as members or Ministers of Dissenting Congregations." Also,
the lack of a bishop deprives us of "the great benefit of
Confirmation the usefulness whereof we preach." As things
now stood, the clergymen reported, they were the butt of
jokes: on the one hand, from Canada's Roman Catholics
who already had their bishops, and on the other hand, from
America's dissenters who didn't believe in them; both
groups "upbraid us for preaching those things we cannot
enjoy."[15] So far as the bishop of London was concerned,
the New England Anglicans knew that he was already on
their side; they contented themselves, therefore, with noting
that we have "room to think that the Arguments for the
Necessity of a Bishop in this Country will have a due Consideration with your Lordship."[16] Gibson had, in fact,
strenuously argued that several bishops, a few bishops,
surely at least a single bishop, should be dispatched to the
American colonies, but thus far all to no avail.[17]

These earnest pleas came from Honeyman in Newport,
Cutler in Boston, Johnson in Stratford, and three others:
James McSparran, missionary in the Narragansett country
of Rhode Island; George Pigot, the Society's appointee in

15. SPG Archives, Letter Books, Series A, 19: 234-37 (July 21, 1725).

16. Fulham Papers, 8: 195-96 (July 21, 1725). As early as 1709, when the
Society had been in existence only eight years, the SPG missionary in New
Jersey, John Talbot, wrote in the strongest terms of the absolute necessity
that a bishop be sent without delay to America. He even suggested that the
Society recall all of its missionaries and suspend all of its operations until
that essential step be taken. There will never be a Church in America "till a
propagator comes over to plant and build it up." Merely to send missionaries
who are supposed to keep "planting the gospel is like Indians planting gun-
powder" SPG Archives, Minutes, 2: 4).

17. Norman Sykes, *From Sheldon to Secker* (Cambridge, England, 1959),
pp. 207-08.

Providence; and, Matthias Plant, minister in Newbury, Massachusetts. Aging Samuel Myles of Boston had been excused
from the meeting because he could not undergo "the Fa-
tigue of a Journey" to Newport. But Harris and Mossom,
who had not been excused, wrote to Bishop Gibson the
following December to explain that they objected to meeting in "a Quaker Province." There was, of course, more to
the story than that, and the internal tensions and disagree-
ments among the Society's remote and underpaid employees
only illustrated one further need for "a worthy Bishop with
us."[18]

While Rhode Island might be loosely styled "a Quaker
province"–Quakers did by this time hold high political
office–this hardly constituted a valid excuse for Anglicans
to avoid meeting in Rhode Island. For in fact they fared
better in that tiny colony than in either Connecticut or
Massachusetts, where wrangles over the payment of ecclesiastical taxes to support Congregationalism were protracted
and abrasive. True, Rhode Island may not have provided
Honeyman (or any other clergyman) with house and glebe;
at the same time, however, it presented neither barrier nor
hindrance to the development and advancement of the
Church of England. Harris and Mossom notwithstanding,
once Trinity parish's commodious church was erected, Newport served with even more aptness as an unofficial diocesan
center for New England.

At the end of 1727, the Anglican clergy therefore gathered
once more in Newport, this time to pledge their "Loyal &
Unfeigned Congratulations" to their new king, George II,
and to petition yet again for only one thing: a bishop.
"Your Lordship will forgive the Zeal we express for a
Bishop resident with us," they wrote, explaining that loyalty
to king and to country would be neither divided nor di-

18. Fulham Papers, 4: 174-75 (Dec. 7, 1725).

minished by the presence of bishop, only strengthened and
enhanced. This being the case, "we humbly hope for your
Lordship's Concurrence and Approbation."[19]

But while praying for a bishop, what these Newport petitioners soon received was a dean. On January 23, 1729,
after an unusually long and difficult voyage, George Berkeley
and party arrived in Newport harbor. Having left Greenwich,
England, for Rhode Island on the sixth of September, 1728,
the privately commissioned *Lucy* (Captain Cobb, Master)
was forced after four and one-half months at sea to put in at
Virginia "for want of Provisions." We were, Berkeley later
wrote, "a long time blundering about the ocean." Hosted
in and around Williamsburg by Governor William Gooch,
Berkeley bid a temporary farewell to two of his traveling
companions, John James and Richard Dalton, who understandably decided to make the rest of the journey overland.
Then Berkeley, his wife, her companion, and the artist John
Smibert, after a ten-day stay in Virginia, sailed on up the
coast to Newport, their original destination.[20] Greeted by a
Rhode Island January, Berkeley, whether he appreciated
James Franklin's prescription or not, must have gladly

19. Fulham Papers, 8: 220 (Dec. 12, 1727). The Anglicans' zeal for a bishop
was more than matched, of course, by the dissenters' determination to keep all
bishops forever out. See A. L. Cross, *The Anglican Episcopate and the
American Colonies* (Cambridge, Mass., 1902); and Carl Bridenbaugh, *Mitre &
Sceptre* (New York, 1962). In England, the church authorities generally
favored the sending of a bishop to the colonies, while the political leaders—
knowing the divisive effect of such a move—generally opposed it.

20. "Diary of John Comer," manuscript at Rhode Island Historical Society,
2: 2: "This day [January 23, 1729] Dean George Berkeley arrived here with
his spouse and a young ladie in companie . . . he was 4 months and 16 days to
Virginia. . . ." See also the letter from Gov. William Gooch to Bishop Gibson,
Fulham Papers, 12: 136-37 (June 29, 1729); Society for Promoting Christian
Knowledge (hereafter SPCK), New England Letters, vol. 3, Henry Newman to
John Boydell, August 24, 1728.

exchanged a Newport winter for continued confinement and buffeting at sea.[21]

Though not a bishop, George Berkeley as dean of Derry (in northern Ireland) was the highest-ranking ecclesiastical dignitary to visit New England shores up to that point. Quite apart from his status as an Anglican, however, he was an international celebrity since his major philosophical work was already behind him when, at the age of forty-three, he stepped onto Newport's busy docks. If the local populace was not immediately blinded by his eminence, later myth-makers have tended to be.[22] But New England's

21. James Franklin (1697-1735), brother of Benjamin, launched his *Rhode-Island Almanac* in 1728. Irreverent, satirical, and ready to burlesque everything from science to religion, Franklin wrote for the widest market possible. He predicted the weather, but not too seriously: on Feb. 14, 1730, he forecast that the weather would be of "all sorts"; by that year's entry for Sept. 26, he wrote that "It would have rain'd the 15th Day, but I had not room to write it." He listed the major meetings scheduled for the year (civil and religious), noted the eclipses, offered homey advice and gentle mockery. James used the pseudonym "Poor Robin" in 1728; five years later in Philadelphia, his younger brother followed the example set in Newport by issuing an almanac under the name of "Poor Richard." Something of James Franklin's tone can be seen in these concluding lines from his 1728 almanac:

> Here are Days for your Feasting and Fasting
> And Days to drink Punch or [*sic*] October
> The Days of all Courts
> And the Days for your Sports
> To be drunk when you cannot keep sober

On the relationship between James's and Benjamin's almanacs, see James A. Sappenfield, *A Sweet Instruction: Franklin's Journalism as a Literary Apprenticeship* (Carbondale, Ill., 1973), p. 128.

22. The most familiar story is that Berkeley arrived to send a letter to Honeyman who, at that moment holding a service in his church, dismissed the congregation, which immediately made its way to the "ferry wharf" in time to welcome the dean onto New World soil. See, for example, Benjamin Rand, *Berkeley's American Sojourn* (Cambridge, Mass., 1932), pp. 17-18, citing Wilkins Updike, *A History of the Episcopal Church in Narragansett Rhode*

churchmen could only be cheered by the presence of this
dean who possibly was an augur of things to come, while
even dissenters took solace in Berkeley's reputation as "a
man of moderation."[23]

Like other wayfarers and immigrants before him, the dean
first busied himself in providing for the immediate needs of
his family and in learning his way around a strange community. Berkeley's marriage to Anne Forster was a recent
one, having taken place only a few weeks prior to the sailing
from Greenwich.[24] A Dubliner of education and religious
sensitivity, the twenty-eight-year-old bride (whose courage
and trust could hardly be questioned) willingly joined her
new husband in a new venture as together they sailed for a
new land. The first product of that marriage, Henry, born
six months after the couple's arrival in Newport, was baptized by the father in Trinity Church in September of 1729.
Shortly after Henry's birth in June, Berkeley wrote to his
close friend in Dublin, Thomas Prior, "I have got a son who,
I thank God, is likely to live."[25] The son did live, but a

Island . . . (New York, 1847). Updike, in turn, is merely reprinting Henry
Bull's "Memoirs of Trinity Church from 1689 to 1810"; Bull acknowledged
that this "tradition" was passed on just as he received it, "but other traditions
vary a little from that . . ." (Updike, p. 395). The day of Berkeley's arrival in
Newport was neither a Sunday nor a holyday, and no contemporary record
indicates either the precise moment or spot of his debarkation.

23. "Diary of John Comer," 2: 2; in July, 1729, Comer, a Baptist minister,
visited Berkeley at Whitehall and happily reported that he was "kindly treated".
(2: 8).

24. A. A. Luce, *The Life of George Berkeley, Bishop of Cloyne* (London,
1949), p. 111. This, the standard biography of Berkeley, is referred to hereafter
as Luce, *Life*. Anne Berkeley's companion, "Miss Handcock," remains an
obscure figure, though her likeness survives in Smibert's famous "Bermuda
Group" discussed below, p. 72.

25. A. A. Luce and T. E. Jessop, *The Works of George Berkeley, Bishop of
Clone*, 9 vols. (London, reprinted 1964), 8: 198; referred to hereafter as GB
Works. Luce edited vols. 1, 4, 7, and 8, while Jessop edited vols. 2, 3, 5, and 6;
together, they edited vol. 9. Luce, in his *Life*, gives the date of Henry's baptism

daughter, born two years later, still lies in Trinity's burial
ground where she was laid on September 5, 1731, less than
two weeks after the dean baptized her.[26] Despite that tragic
loss, Berkeley's family responsibilities in Newport generally
proved more a delight than a burden, as he described his
son as "the most perfect thing we ever saw of its kind,"
and his wife as one who "loves a country life and books
so well as to pass her time contentedly and cheerfully without any other conversation than her husband and the
dead."[27]

For several weeks after their arrival, George and Anne
Berkeley accepted the hospitality of the Honeymans in
their rented house. Within a month, however, Berkeley had
purchased a farm of ninety-six acres for £2,500 from Joseph
and Sarah Whipple. This parcel of land, consisting of "one
orchard . . . arable pasture and meadow and woodland,"
lay about three miles northeast of Trinity Church and of
Newport's docks; very much in the country (as it still is),
the farm was located in what would later be called Middletown—between the two older island towns of Portsmouth
and Newport. A house already existed on the land, but
when Berkeley moved his family out there in May he built
or rebuilt a sturdy two-story farmhouse which he named
Whitehall.[28] Colonial dissenters who constantly worried

as September 1, but the records of Trinity Church show the baptism to have
been on September 25; George C. Mason, *Annals of Trinity Church, Newport,
Rhode Island 1698-1821* (Newport, 1890), p. 48.

26. Luce, *Life*, p.125; Mason, *Annals*, p. 52.

27. Luce, *Life*, p. 125. In a letter to Percival (GB *Works* 8: 188), Berkeley
observes that he has provided his wife with a spinning wheel and that they plan
to buy no finished goods.

28. Ibid., pp. 123-24; also Appendix 3 (a). The name "Whitehall" was not
chosen to honor the British government or in memory of the royal palace
which dated from the time of Henry VIII (who took over "York Palace"
from Cardinal Wolsey and renamed it) and went up in the flames of the great
fire of 1698. Almost certainly, Berkeley chose that appellation in honor of

about episcopal "palaces" (were bishops ever to be allowed
into America) should have been reassured by the modesty
of the dean's design.[29] It was a home, not a palace, and
Berkeley presided there merely as the head of a household,
not a diocese.

While the isolation and bucolic character of Berkeley's
Whitehall—the only home he ever owned—can be exaggerated, clearly the recently transplanted couple both accepted
and appreciated what their new surroundings had to offer.
The winter, Berkeley acknowledged, was "sharper than the
usual winters in Ireland, but not at all sharper than I have
known them in Italy." Summer on the other hand, he
noted, was "exceedingly delightful" and autumn "is said
to be the finest in the world." Of the island of Aquidneck
generally, Berkeley wrote:

> This island is pleasantly laid out in hills and vales and
> rising grounds; hath plenty of excellent springs and
> fine rivulets, and many delightful landscapes of rocks
> and promontories and adjacent islands. The provisions
> are very good; so are the fruits, which are quite neglect-
> ed, tho' vines sprout up of themselves to an extraordi-
> nary size, and seem as natural to this soil as to any I
> ever saw. The town of Newport contains about six
> thousand souls, and is the most thriving flourishing
> place in all America for its bigness. It is very pretty and
> pleasantly situated.

------

the "Chapel Royal, Whitehall" presided over at that time by his good friend
Edmund Gibson, bishop of London. Gibson was automatically dean of the
chapel and may even have had a small apartment there, since Fulham was
thought of as way out in the country. See Norman Sykes, *From Sheldon to
Secker* (Cambridge, 1959), for additional detail on this Whitehall and the
"Whitehall Preachers."

29. For architectural detail, see A. F. Downing and V. J. Scully, Jr., *The
Architectural Heritage of Newport*, pp. 438-40 and plates 85-86.

Berkeley forbore going on "for fear of being thought Romantic."[30]

On May 6, 1729, George Berkeley was "admitted freeman of this colony" in recognition of his status as property owner and his dignity as "Dean of Derry in the kingdom of Ireland."[31] His associations in Newport early extended beyond the Honeymans to include some of the town's leading citizens: Henry Collins, Edward Scott, James Searing, Nathan Townsend, and Daniel Updike. These men, along with James Honeyman, Jr., in 1730 formed "a Society for the promotion of Knowledge and Virtue, by a free conversation." Like Benjamin Franklin's *Junto* in Philadelphia, the Newport society guaranteed to its members the right of full and free debate on any subject whatever, the content of the Monday night meetings not to be divulged "on penalty of a perpetual exclusion." Though Berkeley does not appear to have been a formal member, his residence in Newport may have helped to bring such a group into being. A nineteenth-century descendant of one of the original members claimed, at any rate, that the "learned Dean sometimes encouraged and stimulated their efforts by his presence."[32]

Berkeley also preached regularly in Trinity Church, especially during the months he lived with the Honeymans, somewhat less frequently thereafter. He traveled across Narragansett Bay to see "mainland America" and some of its Indians; bought, instructed, and baptized three slaves;

30. GB *Works*, 8: 198, 196, 194.

31. John Russell Bartlett, ed., *Records of the Colony of Rhode Island and Providence Plantations in New England* (Providence, 1859), 4: 420.

32. Wilkins Updike, *Memoirs of the Rhode-Island Bar* (Boston, 1842), p. 62. Also see George C. Mason, *Annals of the Redwood Library and Athenaeum* (Newport, 1891), p. 13. The famous Abraham Redwood Library, founded in 1747, grew out of this early philosophical club, but of course its connection with George Berkeley is even more remote and tenuous.

received visitors, sometimes for days, at Whitehall; maintained contacts with his former shipmates (Messrs. James,
Dalton, and Smibert), now removed to Boston ("the great
place of pleasure and resort in these parts"); and kept his
friends and supporters back home informed of unfolding
events in the New World.[33] But for none of this had
Berkeley set out on a "tedious winter voyage" nor left his
charge at Derry nor challenged the panjandrums of both
politics and religion in old England.

After a few months in Rhode Island, Berkeley wrote to a
fellow churchman in Britain, "I do not think I could be so
useful in any part of the world as in this place."[34] Neither
whim of fancy nor accident of navigation had brought
George Berkeley to America: nothing less than a certain
vision of history had drawn him there.

33. GB *Works*, 8: 202, 205.
34. Ibid., p. 194; to Bishop Martin Benson of Gloucester, April 11, 1729.

2 *The Dean of Derry and the Somer Isles*

> If my Wifes Cholick continues and Physitians advise
> warmer climate it is not impossible but we may try that
> Air. For my own particular, as I have no ambitious Views
> to keep me in this part of the World, I form to my Self
> the greatest pleasure that can be in enjoying my family
> with Consumate health in a happy Climate, in Company
> of a Set of ingenious virtuous and pious men, and with
> Relations or other friends whose notions and amuse-
> ments fall in with my own. And I know not why in time
> that little Spot may not become the Athens of the
> World. . . .
>
> Sir John Percival to his brother, February 6, 1725

George Berkeley was born in or near Kilkenny, Ireland, on
March 12, 1685. At the age of eleven, he enrolled in Kilkenny College (the "Eton" of Ireland) and, upon the conclusion of his study there, journeyed to Dublin in 1700 to
enter Trinity College. Receiving a Bachelor of Arts in 1704
and a Master of Arts three years later, Berkeley stayed on
at Trinity as a resident junior fellow and tutor at least until
1713. In 1710 he took Holy Orders in the Church of Ireland.[1]

In this period of his closest contact with the college and
while still a very young man, George Berkeley wrote the
books that ultimately won for him a reputation far beyond
the bounds of the Trinity College Green: *An Essay Toward*

1. See Luce, *Life*, pp. 20, 41 et passim.

a *New Theory of Vision* (1709), *A Treatise concerning the
Principles of Human Knowledge* (1710), and in 1713 *Three
Dialogues between Hylas and Philonous*. Not yet thirty
years of age, the young Irishman had produced works of
such originality and force that, centuries later, they continue to stimulate and provoke.[2] In 1713, Berkeley left
Ireland for the first time to pay a visit to England. If
Dublin had opened up to him the world of the mind, London opened up the worlds of politics, society, and letters.
He enjoyed association with Richard Steele (1672-1729)
and wrote for his *Guardian*; he met and admired Joseph
Addison (1672-1719) and Alexander Pope (1688-1744);
and he established a lifelong friendship with John Percival
(1683-1748), first earl of Egmont and an Irishman then
dividing his time between his homeland and England.[3]
While Berkeley had known Percival since 1709, the London
stay permitted their mutual respect to reach a point where
it never wavered on either side. The climax of Berkeley's
introduction to London society came with his presentation
at court by Jonathan Swift (1667-1745), another Irishman and one with whom he enjoyed the school ties of both
Kilkenny and Trinity. With George Berkeley explicitly in
mind, Swift declared himself ready "to use all my little

2. For a full bibliography, see T. E. Jessop, *A Bibliography of George
Berkeley* (New York, reprint 1968); and, Geoffrey L. Keynes, *A Bibliography
of George Berkeley, Bishop of Cloyne: His Works and His Critics in the Eighteenth Century* (Oxford, 1976). As one measure of Berkeley's continuing
stimulation to the field of philosophy, note C. M. Turbayne and Robert Ware,
"A Bibliography of George Berkeley, 1933-62." *Journal of Philosophy* 60,
no. 4 (Feb. 14, 1963). Berkeley's philosophical impact in America is considered
below, chapters 3, 7, and 8.

3. John Percival, a native of the county of Cork in Ireland, served as a
member of the privy council in Ireland under both George I and II, as well as
during the earlier reign of Queen Anne. A member of both the Irish and the
British House of Commons at varying times, Percival exhibited great public
spirit and an unusual degree of involvement in many "schemes" other than
Berkeley's. (See the *Dictionary of National Biography* where the spelling is
"Perceval"; I have followed A. A. Luce and Benjamin Rand.)

credit towards helping forward men of worth in this world."[4]

Berkeley's chatty letters to Percival (when the latter was in Dublin) revealed a full enjoyment of all that city life had to offer. "On Tuesday last," he wrote in 1713, "Mr. Addison's play entitled Cato was acted the first time. . . . I was present with Mr. Addison, and two or three more friends in a side box, where we had a table and two or three flasks of burgundy and champagne, with which the author (who is a very sober man) thought it necessary to support his spirits in the concern he was then under; and indeed it was a pleasant refreshment to us all between the acts." The play dealt with "virtue and religion" which in this eleventh (and penultimate) year of the reign of Queen Anne meant that it dealt with politics as well. The prologue, some parts of which were written by Alexander Pope "a Tory and even a Papist," were hissed, "being thought to favour of whiggism." But on the whole, applause covered the hisses, even the peerage declining to condemn a play or an author just "because his hero was thought to be a Roman whig."[5]

After sipping from London's cultural fountains, nothing remained for Berkeley's full maturing but the continental tour. This he undertook not once but twice, and not for a single year but for five. On his first journey, from October 1713 to August 1714, Berkeley served as chaplain to the earl of Peterborough, military hero and diplomat. His second tour, as tutor for St. George Ashe (son of the bishop of Clogher), lasted from 1716 to 1720. All of this time, Berkeley still held titles at Trinity College; when in 1717 he was elected senior fellow, his repeated leaves of absence provoked some grumbling. Also, all of this time, while absorbing the art, literature, religion, philosophy, and

---

4. Quoted in Luce, *Life*, p. 65.

5. On Percival and Berkeley's long friendship and extensive correspondence, see Benjamin Rand, *Berkeley and Percival* (Cambridge, Eng., 1914); hereafter, Rand *B & P.* Quotation is from pp. 113-14, letter dated April 16, 1713.

politics of Europe, Berkeley kept up with developments
in England and Ireland. The accession of George I in 1714
brought a new dynasty to England, even as it brought dis-
comfort to the Tories and increased sympathies for the
Jacobites. Berkeley, however, took a firm stand in favor of
the House of Hanover, rejecting those who plotted for or
engaged in revolution against a throne which they had
sworn to uphold. In a brief tract published anonymously
in 1715, Berkeley warned that perjury and fraud in the
name of loyalty to the church hardly helped to demonstrate
either the validity or the utility of Christianity. "If oaths
are no longer to be esteemed sacred, what sufficient restraint can be found for the irregular inclinations of men?
Common mutual faith is the great support of society."[6]

When, five years later, Berkeley at last returned to
England, the strength and integrity of English society concerned him even more. In a blistering *Essay towards
Preventing the Ruin of Great Britain*, Berkeley expressed
his profound anxiety over the decline of that religion and
virtue with which Addison's play had dealt. Persistent in
preferring private gain to public good, Englishmen had just
been taken for a ride on that speculation roller-coaster
known as the South Sea Bubble, the bursting of which left
reputations no less than fortunes desolated. The financial
crash also left England with enormous instability, as economic standings shifted and all normal rules of conduct
collapsed. All that, however, were mere surface symptoms
of "the corrupt degenerate age we live in." Berkeley added:

> We have long been preparing for some great catas-
> trophe. Vice and villainy have by degrees grown rep-
> utable among us; our infidels have passed for fine
> gentlemen, and our venal traitors for men of sense,
> who knew the world. We have made a jest of public spir-

6. GB *Works,* 6: 54. See T. E. Jessop's brief introduction, pp. 49-50, for
evidence that this tract, *Advice to the Tories who have taken the Oaths,* is
indeed Berkeley's.

it, and cancelled all respect for whatever our laws and religion repute sacred. The old English modesty is quite worn off, and instead of blushing for our crimes we are ashamed only of piety and virtue. In short, other nations have been wicked, but we are the first who have been wicked upon principle.[7]

Taking a long view of history, Berkeley feared that "the final period of our State approaches." We have seen what has happened to other free governments all over Europe; "yet we seemed disposed rather to follow their example than to profit by it."[8]

While reflecting on the course of history generally and of England more narrowly, Berkeley, with an even tighter focus, reflected on the course of his own career. Too long away from Ireland—he had not resided there since 1713—should be now return? But if so, then in what capacity? Should he turn to the life of a clergyman or that of a professor of, if it were possible, to some happy combination of the two? In September, 1721, Berkeley did return to Dublin actively to seek some ecclesiastical appointment that would secure his livelihood but leave him free to continue academic pursuits. Renewing his associations with Trinity, he took further work at the same time that he accepted the post of Divinity Lecturer. With respect to his livelihood within the church, the deanery of Dromore (just south of Belfast) seemed precisely the sort of sinecure—Berkeley's word—that he had in mind. Thus he began the complex, delicate choreography required for appointment to one of the better livings in the Church of Ireland. However, Dromore, "worth about £500 a year," became so tangled in legal dispute and bureaucratic delay that Berkeley despaired of a positive outcome.[9] Another

7. Ibid., 6: 84.
8. Ibid., p. 85.
9. Ibid., 8: 116; Luce, *Life*, p. 86. Charles Dering to Percival, April 11, 1722, in British Museum (BM) Add. Ms. 47029, fols. 106, 114.

deanery, also in northern Ireland, soon appeared on the horizon. To pursue this deanship at Derry, Berkeley resolved to go directly to the center of power, London, where for two months he made his humble solicitation.

Back in Dublin, maneuvers continued at their own predetermined and barely perceptible pace. Finally, in the spring of 1724, the verdict came in: favorable. Among the "Legion of Candidates," "good Sollicitors" all, Berkeley emerged victorious though chagrined by the whole procedure. He "was ashamed to be seen among" all those good solicitors at Dublin Castle, Philip Percival informed his brother, "and us'd to retire to the Garden."[10] At last, however, three years after his return to Ireland and to Trinity, Berkeley had a secure office ("the best Deanery in this kingdom . . . said to be worth £1,500 p. ann."),[11] a solid reputation, and a serene future. In his fortieth year, the brilliant philosopher-dean, blessed with both lectureship and sinecure, could look ahead to an orderly, rational, cultivated, calm life sure to win universal approval and acclaim.

Except that Berkeley had for some time entertained a few rather different thoughts. At least as early as 1722, appointments to Dromore or Derry or whatever were seen as but a means to another end. For Berkeley, at this point in the history of the world and in the decline of Great Britain, a quiet deanery represented not an anchorage but a port of embarkation. It remained to be demonstrated that bold philosophical speculation could be matched by even bolder personal participation. The seeds of Berkeley's dream lay in that 1721 essay concerning Britain's "ruin." The tides of history moved relentlessly if slowly, and they were moving against England. If public spirit were to prosper anywhere, if religion and virtue were to guide a people

10. Letter, April 24, 1724, in BM Add. Ms. 47030, fol. 64; also, Rand, *B & P* p. 216.

11. Rand, *B & P*, p. 217.

once again, if society were to strive for the noble rather than settle for the base, then one must ride those tides wherever they might lead.

One year after that gloomy essay was written, Berkeley's plan began to take shape as the geography became explicit, the means clearer, and the goals more urgent. At the end of 1722, Berkeley dropped his first hint in a letter to Percival who, along with his wife, had been taking the cure in Bath. "If the Bath does not perfect her cure," Berkeley wrote, "I know a place within a thousand leagues that I am persuaded will, if I can persuade her Ladyship to go thither."[12] Then, three months later in another letter to his friend, the grand plan unfolded. Not yet seated as dean of Derry, Berkeley was nonetheless determined to execute his design "whatever happens," even at "the risk of being thought mad and chimerical."[13]

"It is now about ten months [i.e., roughly May of 1722]," Berkeley began, "since I have determined to spend the residue of my days in the Island of Bermuda, where I trust in Providence I may be the mean instrument of doing good to mankind." As the mean instrument, Berkeley would organize a college—inevitably fashioned somewhat after Trinity—to provide "pastors of good morals and good learning, a thing (God knows!) much wanted," for the churches of the Western world. And in that same college, studying alongside "the English youth of our plantations," would be "a number of young American savages." These Indians, trained in the liberal arts, the Christian religion, and "early endued with public spirited principles" would "become the fittest missionaries for spreading religion, morality, and civil life among their countrymen." The Indians, understandably suspicious of white English mis-

12. GB *Works*, 8: 126; letter dated Dec. 16, 1722.
13. Ibid., 8: 127-28; letter dated March 4, 1723. Here and throughout the book, year dates given in Old Style or given as, for example, 1722/3 have all been changed to conform to modern dating.

sionaries and white English imperialists, "can entertain no suspicion or jealousy of men of their own blood and language."[14]

The letter's first sentence raised the first and most persisting question about the whole idea: why Bermuda (or the Somer Isles, then Summer Islands)?[15] Recognizing that location was hardly peripheral to his plan—"utopia" despite its etymology does demand a place—Berkeley listed seven reasons for his choice.

> 1. It is the most equidistant part of our plantations from all the rest, whether in the continent, or the isles.
> 2. It is the only Plantation that holds a general commerce and correspondence with all the rest, there being sixty cedar ships belonging to the Bermudians . . .
> 3. The climate is by far the healthiest and most serene, and consequently the most fit for study.
> 4. There is the greatest abundance of all the necessary provisions for life, which is much to be considered in a place of education.
> 5. It is the securest spot in the universe, being environed round with rocks all but one narrow entrance, guarded by seven forts, which render it inaccessible not only to pirates but to the united force of France and Spain.
> 6. The inhabitants have the greatest simplicity of manners, more innocence, honesty, and good nature, than any of our other planters, who many of them are descended from whores, vagabonds, and transported

14. Ibid.

15. In 1609, Sir George Somers was shipwrecked off the islands known collectively as Bermuda. When England assumed sovereignty, the islands naturally came to be called the Somer Isles, then, even more naturally, the Summer Islands. Eventually the earlier name (from the Spanish mariner, Juan de Bermúdez), resumed its favored status. For a general history of the islands in the eighteenth century, see Henry C. Wilkinson, *Bermuda in the Old Empire* (Oxford, 1950).

criminals, none of which ever settled in Bermudas.
7. The Islands of Bermuda produce no one enriching
commodity, neither sugar, tobacco, indigo, or the like,
which may tempt men from their studies to turn
traders, as the parsons do too often elsewhere.[16]

After this more or less restrained delineation of Bermuda's
virtues, Berkeley then broke into rhapsody about the islands' beauty: the sky "blue as sapphire"; the earth "eter-
nally crowned with fruits and flowers"; the woods "always
fresh and blooming"; "the finest weather and gentlest
climate in the world"—and more, more, more. Friends
would flock there for their health; "English men of quality,
and gentlemen" would retire there; persons of limited
means would discover that in those enchanted isles their
money would go farther. In sum, Bermuda was a land
"where men may find, in fact, whatsoever the most poetical imagination can figure to itself in the golden age, or
the Elysian fields."

Poetical imagination had clearly already been at work.
Berkeley recognized that his enthusiasm needed to be
checked, but on the other hand he also knew that he must
encourage others to dream his dream too. "If I can make a
convert of your Lordship—" And if then I can convert
other lords and bishops, politicians and professors, sea
captains and plantation owners, and yes even savages, well
if I can do all that, then my dream will become my world.

In the ten months before writing to Percival, Berkeley
had busily sought just such converts in Dublin, apparently
with considerable success. Daniel Dering, one of Percival's
cousins living in Dublin, told his kinsman: "you will be
surprised when you hear the company he has engaged to
go with him. Young and old, learned and rich, all desirous
of retiring to enjoy peace of mind and health of body, and

16. GB *Works*, 8: 128.

of restoring the golden age in that corner of the world."[17]
Though Dering indicated that he was "not allowed till I
see you to name names," it was already known that several
of the younger Fellows at Trinity had indeed "signed up."
Three, in fact, were specifically named in the charter being
prepared for royal approval; William Thompson, Jonathan
Rogers, and James King.[18] For his own part, Dering concluded that the plan "certainly in its foundation is truly
Christian and noble, and so I heartily wish him success in
it."

Percival also found it a "noble scheme," but voiced a
significant word of caution: namely, that Berkeley must be
sure to have "the protection and encouragement of the
government." Otherwise, Percival warned, all kinds of
difficulties and delays would emerge from that complex,
overlapping morass of offices bearing some responsibility
for colonial affairs.[19] Petty bureaucrats and powerful lords
might not deliberately or openly block the plan, Percival
observed prophetically, but "they may perplex you in the
manner of carrying it on." Percival's best wishes nonetheless "attend you," as they continued to do through years
of preparation and frustration. His increasing anxiety over
his wife's health (her colic was treated with daily doses of
labdanum) brought Percival to look upon Bermuda's

17. Rand, *B & P*, p. 207.
18. GB *Works*, 7: 360.
19. Percival himself refers to the "Commissioners of the Plantations," the
SPG, and the bishop of London, but that only started to unravel the tangle of
authorities vaguely responsible somehow and in some way for colonial affairs.
After various royal experiments with the Privy Council and with special officers
or committees, William III in 1696 appointed the "Lords of Trade and Plantations," usually known as the Board of Trade. While all leading ministers were
members of the board, its center of skill and strength lay in eight paid commissioners (and it is to this group that Percival referred). The board had only advisory powers, but because often only the board really knew in any detail the
precise circumstances within the colonies, its advice tended to be taken most
seriously.

reputed therapeutic powers with growing favor. By early 1725 the brothers John and Philip Percival gave serious consideration to removing their entire families from England and Ireland to Bermuda. While John was writing that "we may try that air,"[20] Philip in that same February observed that several of his family were "eager and pressing to go" to "so delightfull and healthy a place as the Summer Islands." To Philip's obvious mystification, a close family friend "point blank declares against Sun Shine and a Clear Sky, to which she greatly preffers a dirty Winter in Sweet Dublin."[21]

In sweet Dublin, some others revealed themselves unpersuaded by promises of healthy climes and sapphire-blue skies. As Berkeley himself had predicted, a few found the whole scheme to be indeed "mad and chimerical." Even before any public announcement had been made, Dublin wits and rowdies, having heard the rumors, decided that they were too good to let lie. Late in 1723, a young child called at Berkeley's rooms in Dublin to present him with some satirical verses indicative of another sort of reaction to Bermuda.

The Humble Petition of a beautiful young Lady

To the Reverend Doctor B_rkl_y

Dear Doctor, here comes a Young Virgin untainted
To your Shrine at Bermudas to be Married and Sainted;
I am Young, I am Soft, I am Blooming and Tender,
Of all that I have I make you a Surrender;
My Innocence led by the Voice of your Fame
To your Person and Virtue must put in its Claim:
And now I behold you I truly believe,

---

20. Rand, *B & P*, pp. 209-10, 225; letters dated June 30, 1723, and Feb. 6, 1725.
21. BM Add. Ms. 47030, fol. 135; letter dated Feb. 24, 1725.

That you'r as like Adam as I am like Eve:
Before the dire Serpent their Virtue betray'd,
And taught them to Fly from the Sun, to the Shade:
But you, as in you a new Race has begun,
Are Teaching to Fly from the Shade to the Sun;
For you in Great Goodness your Friends are Persuading
To go, and to live, and to be wise in your Eden.
Oh! let me go with you, Oh! Pity my Youth,
Oh! take me from hence let me not loose [*sic*] my
Truth;
Sure you that have Virtue so much in your mind,
Can't think to leave me who am Virtue behind,
If you'll make me your Wife, Sir, in Time you may filla
Whole Town with your Children and likewise your Villa;
I famous for Breeding, you Famous for knowledge,
I'll Found a whole Nation, you'll Found a whole
Colledge;
When many long Ages in Joys we have Spent,
Our Souls we'll resign with utmost content:
And gently we'll Sink between Cypress and Yew,
You lying by me, and I lying by you.[22]

22. The Broadside bears neither date nor place of publication, but judging
from the contemporary correspondence, it was probably printed in Dublin in
1723. Also see Philip Percival's letter to his brother (November 9, 1723) in
Rand, *B & P*, pp. 213-15. The "beautiful young lady's" petition was followed
by the Reverend Dr. Berkeley's purported response, which begins and ends as
follows:

> Dear Miss, I thank you for your kind Surrender,
> I doubt not but you'r Soft, and young and Tender,
> As for your Dex'trous Faculty of Breeding,
> Your Species seldom fail of well succeeding:
>
> *   *   *
>
> Since Eden once was lost by Woman's base Device,
> Who'd bring a Woman to his Paradise?
> I live an Easy, Sweet, and Graceful Life,
> My Study my Companion, my Books my Wife.

As long as scurrility was confined to Dublin's pubs, no serious cavil threatened the Bermuda scheme. Yet that plan must have a hearing in the higher echelons (London's more than Dublin's) in order to win something of that official "protection and encouragement" necessary for its execution. At this critical juncture in 1724, an old friend once more intervened. Jonathan Swift in a timely letter to Lord Carteret, now lord lieutenant of Ireland, cajoled and mocked in serious Swiftian fashion on behalf of George Berkeley and his dream. "For three years past," Swift wrote, Berkeley "hath been struck with the notion of founding an university in Bermuda, by a charter from the Crown." And even though he holds "the best preferment among us," "his heart will break, if his deanery be not taken from him." Swift acknowledged that he had tried to discourage his fellow dean "by the coldness of courts and ministers who will interpret all this as impossible and a vision; but nothing will do." Thus, concluded the master satirist, one had a choice: either to encourage "one of the first men in this kingdom" to stay quietly at home, or else help him "to compass his romantic design."[23]

In his letter Swift happened to mention that Berkeley had "shewed me a little tract which he designs to publish" where he will lay out "his whole scheme of a life academico-philosophical." Just a few months later that little tract emerged under the title, *A Proposal For the better Supplying of Churches in our Foreign Plantations, and for Converting the Savage American to Christianity.*[24] Some of

23. In Luce, *Life*, pp. 100–01; letter dated Sept. 3, 1724. Carteret's ability to assist Berkeley, should he have desired to do so, was limited by his recent feuding with Robert Walpole, who had maneuvered him out of London back into Ireland and out of the position of secretary of state; J. H. Plumb, *England in the Eighteenth Century* (Middlesex, 1950, 1963), pp. 61-62.

24. London, 1724. Probably the tract was published in January or early February, 1724 Old Style, but 1725 New. In Berkeley's *Miscellany* (published

the detail resembled that already spelled out in Berkeley's earlier letter to Percival, but other items discussed in these twenty-two pages found themselves new or more fully clothed. In addition to explaining the advantages of Bermuda as before, Berkeley now described the disadvantages of locating the college elsewhere—especially on the mainland of America. Revealing a surprising degree of misinformation, Berkeley wrote of the continent that it possessed "little sense of religion"; rather, "a most notorious corruption of morals prevailed." Many Anglican clergymen there, "very meanly qualified both in learning and morals," have "quit their native country on no other motive, than that they are not able to procure a livelihood in it." Churches in America "are now a drain for the very dregs and refuse of ours." Harvard and Yale exist "to little or no purpose," an unwarranted criticism that Berkeley quietly dropped from the second edition of the *Proposal* published later in the same year. And native Americans, the author noted, were eminently educable, "not being violently attached to any false system of their own."[25]

Apart from his scanty or wrong information about the mainland (chiefly negative) and his misinformation about Bermuda (wholly positive), Berkeley correctly saw sea travel in the 1720s as the chief means for bringing together all of Britain's western colonial empire. And Bermuda, virtually alone of that empire, maintained commercial contact not primarily with Europe but with the American continent and the Caribbean islands. Unlike Barbados, which was virtually a part of South America and which, in

---

in 1752), publication date for the *Proposal* is given as 1725. Percival had a copy by February 6, 1725 New Style. The first edition, whose wording is followed here, is available in a facsimile reprint under the title *British Imperialism: Three Documents* (New York, 1972).

25. 1724 edition, pp. 3, 4, 5, 16, 19.

addition, had too much trade, wealth, and corruption, Bermuda was just remote enough to allow a quiet, controlled development. Furthermore, not subject to "the inroads of savages" as backcountry America was, nor hindered by the necessity to travel great distances overland (as on the mainland where there were "neither inns, nor carriages, nor bridges over the rivers" to facilitate travel), Bermuda remained the "one spot" that met all criteria.[26]

Since the *Proposal* (unlike Berkeley's letter to Percival) was a public document, it included a public appeal—indeed, several appeals: to nationalist pride, to Roman Catholic phobias, and to prospective contributors. In the spirit of Richard Hakluyt a century and a half earlier, Berkeley declared that the fate of the empire might hang upon the encouragement of this design; if her colonies should fall under the influence of other nations, then Britain's wealth and "so considerable a branch of his majesty's revenue" would fall too. Likewise in the spirit of Hakluyt and Samuel Purchas, Berkeley reminded his readers that "the protestant religion hath of late years considerably lost ground, and America seems the likeliest place, wherein to make up for what hath been lost in Europe, provided the proper methods are taken." If the proper method (namely, that described in this very *Proposal*) be not taken, then Spain in the south and France in the north "may one day spread the religion of Rome, and with it the usual hatred to protestants, throughout all the savage nations in America."

26. Ibid., pp. 9, 10. Berkeley's highly favorable and unfortunately outdated impressions of Bermuda were probably drawn from the enthusiastic reports of The Reverend Lewis Hughes, written a century earlier: *A Letter, Sent into England from the Summer Ilands* (1615); and, *A Plaine and True Relation of the Goodnes Of God towards the Sommer Ilands* (1621). See Louis B. Wright, *Religion and Empire: The Alliance between Piety and Commerce in English Expansion 1558-1625* (Chapel Hill, N. C., 1943; reprinted New York, 1965), pp. 105, 113-14.

For fear that some may have missed the point, Berkeley
would make it ringlingly clear that "the honour of the
crown, nation and church of England" does depend on the
successful prosecution of his Bermuda plan. And success-
fully prosecuted, "it will cast no small lustre on his
majesty's reign, and derive a blessing from heaven on his
administration." And now the solicitation: £10, which
would be enough to lodge, feed, clothe, and educate a
student for one year, or £200 which would become an
endownment to maintain "one missionary at the college
for ever."[27]

A second edition of the *Proposal* which appeared a few
months later (and was published in both Dublin and
London) provided an opportunity to correct minor errors,
to add some more lines on the acknowledged difficulty of
converting the Indians, to insert a paragraph emphasizing
that "gospel liberty" need not require immediate emancipa-
tion for baptized blacks, and to issue a forceful declaration
that the English, too, have "spiritual Wants" not now
being met in the New World (instead of gaining converts,
the English are often "themselves degenerated into
Heathens").[28] But the main reason for sending forth a second edition so quickly was to announce the great good
news: Berkeley's college now possessed a royal charter.[29]

For a month or more Berkeley's request for a charter had
been bouncing about the cavernous halls of government.
Presented in the name of "George Berkeley Doctor in
Divinity & Dean of Derry" as well as in the names of "William
Thompson, Jonathan Rogers, & James King Masters of

27. *Proposal*, pp. 17, 18, 21. In his appeal for funds, Berkeley even offered
a kind of Protestant indulgence: "whoever would be glad to cover a multitude
of sins by an extensive and well-judged charity—" p. 21.
   28. For the later editions of the *Proposal*, see GB *Works*, 7: 337-61, with
editorial introductions. Quotations are from pp. 346, 358-59.
   29. Ibid., 7: 360-61.

Arts & Fellows of Trinity College near Dublin," the petition briefly outlined the plan for "a College or Seminary in a proper place where Students may be safe from the Contagion of Vice and Luxury." After naming Bermuda as such a place, the petition offered rules and procedures for the operation of the school. Berkeley not surprisingly was named president, with nine fellows to be appointed (Thompson, Rogers, and King were only the first third of the full complement). Regular reports were to be made to the bishop of London (named official Visitor) and to the secretary of state (designated chancellor). Permission was sought for the President and Fellows to "hold their Preferments for a year & a half after their arrival in Bermuda," and for the college to enjoy a pedagogical monopoly: namely, that no one else "teach the Liberal Arts in the Islands of Bermuda" except by royal license. And for an institution dedicated to training missionaries, the choice of name was foreordained: St. Paul's College.[30]

When the petition was first submitted on February 16, 1725, the duke of Newcastle informed the bishop of London that the king "is very well inclined to give all due encouragement to so good and usefull an undertaking."[31] On February 24, the Board of Trade and Plantations informed Berkeley of the board's "desire to speak with him on Friday morning next," requesting also the presence of the bishop of London at that meeting. Two days later, Berkeley and Bishop Gibson attended, the board listened, and, on March 2, gave its blessing: "Having discoursed with Dean Berkley [*sic*] upon his petition, we have no objection to so laudable an undertaking, provided the said Colledge

30. Ibid., pp. 363-65. Also see Calendar of State Papers, Colonial Series, *America and West Indies, 1724-5* (London, 1936), pp. 328-29 (document 506); (hereafter *Amer. and West Ind.*).

31. *Amer. and West Ind.*, p. 327 (document 505).

be not impowered to purchase or receive above 1000 acres
of land in the Bermuda Islands, and that their revenue in
any other part of your Majesty's Dominions do not exceed
£2,000 a year."[32] On March 15, the attorney general
approved the design as being "of a very usefull Tendency";
he expressed some concern, however, about the lack of an
endowment and further offered the opinion that granting a
monopoly on the teaching of liberal arts was "contrary to
law."[33] On the matter of endowment, Berkeley had suggested that the will of Sir Nathaniel Riche of Bermuda,
which provided for land to be set aside for a "free school,"
might be decided in favor of St. Paul's College, but the
legal issue had not been resolved. By the end of April, the
charter reached its final form and, on June 3, Berkeley
could report that the "Charter hath passed all the seals,
and is now in my custody."[34] In May of 1722, all of this
had been but an idea perceived in the mind of one man;
now, three years later, the highest officers of church and
state had given substance to that spirit. If now some
financial substance could be added, then perhaps the President and his Fellows could indeed sail for Bermuda "next
spring."

While England in the early eighteenth century did in-
dulge in luxury and vanity, as Berkeley and others charged,
the nation also indulged in philanthropy—often on a grand
scale. Not all fortunes evaporated in reckless speculation or

32. *Journal of the Commissioners for Trade and Plantations . . .* (London,
1928), pp. 151-52; *Amer. and West Ind.*, p. 346 (document 540).

33. GB *Works*, 7: 365-66.

34. *Amer. and West Ind.*, p. 364 (document 586); GB *Works*, 8: 137-38
(letters to Thomas Prior, June 3 and June 12, 1725). On April 20, Berkeley
had written to Prior: "I have obtained reports from the Bishop of London, the
Board of Trade and Plantations, and the Attorney and Solicitor General, in
favour of the Bermuda scheme, and hope to have the warrant signed by his
Majesty this week." Also see David Berman, "Some New Bermuda Berkeleiana," *Hermathena* 110 (1970): 25.

in conspicuous consumption. Two private societies originating around the turn of the century illustrate this philanthropic drive; moreover, they both bore directly on Berkeley and the Bermuda plan. In 1699, Thomas Bray (1656-1730), Anglican clergyman and briefly commissary to Maryland, founded the Society for Promoting Christian Knowledge (SPCK). Two years later he brought into being the Society for the Propagation of the Gospel in Foreign Parts (SPG).[35] These two societies, both heavily dependent upon philanthropic giving, played vital roles in extending to many parts of the world that "protestant religion" with which Berkeley was so concerned. George Berkeley joined the SPCK early in 1725 and the SPG immediately upon his return from the New World. To many of the patrons of Bray's two societies, Berkeley also made his own financial appeal.

His first gift, however, seemed more heaven-sent than solicited. At least, it arrived without warning and even before the project had received royal approbation. Jonathan Swift's special friend, Esther van Homrigh or "Vanessa," died in Dublin on June 4, 1723. In her will, prepared only a month before, she left half of her estate (some £2,000 to £3,000) to an astounded if grateful George Berkeley. In reporting the news immediately to Percival, Berkeley declared that it "probably will surprise your Lordship as much as it does me . . . having never met [the Lady] in the whole course of my life."[36] Because Vanessa's relationship with Swift was uneven at best, his biographers have speculated that Vanessa left this large sum to Berkeley rather than

35. See H. P. Thompson, *Thomas Bray* (London, 1954), as well as his history of the SPG, *Into All Lands* . . . (London, 1951); also, Bernard C. Steiner, ed., *Rev. Thomas Bray* (Baltimore, 1901; reprint New York, 1972).

36. GB *Works*, 8: 130.

Swift both out of spite[37] or affection.[38] In either event,
Berkeley, whose plans were known outside of Dublin's
pubs as well as within them, could only be cheered by
Percival's enthusiastic response: "We all conclude that you
will now persist in your thoughts of settling in Bermuda,
and prosecute the noble scheme which . . . may in some
time exalt your name beyond that of St. Xavier."[39]

Not until the royal charter was granted, however, did the
active solicitation of private gifts begin. By that time,
Berkeley had managed to enlist an impressive group of
trustees or overseers for funds received: the duke of Newcastle who had general jurisdiction over the colonies, the
archbishop of Canterbury, the lord high chancellor, and of
course the bishop of London. To this distinguished quartet,
Berkeley added a much longer list of persons scattered
throughout the kindgom in whose hands "contributions
and subscriptions may be deposited."[40] Percival, naturally,
was among the first to subscribe, pledging £200, as did
even the prime minister, Robert Walpole.[41] The Treasurer
of the SPCK was among the many prepared to accept contributions on Berkeley's behalf. That Society, as represented
so ably in its secretary-treasurer, Henry Newman, became
both champion and clearing house for all information concerning the "romantic Design." In the fall of 1725, Newman
reported that "about 2000 £ has been promis'd or pay'd
into [the] Undertaking."[42] By December of that year,
Berkeley himself reckoned "that the subscriptions amount

37. See, for example, M. M. Rossi and J. M. Hone, *Swift* (New York, 1934),
p. 294.

38. See, for example, Nigel Dennis, *Jonathan Swift* (New York, 1964), p. 113.

39. Rand, *B & P*, p. 209.

40. GB *Works*, 7: 361.

41. Rand, *B & P*, p. 223.

42. SPCK Society Letters, vol. 16; letter from Newman to Percival, Oct. 21,
1725.

to £3400."[43] And the following March, Newman could write that Berkeley "has about 5000 £ promis'd, and is dayly adding to that Sum, which . . . may be so encreased as to enable him to being to make his Settlement the ensuing Summer."[44]

The tides continued to move, bringing Bermuda closer and closer. Yet £5000, even added to Vanessa's legacy (still in litigation) and possible lands marked for a "free school," hardly constituted a firm financial base for the college. Berkeley, however, was learning how to play for even higher stakes. In late 1725 and following, he concentrated on that vital government "protection and support" that Percival had wisely urged. "I am in a fair way," he wrote his classmate Thomas Prior in February, 1726, "of having a very noble endowment for the College of Bermuda."[45] By the terms of the Treaty of Utrecht (1713), Britain had acquired certain lands from France on St. Christopher (St. Kitts) Island in the Caribbean. Those lands were to be sold for public benefit, and what better benefit than an endowment for St. Paul's College? Using all of the "diligence, patience and skill that I was master of," Berkeley worked for weeks to persuade Parliament of the wisdom of just such a use of these lands. The king was favorable, if only Robert Walpole and the House of Commons might see their way clear to following the royal lead.[46] On May 12, 1726, Berkeley, with obvious relief and satisfaction, informed Prior of the happy turn of events.

43. GB *Works*, 8: 145.

44. SPCK Society Letter, vol. 16; letter from Newman to The Reverend William Carey at Bristol, March 22, 1726. For many indications of support for the project, see the SPCK Abstract Letter Book, vol. 13, entries 8435, 8450, 8561, 8564, 8574, 8576, 8577, 8586, 8617, 8636, 8639, 8641, 8655, 8671, 8689, 8711, 8725, 8743—all in 1725-26!

45. GB *Works*, 8: 151.

46. Luce, *Life*, p. 108.

After six weeks' of struggle against an earnest opposition from different interests and motives, I have
yesterday carried my point just as I desired in the
House of Commons, by an extraordinary majority,
none having the confidence to speak against it, and not
above two giving their negative; which was done in so
low a voice as if they themselves were ashamed of it.
They were both considerable men in stocks, in trade,
and in the city: and in truth I have had more opposition
from that sort of men, and from the governors and
traders to America, than from any others. But, God be
praised, there is an end of all their narrow and mercan-
tile views and endeavours, as well as of the jealousies
and suspicions of others . . . who apprehended this
College may produce an independency in America, or
at least lessen its dependency upon England.[47]

Political and commercial opposition notwithstanding,
the long fight seemed over, and perhaps only in time. "I
am heartily tired of soliciting," Berkeley wrote a few days
later,[48] and a munificent grant of £20,000 might make it
never again necessary. Precisely how and when the money
was to be paid had not been specified. Newman the next
year stated that "The King has graciously granted to Dr.
Berkeley 1000 £ p. añ. out of lands belonging to the
Crown at St. Christophers as a perpetual Endowm.ᵗ of the
College to be erected at Bermudas,"[49] but the sad fact is
that much ambiguity about the payment remained. If one

47. GB *Works*, 8: 155. With respect to the anxieties over American independence, even this early in the century, see chapter 7 below.

48. GB *Works*, 8: 156.

49. SPCK Society Letters, vol. 18; letter from Newman to The Reverend
Mr. Paley at Leeds, May 27, 1727. Also see Berkeley's petition to the king,
which he presented as "President of St. Pauls College in Bermuda," *Hermathena*
110 (1970): 25.

were looking for assurance, however, surely the resounding vote left little ambiguity, with two timid "no's" scarcely audible. Perhaps the skies over Bermuda were, after all, really sapphire-blue.

In Britain, on the other hand, the clouds never totally disappeared. Even in the *Proposal* itself, Berkeley recognized that he had opposition. Some will object, he wrote there, that missionary energies should be better spent at home among "papists, infidels and dissenters of all denominations" than being squandered abroad. But two answers suggested themselves: first, "religion like light is imparted without being diminished"; and second, "ignorance is not so incurable as error" (that is, missionaries stand a better chance with the savage Indians than with the wayward English encumbered "with all that rubbish of superstition and error").[50] This in 1724. In 1725 and 1726, Berkeley continued to allude to the discordant chorus, though his mood generally was that expressed to Prior in January of the latter year: the Bermuda plan will "thrive and flourish in spite of all opposition."[51]

As Berkeley indicated above, most of the opposition stemmed from the commercial and merchant classes, with some from the political interests. More serious objections to Berkeley's plans came, however, from persons essentially sympathetic to his goals but highly critical of his means. These persons, moreover, had one clear and telling advantage over George Berkeley: they knew America. All had either lived there at one time or were living there when they voiced their criticisms. Quite apart from the ambitious plans for a college, the descriptions of Bermuda which now flowed into England gave it a sharply different cast from that displayed in the *Proposal*: the political situation

50. 1724 edition, pp. 18-19.
51. GB *Works*, 8: 149.

"mean and ridiculous," "petty communities," "incessant and violent wrangles," and vagabonds, drifters, and beachcombers "living not like animals that are imbued with reason."[52]

In 1726, Benjamin Colman, a respected Congregational minister in Boston, revealed his "surprise at ye news of a designed College upon ye Island of Bermuda, without any Grammar Schools there, or in ye Islands . . . to supply a College." Berkeley was beginning at the wrong end of things, Colman warned; first a number of grammar schools must be established "& then lay ye foundation of a College, & build but a part of it, & let it grow as Students increase."[53] Simon Smith, Anglican clergyman living on Antigua, wrote Bishop Gibson that Bermuda was the "unfittest place in America" for what Dean Berkeley had proposed. Blacks were totally dominated by their masters; Indians would certainly resist being transported all the way to Bermuda; neither Indians nor blacks could contribute anything to their support on this "poor and barren Island." On the whole, South Carolina, Smith concluded, would be "the best place in America for the conversion of Indians." Being numerous and nearby, Indians might actually permit their children to receive religious instruction in a Carolina college, whereas under no circumstances would they part with their children to embark for "another Country."[54]

By far the severest, most damaging criticism in 1727 came from a fellow missionary and Anglican cleric whose interest in and commitment to America was beyond dispute: none other than Thomas Bray. Bray, having visited America almost thirty years before, had the New World much on his mind even before that brief sojourn. In 1695, for

52. *Amer. and West Ind.,* pp. xlvii–xlviii.
53. Colman to the bishop of Peterborough, Sept. 30, 1726; Fulham Papers, 4: 192.
54. Smith to Gibson, May 5, 1727; Fulham Papers, 19: 148–49.

example, he had published *Proposals for Encouraging Learning and Religion in the Foreign Plantations*. So in 1727 Bray was no newcomer to the scene, no amateur, no dilletante. Nor was he a member of that commercial class whose objections could so easily be dismissed as thinly disguised avarice and self-interest. In the same year that he founded the SPG, Bray published *A Memorial Representing the Present State of Religion, on the Continent of North-America* (London, 1701). Two decades before the Bermuda idea was born, Bray observed that "the Bermudas, or Summer-Islands, formerly reckoned very plentiful, as well as pleasant and healthful . . . are now known to be very poor and barren." The radical change came about because great cedars that had protected the islands "from hurtful Winds" had fallen, and because of "a certain Worm or Ant, so much increased upon them, as totally in some places to devour their corn."[55]

In 1727, Bray spoke directly to the Berkeley scheme. Choosing not to communicate quietly by letter to friends or to the bishop of London, Bray in that year published his *Missionalia: Or, A Collection of Missionary Pieces Relating to the Conversion of the Heathen; Both the African Negroes and the American Indians*. One of his "missionary pieces" took the form of a memorial to the Anglican clergy residing in Maryland. That was the form; the substance was a sustained and devasting critique of George Berkeley's *Proposal*. Bray, by frequent references to his own experiences, his personal observations, his knowledge of the geography of America, his familiarity with the different Indian tribes, et cetera, made the point that the good dean of Derry simply did not know whereof he spoke. He did not personally know Bermuda, and what he had learned

55. P. 8. Bray visited America in 1699 as Commissary, spending three months in Maryland.

from others was woefully out of date. He did not know
America, nor its schools, its morals, its religion, nor especially its Anglican clergy, whom he had characterized as
"very meanly qualified both in learning and in morals."
Bray, on the other hand, could "testify from my own
knowledge" to the burden of those clergymen's duties,
the enormity of their parishes, the sincerity of their intentions, and the fruitfulness of their ministry. And at the
very least, you clergymen in Maryland, Bray wrote, with
a bitter jab at the Irish dean, "have not yet Learnt that
Black Art of turning large Parishes having *Cure of Souls*
into *Sine-Cures*, or as some call them *Non-cures*, or utterly
leaving your own Cures to live elsewhere, to no purpose
of your Ministry, but like Lay-Gentlemen, on the Rents
thereof."[56] Who was this dean of Derry to besmirch the
reputation of America's dedicated, hard-working clergy!

Most of all, Berkeley did not know the Indians, nor did
he comprehend what was sensible, possible, and reasonable
with respect to their conversion. If one understood anything at all about either blacks in Africa or Indians in America, one knew that civilizing and Christianizing must go
hand in hand, slowly, moderately, gently. One could not
treat a person's religious state while ignoring his civil state;
one could not plant Christian faith and Christian morality
"upon an unprepar'd Soil." Above all else, one could not
suppose that Indians would voluntarily send their children
to far-off Bermuda, or that Christians would be so cruel as
to agree to taking their children from them by force, either
as prisoners of war or whatever, to that distant and wretched
place. "I shall only pray to God, not to deliver us to such an
Infatuation, as to use the most *Unchristian*, or rather the
most *Anti-Christian* Method to propagate the Gospel."[57] If

56. "Memorial" in *Missionalia*, pp. 63–64.
57. Ibid., p. 73.

Berkeley had bothered to inform himself about the College
of William and Mary, for example, he would have learned
that Indians would not send their children a mere "Forty or
Fifty Miles," even where they "may come and see their
Children, and be satisfy'd by their own Eyes how kindly
they are us'd." How, then, could it "be thought they will
Voluntarily send them Six Hundred Miles, nay from some
Places a Thousand over Sea, thence scarcely ever to hope
for a Return!" The most charitable explanation for Berkeley's setting forth "so crude a Scheme" was his "want of
Experience."[58]

Nonetheless, let us suppose for argument's sake, or for
charity's sake, that Berkeley did eventually acquire some
Indian scholars on his island. What sort of education was
he then prepared to give them? The wrong sort. He actually
planned to award a Master of Arts in liberal studies to these
savages! Colleges no doubt have their place, Bray acknowledged, especially "in Countries already cultivated, and in

---

58. Ibid., p. 72. Bray's own counterproposal included the introduction of
artificers—tailors, carpenters, farmers—into the regions immediately adjacent
to the English settlements. Working gradually with these already somewhat
"more Humaniz'd" Indians, civilizing and Christianizing them, one could
incidentally create "a good Barrier to the English against the Incursions of the
Wild and Savage Indians, and against the French of Canada, who halloo them
to fall upon us in the Out-skirts of our Colonies" (pp. 61–62). In comparing
his plan with Berkeley's, Bray even offered a cost analysis, showing the dean's
endeavor to be vastly, prohibitively more expensive. On the highly questionable
matter of capturing Indian boys for removal to Bermuda, the practical Bray
noted what an expensive (as well as "Anti-Christian") undertaking this would
be. Let us suppose that five Indian lads might finally make it to Bermuda. "If
the five Indian Youths must be Bought, and so brought to the College as
Captives taken in War, I dare scarcely mention what I am told they exact at
New-England for them, if they happen to take any. The Reason of the excessive
Rate . . . is to Ballance that requir'd by the Frenchify'd Indians lying between
New-England and Canada, who will have a hundred Pounds for every English
Person they take, or they will Scalp him. So that from Self-Defence they are
necessitated, I am told, to put no less upon an Indian Boy than a hundred
Pounds" (pp. 82–83).

some Measure Polished; yet among Savages, I cannot conceive, but even a *Charity School* . . . taught tho' by old
Women, would answer the Ends better than by Professors
of Sciences. And the Mechanicks would be more usefull
taught among such than the Liberal Arts.'' [59]

Though Bray maintained a degree of objectivity regarding the plan which the dean had ''spread throughout the
Nation,'' his irritation was evident—and probably war-
ranted. He was irritated by the naïveté, by the lack of con-
sultation, but most of all by the slanders levied against the
Anglican clergy then serving in America. For more than
two decades, Bray's SPG had been sending missionaries to
the British colonies; the calumny reflected, therefore, upon
the SPG and upon Bray himself. Moreover, were Berkeley's
broad charges to be believed, England's entire missionary
enterprise would be threatened. ''You see,'' Bray wrote the
Maryland clergy, ''how he has been pleased to Blacken you
therein [in the *Proposal*] in a very free Way.'' He thinks
that you were sent to America primarily to convert the
Indian, whereas ''you were sent to Preach the Gospel to
the *English* Planters, to prevent their turning Heathen in
Time.'' Now that the slander has been hurled, however,
and to avoid ''pernicious Consequences,'' you who ''live
upon the Borders of the *American Heathen* . . . are better
able to Judge what Method may be taken with best Hopes
of Success, both to *Humanize* and *Christianize* those Bar-
barians.'' So if you will now give your attention to this
matter, we can ''Vindicate your Characters from the Re-
proaches That Gentleman has been pleas'd to load you
withal.'' Among the pernicious consequences which Bray
had every reason to fear was the withdrawal of all royal

59. Ibid., pp. 96–97. While Berkeley in his *Proposal* did suggest that ''a
good tincture of other learning'' be provided (''a practical mathematicks,''
''some skill in physick''), his emphasis for both English and Indian youths
was clearly on the traditional liberal arts.

aid. "For if the Government, which it Costs some Hundred
Pounds Yearly in the Royal Bounty of Twenty Pounds to
every Missionary going over, shou'd take it into their Heads
to save that Charge as bestow'd upon a worthless Set of
Men; Good God! What a Fatal Blow will this Man have
given to the *Propagating the Gospel in Foreign Parts.*"[60]
But if a fatal blow had been struck, it was more by Bray
than by Berkeley.

Bray also indicated that many stood ready to assist the
dean in his enterprise "could they see it set upon a Practi-
cable Method." Among those prepared to help, "perhaps
none could, or would be more ready and Capable to Assist
him therein than our *Religious Societies.*"[61] Certainly
Berkeley had not intended to castigate or to weaken either
of Bray's important societies. Berkeley's subsequent relationship to the SPG was one of continuous good will and
specific financial assistance. With respect to the SPCK,
Berkeley worked in closest harmony with Henry Newman
from 1725 on. But Newman like Bray, though more privately and mildly, wished that the dean had done more
consulting and checking before publishing his *Proposal* in
1724.

Of all Berkeley's potential allies, Newman was in the best
position to advise him about America. Born in Rehoboth,
Massachusetts, in 1670, Newman (despite being orphaned
at the age of eight) entered Harvard in 1683; there he established contacts and friendships that proved of great value in
later life. Initially setting out to follow his father and grand-
father into the Congregational ministry, Newman by the
time he took his first degree in 1687 seemed less interested
in the ministry and less sure of his Congregationalism. After
taking his Master of Arts in 1690, Newman remained on at

60. Ibid., pp. 104–05.
61. Ibid., p. 98.

Harvard as the college librarian from 1690 to 1693. Restless both in mind and in body, Newman engaged in commercial activity for several years, traveled extensively, worked for the duke of Somerset, switched to Anglicanism, and in 1708 became secretary of the SPCK—a post he retained until his death in 1743.[62]

Henry Newman not only knew America, he knew highly placed Americans, both dissenters and churchmen. Berkeley, who knew neither the land nor its people, eventually came to rely upon Newman for all kinds of assistance and advice. Had the "eventually" only been "initially," Berkeley's career in America would have run a far different course. In August of 1725, Newman sent a copy of the *Proposal* to the governor of the Bahamas, stating that "the Project for creating a college at Bermudas is so far advanced that a Charter is already granted for that purpose . . . I can't help wishing the Undertakers could have been persuaded to have settled in your Government, or somewhere else nearer to the Continent for whose benefit it is chiefly intended."[63] The following November, Newman wrote to a clergyman at Leeds that hopes for Berkeley's design were high; yet he added (and then crossed out in his copy and probably in the original) that objections were already raised to the choice of Bermuda: provisions there were sometimes scarce, the distance from the mainland was too great, and difficulties "will attend prevailing upon the Indian Natives of America to leave the Continent for the Benefit of an Education of the advantage of wch they have so little apprehension."[64] In the spring of 1727, one of Newman's correspondents informed him that the scarcity of food in

62. See Leonard W. Cowie, *Henry Newman, An American in London 1708–1743* (London, 1956).

63. SPCK Society Letter, vol. 16; Newman to Colonel George Phenney, Aug. 18, 1725.

64. Ibid.; Newman to The Rev. W. Henry Robinson, Nov. 4, 1725.

Bermuda "grows every year worse"; the advice from Bermuda was "that if Mr. Dean Berkeley's Scheme is not too far gone, he should be persuaded to go to Pensylvania [*sic*] or New York."[65] Two years later Newman still expressed regret that Berkeley had not gone "to America for experience one Summer before he had published his proposal."[66]

Beyond question, the *Proposal* was flawed. By 1727 or 1728 the question was whether, though flawed, it could still be saved. The Indians, after all, were a subsidiary consideration; the main thrust of the plan, as the *Proposal's* lead title made clear, was "the better supplying of churches in our Foreign Plantations." And the choice of Bermuda was not the foundation upon which the whole grand scheme rested—though now a royal charter did specify Bermuda, and that might occasion some awkwardness. What was pivotal, central, and fundamental was saving England from ruin. And this could be accomplished only, or so it seemed, by leaving England to create elsewhere a society purged of luxury and greed, to instill a Christianity both useful and true, and to bring into being an "Athens of the World," a "Utopian Seminary."[67] Just a century earlier, other Englishmen had reacted precisely the same way, as they too believed it necessary to leave England in order to save England, to escape a corrupt church in order to create a pure church. Since that great Puritan migration of the 1630s, England had been torn by revolution, tossed about by Cromwellian adventures, encouraged by a Restoration, dismayed by Jacobean pretensions and plots, transferred

65. SPCK Abstract Letter Book, vol. 14, #9214; William Cary of Bristol, writing April 8, 1727, and quoting "a Gent. who has a good Estate in Bermuda."

66. SPCK Society Letters, vol. 20; Newman to Percival, Sept. 25, 1729.

67. The first phrase was Percival's in a letter to his brother Philip, Feb. 6, 1725; Rand, *B & P*, p. 225. The second was Peter Tustian's, one of those Maryland clergymen whom Bray addressed in 1727; in a letter appended to Bray's "Memorial," in *Missionalia*, p. 117.

to a foreign dynasty, and tempted by strange gods. Who
spoke now for England's morals, for England's church, for
England's destiny? Other nations have been wicked, "but
we are the first who have been wicked upon principle."

> God grant the time be not near when men shall say:
> "This island was once inhabited by a religious, brave,
> sincere people, of plain uncorrupt manners, respecting
> inbred worth rather than titles and appearances, assert-
> ors of liberty, lovers of their country, jealous of their
> own rights, and unwilling to infringe the rights of others;
> improvers of learning and useful arts, enemies to luxury,
> tender of other men's lives and prodigal of their own;
> inferior in nothing to the old Greeks or Romans, and
> superior to each of those people in the perfections of
> other. Such were our ancestors during their rise and
> greatness; but they degenerated, grew servile flatterers
> of men in power, adopted Epicurean notions, became
> venal, corrupt, injurious, which drew upon them the
> hatred of God and man, and occasioned their final
> ruin." [68]

There lay the heart of the 1724 *Proposal*, there the
essence of Berkeley's dream: to create a New World community, to rescue historic Christianity, to purify and preserve Western civilization. Somewhere, and precisely where
did not matter all that much, one must be an evangel for
that "common mutual faith" without which a society cannot survive. Somewhere one must build "a fountain, or
reservoir, of learning and religion" from which rivulets will
go "streaming thro' all parts of America." And if one truly
considers "the divine power of religion, the innate force of
reason and virtue," then the steady streaming, even from a
single source, "must in due time have a great effect." [69]

68. GB *Works*, 6: 84–85.
69. 1724 edition of the *Proposal*, pp. 20–21.

But was it too late? For a time, all had seemed propitious, as the king had granted the charter, Parliament had cast its vote, and supporters had made their pledges. Just as momentum had been so nicely building, however, dissident voices were heard, objections were raised, faults and flaws loudly decried, ridicule and raillery bruited about. Was it possible that the whole grand plan might be scuttled and lost, England's hope destroyed, because of these clouds that momentarily darkened those sapphire-blue skies? Should discouraging words and sharp criticism be allowed to carry the day ("there is hardly an enterprise or scheme whatsoever for the publick good, in which difficulties are not often shewing themselves, and as often overcome by the blessing of God, upon the prudence and resolution of the undertakers")?[70] On the other hand, was it resolution or was it foolhardiness to make one's move before Parliament's £20,000 was actually in hand? Yet, if one made no move at all, did not this seem to betray a faintness of heart and wavering of purpose? What could one do, what must one do?

While time and tide are notoriously impatient, they now and again appear balanced, poised, hesitant—waiting only for that decisive act, that seizing of the helm, which nudges fate and, with a little luck, shapes a destiny. To George Berkeley, the summer of 1728 seemed such a moment. His plan, now six years aborning, showed signs of losing its novelty and zest. Convinced that time no longer worked for him, Berkeley vowed to give that nudge to history or heaven—or to Walpole. He would proceed, "privately," to set out for America, there to lay the foundation for his "Utopian Seminary," there to await the fulfillment of promises made, of hope cherished. Convinced also by now that Bermuda was a mistake, Berkeley wrote from Gravesend on September 5, 1728: "Tomorrow, with God's blessing, I set sail for Rhode Island."[71]

70. Ibid., p. 20.
71. GB *Works*, 8: 189; George Berkeley to Thomas Prior.

3 *Philosopher in Residence*

Already have the Fates your Path prepar'd
And sure Presage your future Sway declar'd:
When Westward, like the Sun, you took your Way,
And from benighted Britain bore the Day . . .
John Dryden, from *Fables Ancient and Modern* (1700)

Almost certainly Henry Newman chose Rhode Island for
George Berkeley. First, Newman recognized that Bermuda
was unsuitable. Second, he knew New England best and
could most readily assist Berkeley in making the initial contacts and adjustments. Moreover, Newman could appreciate
the fact that Rhode Island, unlike Massachusetts and Connecticut, possessed no college. And finally, he saw in Roger
Williams's colony the one spot in New England free from
Puritan establishment. The presence of a Church of Ireland
dean would not embarrass the government of Rhode Island
as it might those of her neighbors; at the same time, Berkeley would be spared possible slights or affronts unwittingly
offered by a dissenting government.

Once Rhode Island had been settled upon, Newman
became even more explicitly Berkeley's consultant, well-
wisher, and expediter. Two weeks before Berkeley sailed
from England, Newman provided him with a rash of letters
of introduction to friends and officials in New England. In
his brief note to Benjamin Colman in Boston, Newman
managed to convey his continuing affection for "our Country" and for Harvard, even while he commended Berkeley
and his "Errand" on which "I am sure he will be welcome
to you and all good men." Newman also mentioned that
two gentlemen joining the dean in his venture, John James

and Richard Dalton, were "men of Honour & Fortune who having travell'd through Europe to Rome now accompany the Dean & honour our Country with their presence, to see how the world look'd at the beginning of it after the Flood." Newman's failure to mention John Smibert so short a time before the party's departure suggests that the artist's decision to accompany them was made almost at the last minute.[1]

To the governor of Massachusetts, William Burnet, Newman recommended "to yr. Protection & advice, the Revd Dr Berkeley Dean of Londonderry who goes hence with His Majesty's Patent for laying a Foundation for Propagating Religion and Learning in America." Similarly, Newman indicated to New Hampshire's lieutenant governor (Benning Wentworth) that "Whatever civilities" he showed to Berkeley "will always be acknowledged as obligation on, s^r, yr. most obed. & humble ser^t." To fellow Anglican, Timothy Cutler of Boston, Newman dared to presume not only civility but friendship and assistance "in whatever may advance so noble a design."[2]

Newman took the greatest pains, however, in his letters addressed to Rhode Island, for here understanding and aid were most critical. It helped, of course, that Newman personally knew the governor, Joseph Jenckes, as he did most of those to whom he wrote. In writing to Jenckes, the SPCK secretary placed Berkeley's errand in the broadest

1. SPCK New England Letters, vol. 3; Newman to Colman, August 24, 1728. On September 5, Berkeley at least knew the passenger list, for he informed Thomas Prior that James, Dalton, and Smibert were all going to be on board; GB *Works*, 8: 189. That Berkeley's departure, and indeed his movements for some weeks prior to the departure, were somewhat secretive is further revealed in Newman's being quite unaware of Berkeley's marriage until he read about it in the *Daily Journal* in October.

2. All of these letters of introduction, dated August 24, 1728, were apparently placed in Berkeley's hands (one speaks of Berkeley as "the Bearer of this"); SPCK New England Letters, vol. 3.

context, speaking of the latter's "Zeal for the service of
Religion & Humanity." And in writing to Rhode Island's
colonial financier, Jahleel Brenton the Younger, Newman
again rose above the particularities of Bermuda and the
specificity of converting the Indians. "His Errand is to
inform himself wherein he can be serviceable to the Interests of Religion & Humanity in America."[3] Newman clearly
intended to leave the door open as wide as possible to mod-
ifications in or even redirection of the Bermuda scheme.
And Berkeley, too, soon revealed a readiness to amend
much of the detail he had so confidently set forth in 1724.

Newman and Berkeley shared another perspective, this
one concerning those shifting tides of history. One of
those many letters given to the dean to ease his way in the
New World, written to John Boydell in Boston, tended to
such mundane matters as arranging for Berkeley to have a
line of credit properly honored in New England. Then
Newman observed that those cosmopolitan travelers, James
and Dalton, "now condescend to honour our wilderness
with their Company." In a more philosophical vein, he
added:

> If these Gent. make a good report of us, other Gent. of
> their Fortunes may follow their Example, and by degrees
> transmit all the pleasures [he crossed out "politeness"]
> of Old to New England. I am sure their time and their
> fortunes would be much better spent than they are by
> many here in all the vanities ["Fox hunting" crossed
> out] that a Luxurious Age can invent. But the danger
> is that when N. Eng.^ld has got the same Temptations
> they'l fall into the same Excesses, and become another
> Old Eng.^ld blemis'd with Masquerades, Italians operas
> &c. of European vanities ["French" crossed out] w^ch

3. Ibid.

our forefathers knew nothing of, from wch only the
Grace of God can defend us. [4]

Here again, but from another pen, the "ruin of Great Britain" theme is heard. Perhaps in escaping from "benighted
Britain" one escaped England's ordained fate—especially if
"Zeal for the service of Religion & Humanity" should in a
wilderness prove contagious.

In that agonized decision to leave England (if "I continued there, the report would have obtained . . . that I had
dropped the design"; if "I had taken leave of my friends,
even those who assisted would have condemned my coming
abroad before the king's bounty was received"), Berkeley
confessed that he felt obliged to "come away in the private
manner that I did." [5] But within a month's time, the world
—at least Berkeley's world—knew. London's *Daily Journal*
(October 12, 1728) carried a story which, though inaccu-
rate in some details, did make a private matter now public.

> The Rev. Dr. Barkeley [*sic*] . . . sailed a few weeks since
> for the West-Indies in a Ship of 250 Tons, which he
> hired. . . . The Dean married an agreeable young Lady,
> about six Weeks before he set Sail. . . . They sail'd
> hence for Rhode Island, where the Dean intends to
> Winter, and to purchase an Estate . . . particularly for
> supplying Bermudas with Black Cattle and Sheep. The
> Dean's Grant of 2,000 £ [*sic*] on St. Christopher's is
> payable in two Years Time, and the Dean has a year
> and a half allow'd him afterwards, to consider whether
> he will stick to his College in Bermudas, or return to
> his Deanery of Derry. [6]

---

4. Ibid. Newman had planed to write even more letters "if a violent headache
had not prevented me."

5. GB *Works*, 8: 199; Berkeley to Percival, June 27, 1729.

6. *The Daily Journal*, Saturday, Oct. 12, 1728; British Museum Burney Collection, #2422. The £2,000 figure was probably only a typographical error.

In his first letter addressed to Berkeley in Rhode Island, Newman sent word that the news was now out, but granted that "I wonder you have been so long spar'd by our News writers this being the first acc! they have given of you since you went." He added, somewhat cryptically, "and some things being awkward represented I suspend my belieffs of them till I hear from you." In all probability the principal awkwardness lay in the *Journal*'s assertion that Berkeley planned to purchase land in Rhode Island (even if for Bermuda) and in the tentativeness implied in the dean's suspended judgment over whether to stay or return.

In any event, partly informed and partly misinformed, "the town" (as Newman referred to London) had been told; from that capital the word spread quickly into the surrounding country. In that other somewhat smaller town, Newport, news also reached out into the neighboring provinces. There the excitement centered not on Bermuda or black cattle or St. Christopher's, but on the person and presence of Berkeley himself. Anglicans were still a rarity in New England, and dignitaries of any rank an utter nonpareil. Headiest of all, here now in our midst would reside a world traveler, an intimate of London high society, and a scholar of great note. That Newport and New England should be so graced!

With regard to his scholarly reputation, Berkeley's acclaim in 1729 had not ascended to the heights that it would later reach. Early neglected in England itself, Berkeleyan ideas found greater receptivity in Scotland; Edinburgh's Rankenian Club corresponded with and discussed the Trinity scholar and his immaterialism from around 1717 on.[17] David Hume, a member of that club (as was John Smibert), read Berkeley and was much influenced by him, though in a direction

7. See Harry M. Bracken, *The Early Reception of Berkeley's Immaterialism 1710–1733* (The Hague, rev. ed., 1965).

quite different from that which Berkeley intended.[8] Hume
found the Irish philosopher to be chief of all the skeptics:
"all his arguments . . . admit of no answer and produce no
conviction. Their only effect is to cause that momentary
amazement and irresolution and confusion which is the
result of skepticism."[9] Yet skepticism was furthest from
Berkeley's mind as he sought, rather, "to demonstrate the
existence and attributes of God, the immortality of the
soul, the reconciliation of God's foreknowledge with freedom of men, and . . . to reduce [lead] men to the study of
religion and things useful. How far my endeavor will prove
successful, and whether I have been all this time in a dream
or no, time will manifest."[10]

An Essay Towards a New Theory of Vision (1709), shortly
followed by *A Treatise Concerning the Principles of Human
Knowledge* (1710), were intended to serve religion and
morality, not subvert them. Berkeley hoped to give the lie
to the swaggering materialists and to the new science in so
far as the latter found reality chiefly or solely in physical
stuff. In general, however, Berkeley's English audience
failed to get the point. Your *Principles* are treated here
with ridicule, Percival candidly reported to Berkeley in
Ireland: physicians deem you mad and clerics pity you
because you revel in novelty. And my wife even has cause
to wonder how a world consisting of only spirit and idea
can possibly be reconciled with the Genesis account of
creation.[11]

8. On the matter of Hume's relationship to and reading of Berkeley, see the
notes and communications in the *Journal of Philosophy* 56 (1959): 533–35,
535–45; 58 (1961): 50–51, 207–09, 327–28; and, 61 (1964): 773–78.

9. David Hume, *Enquiry concerning Human Understanding* (section 12,
part 2), quoted by R. H. Popkin in S. C. Pepper et al., *George Berkeley:
Lectures Delivered Before the Philosophical Union of the University of
California* (Berkeley, 1957), p. 18.

10. GB *Works*, 8: 31; Berkeley to Percival, March 1, 1710.

11. Rand, *B & P*, 80–81; letter dated August 26, 1710.

Berkeley acknowledged that one must proceed with caution when contradicting "vulgar and settled opinion." For that reason, he explained, "I omitted all mention of the non-existence of matter in the title-page, dedication, preface and introduction, that so the notion might steal unawares on the reader." [12] Regarding the canard that his little book was intended either as a joke or a lie, "God is my witness that I was, and do still remain, entirely persuaded of the non-existence of matter." "As to your Lady's objection," Berkeley would make it clear that no contradiction existed once one understood what creation consists of: namely, "in God's willing that those things should be perceptible to other spirits, which before were known only to Himself." After some more words designed to comfort Percival's wife and allay her uneasiness, Berkeley gently added, "I know not whether I express myself so clearly as to be understood by a lady that has not read my book." [13]

Berkeley felt a good deal more strongly about those who, having not read his book or who, reading it wrongly, concluded that he was a skeptic. Since "I question not the existence of anything that we perceive by our senses," how is it that I am categorized among the skeptics? As Richard Popkin has pointed out, skepticism arises when an attempt is made to distinguish between appearance and reality, between ideas and things. Berkeley labored to remove that distinction, arguing that what one observes is what actually exists; what one perceives is what is real. Berkeley emerged, then, not as chief of the skeptics but as champion of common sense, getting rid of some phantom "Reality" for philosophers to worry about. "Immaterialism was not intended as fanciful speculation, but, with regard to the physical world, as downright hard-headed common-sense realism, that any Irishman could believe." [14]

12. GB *Works*, 8: 36; letter dated Sept. 6, 1710.
13. Ibid., pp. 37–38.
14. Popkin in S. C. Pepper et al., *George Berkeley*, pp. 7–10.

Yet, because Irishman and Englishman alike continued
to have trouble with "to be is to be perceived," Berkeley
in 1713 published *Three Dialogues between Hylas and
Philonous . . . in opposition to Sceptics and Atheists* (the
latter phrase being added for those who never got beyond
the title page). Determined "plainly to demonstrate" the
principles of human knowledge, the author endeavored
with artistry and consummate skill to make metaphysics
both popular and palatable, an effort that enjoyed only
limited success.[15] Percival commended the "new method
you took by way of dialogue," agreeing that the novelty of
Berkeley's immaterialism aroused the natural prejudice
against any new idea and therefore made this stylistic tech-
nique "the properest course you could use." Percival also
approved of the author's fairness in presenting so many
objections to his own position, and of his skill in then providing so many "satisfactory answers." Percival, though
perhaps not his wife, found himself "much more of your
opinion than I was before." At the very least, "your notion
is as probable as that you argue against"—words which
brought only limited comfort to the twenty-eight-year-old
author.[16] Swallowing hard, Berkeley responded that it
pleased him to know his good friend did not "dislike the
notions . . . the more from having attended to them."[17]

Though a man of broad interests and lively curiosity,
Percival was no philosopher, nor did he ever pretend to be.
A new friend and new correspondent assumed the place
which Percival was not prepared to fill, and that friend was
neither Irish nor English but American. Samuel Johnson,
born in Connecticut in 1696, turned from the Congregational ministry to Anglicanism in that "defection" which
wracked New England generally and Yale specifically.[18]

15. Twelve years after its initial printing in 1713, many copies remained
unsold; Geoffrey L. Keynes, *A Bibliography of George Berkeley*, p. 27.
16. Rand, *B & P*, pp. 120–21; letter dated July 18, 1713.
17. GB *Works*, 8: 70; letter dated August 7, 1713.
18. See above, pp. 7–8.

When Berkeley arrived in Newport in 1729, no one greeted the news of his coming more eagerly than Samuel Johnson. Only the year before, Johnson had read with fascination Berkeley's *Principles of Human Knowledge*. When the dean settled a mere hundred miles from Johnson's home in Stratford, Connecticut, the opportunity for philosophical dialogue as well as book borrowing was not to be missed. Years later Johnson recalled that he very quickly paid a visit to Newport so that he "might converse with so extraordinary a genius and so great a scholar."[19] Newport's rector, James Honeyman, provided the introductions, as Johnson "was received by the Dean with much kindness and condescension and gladly put" himself under Berkeley's instruction.[20] The relationship was not all that passive, however, as Johnson also carried on a vigorous correspondence with Newport's distinguished resident, his letters containing "the earliest known criticism of any length and weight of Berkeley's theory."[21]

Writing to Berkeley some months after that hurried visit, Johnson indicated that he was moving closer and closer to the dean's philosophical position. Now (in the summer of 1729) reading *A Theory of Vision* and the *Three Dialogues* for the first time as well as quickly rereading the *Principles* had "almost convinced me that matter . . . is but a mere non-entity." Johnson had little leisure in which to absorb this whole novel world-view because his friends kept pressing for the books. "Indeed I had not opportunity sufficiently to digest your books; for no sooner had I just read them over, but they were greedily demanded by my friends who live much scattered up and down . . . The *Theory of Vision* is still at New York and the *Dialogues* just gone to

19. Herbert and Carol Schneider, eds., *Samuel Johnson . . . His Career and Writings,* 4 vols. (New York, 1929), 1: 506; hereafter Johnson, *Writings.*
20. Johnson, *Writings*, 1: 25; from his "Autobiography" written in 1786-70.
21. GB *Works*, 2: 267; the words are those of editor T. E. Jessop.

Long Island." But Samuel Johnson had grasped enough to
exclaim to Berkeley that his speculations were "the most
surprisingly ingenious I have ever met with." He and his
friends, nonetheless, had a few difficulties. Asking the
dean's pardon for "writing like a man something bewil-
dered, since I am, as it were, got into a new world," Johnson raised issues that troubled him both as theologian and
philosopher.

From one point of view, Berkeley's philosophy did confound the skeptics and the atheists because it required the
presence of a "Great Mind" who continuously perceived
objects in the sensible world. Citing Berkeley's *Three Dialogues*, Johnson wrote "that, e.g., a tree, when we don't
perceive it, exists without [outside] our minds in the infinite mind of God." Now this to be sure was a handy way of
making God useful and maybe even necessary, since few
are prepared to believe that the sensible world is forever
popping in and out of existence. On the other hand, however, the God whose existence one has in this fashion demonstrated is a God obliged at every moment to sustain the
world and keep it going, "to stand by it and influence and
direct all its motions." Is not this God somehow inferior
to, weaker than the deists' God who, when he set the world
going, did so with such firmness of purpose and fixity of
law that he does not have to keep tinkering with the machinery? When the watchmaker lets go of his product, it
should not thereafter require his constant attention and
repair. [22]

Berkeley assured his new intellectual companion that he
did not find his own notion of God in any way inferior to
that of the deists. For one thing, the deist idea of God as

22. Ibid., pp. 285, 276, 272–73. The dates of this intriguing correspondence
are as follows: Johnson's first letter to Berkeley, Sept. 10, 1729; Berkeley's first
reply, Nov. 25, 1729; Johnson's second letter, Feb. 5, 1730; and, Berkeley's
second reply, March 24, 1730.

creator and conservator of the world was singularly unorig-
inal, having been anticipated by the Stoics, the Platonists,
and the medieval scholastics. The watchmaker argument,
moreover, lacked logical force since, when the watchmaker
lets go of his watch, he depends on other powers (e.g.,
gravity) to keep the watch going: "the artificer is not the
adequate cause of the clock; so that the analogy would not
be just to suppose a clock is in respect of its artist what the
world is in respect of its Creator." Besides, in what way
does it diminish or demean God to suppose "Him to act
immediately as an omnipresent infinitely active Spirit"
rather than to suppose Him to work only through other
agencies or laws or "subordinate causes"? "For aught I can
see," Berkeley asserted, "it is no disparagement to the
perfection of God to say that all things necessarily depend
on Him . . . and that all nature would shrink to nothing, if
not upheld and preserved in being by the same force that
first created it." This view, moreover, was "agreeable to
Holy Scripture as well as to the writings of the most
esteemed philosophers."[23]

While Johnson's friends were especially pleased to have
their religious anxieties laid to rest, Johnson himself continued to be troubled over some more technical philosophical issues. Even after Berkeley's initial effort to satisfy his
Connecticut correspondent ("this intercourse with a man
of parts and philosophic genius is very agreeable," Berkeley wrote in November of 1729), Johnson still experienced
difficulty concerning "archetypes, space and duration, and
the *esse* of spirits." These sources of perplexity "yet lie in
the way of our entirely coming into your sentiments."
Immaterialism itself, however, had ceased to be a sticking
point: "I am content to give up the cause of matter," to
abandon "that sandy foundation."[24]

23. Ibid., pp. 280–81
24. Ibid., pp. 284–85.

With respect to archetypes, however, "some of us are at a loss to understand your meaning," Johnson wrote in his earlier letter. "You say the being of things consists in their being perceived. And that things are nothing but ideas, that our ideas have no unperceived archetypes, but yet you allow archetypes . . . when things are not perceived by our minds": that is, they exist in or are perceived by some other mind. Pushing Berkeley in a Platonic direction, Johnson inquired whether "real and permanent archetypes (as permanent and stable as ever matter was thought to be)" do not exist in "the all-comprehending Spirit?" Writing only as a humble learner "bred up under the greatest disadvantage," Johnson would know: "Do I understand you right?" Berkeley replied that he had no objection to the use of the term *archetype* to stand for ideas in the mind of God, just as long as one did not suppose these ideas to be "real things, and to have an absolute rational existence distinct from their being perceived by any mind whatsoever."[25] For Berkeley could allow no distinction between what is intelligible and what is real. That distinction, "a most groundless and absurd notion, is the very root of skepticism."[26]

Like many another philosopher before him, Johnson found himself baffled by the concepts of space and time. I tried hard, Johnson reported, to convince myself that external space is nothing but an idea in my mind, but "in spite of my utmost efforts" I concluded that "there must be, there can't but be, external space." In fact, if I could only get rid of external space—such as that between Newport and Stratford—then I would not be such a dullard and could "more nearly enjoy the advantages of your instruction." In response, Berkeley conceded that Isaac Newton presupposed

25. Ibid., pp. 274–75, 292.
26. Ibid., p. 78; from *Principles*, section 98.

an absolute space (and Johnson was loathe to disagree with "that great man"), but the dean baldly asserted that he differed with Newton on this point. "I make no scruple to use the word Space . . . but I do not thereby mean a distinct absolute being." Similarly, Johnson wished to hold onto the notion of time as at least an attribute of God, but again Berkeley differed with his predecessors. While Locke thought that the succession of our ideas takes place in time, this very succession "I take to *constitute* Time, and not to be only the sensible measure thereof."[27]

Finally, Johnson would understand the true nature or essence of spirits. Berkeley conceived of human knowledge as being of only two sorts: knowledge of ideas (unthinking things), and knowledge of spirits or souls or minds that were always thinking ("whoever shall go about to divide in his thoughts, or abstract the *existence* of a spirit from its *cogitation* will, I believe, find it no easy task").[28] Johnson, still perturbed, saw the mind sometimes at rest, or surely undeveloped as in an infant, or asleep without dreaming. If the very essence of a spirit "be nothing else but its actual thinking, the soul must be dead during these intervals." And that just doesn't make much sense; besides, noted Johnson, who had trouble sorting out his authorities, "I thought Mr. Locke had sufficiently confuted this notion."

Berkeley's response was terse if not fully persuasive: Locke "holds an abstract idea of existence; exclusive of perceiving and being perceived. I cannot find I have any such idea, and this is my reason against it." To soften the abruptness of that reply, Berkeley referred Johnson to what he had published but even more graciously suggested

27. Ibid., pp. 275-76, 272, 292-93.
28. Ibid., pp. 83-84; from *Principles*, section 98.

that his Anglican friend pay a visit to Whitehall in Newport. "Four or five days' conversation would set several things in a fuller and clearer light than writing could do in as many months."[29] If Johnson could not understand space, perhaps he could conquer it, or at least one hundred miles of it.

A man who could think of conversations as of four or five days' duration was a man eager to be understood by others. Berkeley wanted Newporters and others to understand not only the technical niceties of his philosophy, but he would have them understand the whole philosophical quest as well. Johnson had expressed the hope that the usefulness of Berkeley's philosophy might be "more particularly displayed in the further application of it to the arts and sciences."[30] And whether or not the application of those first principles was always or even often evident, what did come through clearly was the catholicity of Berkeley's intellectual interests: in art and architecture, in education and economics, in literature and language, in medicine and mathematics, in politics and science. Many years earlier in writing to Percival, this Irish lover of all wisdom revealed what he believed a philosopher should be about. Socrates served as the model, "reasoning on the most noble and important subjects . . . painting vice and virtue in their proper colours, deliberating on the public good." "In short his whole employment was the turning men aside from vice, impertinence, and trifling speculations to the study of solid wisdom, temperance, justice, and piety, which is the true business of a philosopher."[31] During his thirty-three months in North America, Berkeley sought to be just such a philosopher.

Since a commitment to education had prompted Berkeley's

29. Ibid., pp. 288–89, 293–94.
30. Ibid., p. 277.
31. Ibid., 8: 28; letter dated Dec. 27, 1709.

interest in the New World, it is not surprising that he found
occasion to indicate his views on that subject. Even before
the Bermuda idea was born, in that bon-vivant year in London (1713), Berkeley offered an early hint of his philosophy
of education in a piece written for the *Guardian*. [32] Nature,
he noted, prepares us for the enjoyment of differing pleasures at successive stages of life. By "gentle degrees, we
rise from the gratifications of sense to relish those of the
mind." Life properly moved, then, from the lowest pleasures, "sensual delights," to those "sublimer pleasures of
reason, which discover the causes and designs, the frame,
connexion, and symmetry of things." The purpose of the
university or college, therefore, was "to raise the mind to
its due perfection." In fulfilling that purpose, the educational institution not only transmitted the learning of the
ancients but, more constructively, saw to it that learning
"receives a daily increase." And graduates of these institutions bore the responsibility to spread "knowledge and
good taste throughout the land." The young Berkeley also
indicated his conviction—one never abandoned—that religion and learning are allies, never enemies, the Reformation
being a clear instance where the two worked together for
the benefit of both. Deism, not Christianity, threatened
Britain's universities; if we permit ourselves to be led astray
by the former, then we shall collapse into that "same state
of barbarism which overspread the northern nations before
they were enlightened by Christianity." [33]

Like Dublin's Trinity College, Berkeley's St. Paul's would
preserve and propagate the liberal arts, elevate morals,
rescue religion, and cultivate good taste. Faculty must be
"able and worthy men" prepared to give themselves unre-

32. Here I follow A. A. Luce's careful collation determining which of the
anonymous essays in Steele's short-lived magazine are truly Berkeley's; GB
Works, 7: 173-75.
33. Ibid., 7: 203-05.

servedly to the teaching of the young. If the faculty were
unprincipled, all would be rotten. But if the foundation
were solid, then students instructed in the liberal arts would
also be rooted in religion and morality. The young Indians,
too, as part of their preparation for higher studies, should
be instructed in history, rhetoric, practical mathematics,
and "some skill in physick." [34] As John Smibert's presence
aboard the *Lucy* clearly demonstrated, Berkeley also hoped
to offer some instruction in the arts. And Berkeley's wife
Anne later stated that "one of the first composers & per-
formers in Music of that time had engaged to come there
[i.e., Bermuda] as soon as he was settled." The entire intellectual community in that New World should offer only
the wheat from the Old, leaving behind its chaff. In Anne
Berkeley's words once more: "This place was therefore to
be the retreat for Men of fine taste & Learning who had
seen much of the World & therefore was [*sic*] tired of it
and yet intended to carry everything laudable & lovely
with them." [35] Since St. Paul's never came into being, its
precise curriculum cannot of course be determined, but it
would probably have been as earnest an effort to recreate
Trinity College as young Harvard's was to recreate Cambridge. Trinity's curricular emphasis at this time included
logic, rhetoric, classics, physics, natural and moral philosophy, sacred and profane history, and "divinity." [36]

34. 1724 edition of Berkeley's *Proposal*, 15, 6.

35. Anne Berkeley's interleaved commentary to Joseph Stock, *Account of the Life of George Berkeley* (London, 1776). This unique copy, now in Trinity College's library, was not known to exist until 1972. Quotations are from leaf opposite page 20 of Stock. Anne Berkeley comments more extensively on the Bermuda plan and her American stay than on any other phase of her husband's career.

36. The divinity lectureship which Berkeley held at Trinity had been created only shortly before—in 1718. In 1724, the college added two other professor-ships: one in "Natural and Experimental Philosophy," the second in "Oratory and History." Not until 1785 were professorships added in chemistry and

Most of Berkeley's ideas concerning universities and the
education they offered remained the same after his residence in Rhode Island, but in one particular he changed:
namely, his assessment of Harvard and Yale. Earlier, he
had stigmatized both schools as having "so long subsisted
to little or no purpose." Now, he not only appreciated
their instruction in the liberal arts, he sought even to
encourage it in a variety of ways. The better the education,
the more fair-minded the attitude toward Anglicanism.
And even though "you have to do with a people of no
very easy or tractable spirit" at New Haven, Berkeley wrote
Johnson, one can take hope now that "learning and good
sense are gaining ground among them." [37] When Samuel
Johnson a few years later called upon Berkeley for additional advice in educational matters, Berkeley complied
with a "few crude thoughts" thrown together "for you to
ruminate on and digest." Such ruminations, filtered through
the prisms of Trinity College, continental tours, Bermuda
plans, and a Rhode Island sojourn, left their mark on New
World education. [38]

Berkeley's ever active mind also turned to the field of art
and architecture. Since the years of his two grand tours, he
attentively perceived and reflected upon the peculiar com-
binations of style, form, balance, taste, and function that

---

botany. Constantia Maxwell, *A History of Trinity College Dublin 1591–1892*
(Dublin, 1946), 52, 148–49.

37. GB *Works*, vol. 8; all quotations are from letters to Samuel Johnson:
241 (June 11, 1735), 247 (May 11, 1738), and 243 (May 12, 1736).

38. On Berkeley's influence in the founding of what later became Columbia
University and the University of Pennsylvania, see below, chapter 7. Also see
Graham P. Conroy, "Berkeley and Education in America," *Journal of the
History of Ideas* 21, no. 2 (April–June, 1960): 211–21; and Norman J. Catir,
Jr., "Berkeley's Successful Failure; A Study of George Berkeley's Contribution
to American Education," *Historical Magazine of the Protestant Episcopal
Church* 33 (March, 1964): 65–82.

somehow make up works of art.[39] No mere frill, art rendered elemental service to the condition and the quality of life. "Those noble arts of architecture, sculpture and painting," Berkeley wrote in 1721, "do not only adorn the public but have also an influence on the minds and manners of men, filling them with great ideas, and spiriting them up to an emulation of worthy actions."[40] "I pretend to an uncommon skill in architecture," Berkeley wrote while visiting Rome; yet, "there is not any one modern building in Rome that pleases me . . . the old Romans were inferior to the Greeks, and . . . the moderns fall infinitely short of both in the grandeur and simplicity of taste."[41] One of Ireland's wealthiest landowners, William Conolly, sought the returned traveler's advice in 1722 for the building of what Percival predicted "will be the finest [house] Ireland ever saw . . . fit for a Prince." While Berkeley hoped Conolly's home would be "an ornament to the country," he soon discovered that his advice was only one counsel among many: "as I do not approve of a work conceived by many heads so I have made no draught of mine own."[42]

With so profound an interest in the subject, the Bermuda plan might be expected to have an architectural as well as educational dimension. Influenced especially by the sixteenth-century Italian architect Andrea Palladio, Berkeley (like the similarly influenced Thomas Jefferson) paid attention to scale and proportion with geometric precision. Each building, moreover, should relate in harmony to its natural environment as well as to the surrounding structures. "I

39. See, for example, his letter to Percival, March 1, 1717; GB *Works*, 8: 101–02.

40. In his *Essay towards Preventing the Ruin of Great Britain;* GB *Works*, 6: 80.

41. GB *Works*, 8: 111; letter dated July 28, 1718.

42. Rand, *B & P*, 195–96; letter dated Aug. 5, 1722. Berkeley's letters to Percival are dated July 29, 1722 and Sept. 7, 1722; GB *Works*, 8: 123–25.

have seen the plan of the College & Town of Bermuda
drawn by the Dean," Anne Berkeley wrote in her later
years, and it looked like this:

> in the midst of a large Circle stood the College—and
> this Circle was formed by the Houses of the Fellows at
> proper distances to Allow a good Garden to each house.
>   Another circle without this one was formed of houses
> for Gentlemen who had requested of the Dean to build
> such & erect such houses for them. The Models of these
> houses I have seen in various tastes of truest Architec-
> ture. An Outward Circle was composed of shops &
> houses for Artificers of various denominations. He had
> a great dislike to the contaminating Churches with *dead
> bodies*—& for this reason a walk called the Walk of
> Death planted with Cypress trees was Appropriated for
> the purpose of interment, where Monuments and Urns
> might be erected.[43]

Since all of this never proceeded beyond the sketchpad,
Berkeley's one architectural achievement in the New World
was Whitehall, and even that modest structure has a clouded
ancestry.[44] Whether Berkeley only remodeled an earlier
structure or built this home entirely on his own design, the
result cannot compete with Ireland's princely homes or
with Jefferson's achievement at Monticello. In the end, it
may be fair to say that Whitehall enjoys architectural prominence more for what Berkeley wrote there than for what he
built there. His only book written in Rhode Island, discussed

43. Anne Berkeley's commentary on Stock's *Life*, opposite page 18. Also
see J. M. Hone and M. M. Rossi, *Bishop Berkeley: His Life, Writings and
Philosophy* (London, 1931) where a sketch of the plan may be found opposite
page 134.
44. On Berkeley's contribution to the field of architecture, see Marcus Whiffen, "Bishop Berkeley," *Architectural Review* 123, no. 733 (February, 1958):
91–93. Whiffen argues that Berkeley—well before Hogarth, Hume, and Burke—
contributed to "the overthrow of the Renaissance tradition in aesthetic theory."

below,[45] paid remarkable tribute to the role of architecture. In one dialogue of that work, the conversation centered on the idiocy as well as the occasional glory of fashions in art, clothing, and architecture. The latter stood out among all the arts as the one most capable of leading mankind into the very heart of the aesthetic experience. In its concern with order, proportion, symmetry, and purpose, architecture—"the noble offspring of judgment and fancy"—rose above all the other arts, helping us to perceive the true nature of beauty.[46]

Whitehall's and Berkeley's contribution to New World painting was similarly indirect. Berkeley brought with him to America John Smibert, "the best trained and most skillful painter who had ever come to the Colonies."[47] Smibert stayed for a time in and around Newport, but within a year of that cold January debarkation he had made his way to Boston, where he remained until his death in 1751.[48] The dean continued, however, to be both his patron and his friend. Smibert painted six portraits of Berkeley (one a

45. See below, chapter 6.

46. *Alciphron*, Third Dialogue, section 8; GB *Works*, 3: 125-28. Berkeley observed (via Euphranor) that in the matter of clothing the Greeks and Romans, unlike northern Europeans and the English, knew how to "cover the body without encumbering it, and adorn without altering the shape." The East, along with classical civilization, solved the problem of dress quite rationally "while our Gothic gentry, after so many centuries racking their inventions, mending and altering, and improving, and whirling about in perpetual rotation of fashions, have never yet had the luck to stumble on anything that was not absurd and ridiculous" (pp. 125-26).

47. Henry Wilder Foote, *John Smibert Painter* (Cambridge, Mass., 1950), p. 112.

48. On March 9, 1730, Berkeley wrote that "Messrs. James, Dalton and Smibert, &c. are at Boston, and have been there these four months." By that accounting, Smibert would have remained in Newport most of 1729; yet, his notebook indicates that he began painting some pictures in Boston as early as May of 1729. It is quite possible, of course, that he divided his time for some months between the two towns. For further biographical detail on Smibert, see the excellent sketch by Theodore Sizer in the *Dictionary of American Biography*, as well Foote's volume noted above.

copy), five of which seem to have been at Berkeley's direct initiative. The sixth, the famous "Bermuda Group" (see Frontispiece), was commissioned by John Wainwright of Dublin and London, a close friend of Berkeley's who had even considered accompanying him to America. Smibert drew the patron as well as himself into this, the largest as well as the finest of all his paintings.[49] Popular and prolific as a portrait artist,[50] Smibert painted some 241 portraits on this side of the Atlantic,[51] provided the design for Faneuil

49. The misidentification of the "other man" in this group portrait as Thomas or John Moffat (Thomas in Foote, John in Luce) represents an earnest effort to give that mystery figure some fleshly reality. But either Moffat's only relevance to the other members of the Bermuda Group was his kinship to Smibert. Fortunately, Smibert's recently published notebook solves the confusion by clearly identifying Wainwright. A long-time friend of Berkeley's who helped him politically after his return to Britain, Wainwright served as Baron of the Exchequer in Dublin from 1732–41. Berkeley wrote the memorial inscription for his close friend, who is buried in Chester Cathedral. GB *Works*, 7: 377, 399; and 9: 89–90. Also, David Evans et al., *The Notebook of John Smibert* (Boston, 1969), 89, 107–08. At least two of the portraits listed in this notebook (#49 and #60) appear not to have been known to Luce (*Life*, Appendix 4) and may be lost. One of those, a portrait of "The Revd. Dean Berkeley his Lady and son," earned Smibert the highest commission recorded anywhere in his records: £120! Smibert's six portraits of Berkeley, as listed in the *Notebook,* are as follows:

1.	(p. 83)	"Mr. Dean Berkeley"	June, 1726 (London)
2.	(p. 84)	"Doctor Berkeley Dn. of Dy."	
		copy	June, 1727 (London)
3.	(p. 89)	"Dean Berkeley"	April, 1730 (Boston?)
4.	(p. 89)	"John Wainwright Esqr., Revd. Dean Berkeley his Lady, and son, John James Esqr., Ricd. Dalton Esqr., Ms. Hendcock, John Smibert"	Nov. 1730 (Boston?)
5.	(p. 90)	"The Revd. Dean Berkeley his Lady and son for him selfe in one clothe half lenths" /	Jan., 1731 (Boston?)
6.	(p. 90)	"Dean Berkeley"	March, 1731 (Boston?)

All portraits marked "Boston" may with equal or greater probability have been painted, at least in part, in Newport. See note 51, below.

50. See Andrew Oliver's comment to that effect in *The Notebook of John Smibert*, p. 23.

51. Not all of the 241 portraits were painted in Boston, for Smibert indicated

Hall, served as "stimulating example" to his son Nathaniel, as well as to Robert Feke, John Greenwood, and John Singleton Copley, and kept a studio and "colour shop" to which America's best-known painters gravitated long after his death.[52] When Berkeley invited Smibert aboard his ship at Gravesend, he brought with him more than his own cultivated taste and continental experience: through Smibert he gave substance to his perceptions.[53]

Neither his immaterialism nor his aestheticism, however, brought Berkeley to America. That feat was accomplished by his philosophy of history. As already noted, Berkeley saw England as a nation that blushed not for its crimes but only for its virtues. If it is a "corrupt degenerate age we live in," then, in the given order of things, as one nation stumbled and fell, another arose to take its place.[54] If Britain set her face toward ruin, others must set their faces toward another land, another country. And where did such a land lie? "Westward, like the Sun," John Dryden had written at the turn of the century, in lines that likely influenced Berkeley's one serious poetic effort.[55] The results of

---

trips to New York, Burlington, N.J., and Philadelphia. He probably also traveled often to nearby Newport, where "The Bermuda Group" is most likely to have been painted or at least largely sketched, for Anne Berkeley specifically stated that Berkeley "avoided going to Boston" and did not do so until his departure in 1731.

52. Foote, *John Smibert Painter*, pp. 117–18, 126. Speaking of "The Bermuda Group," Foote observed that "Smibert's masterpiece was, indeed, his one picture which had a marked influence on the younger painters in America" (p. 120). Visitors to Smibert's home in Boston also included John Trumbull and Charles Willson Peale.

53. See Padraic Colum, "Berkeley and the Modern Artist," *Saturday Review of Literature* 12, no. 7 (June 15, 1935): 3–4, 14–15. Berkeley's continuing interest in art is evident in the collection amassed in his official residence in Cloyne; GB *Works*, 8: 300.

54. GB *Works*, 6: 83–84.

55. John Dryden, *Fables Ancient and Modern . . .* (London, 1700); poem addressed "To Her Grace the Dutchess of Ormond. . . ." See also Historical

that effort Berkeley sent to Percival in 1726, noting that it
was "wrote by a friend of mine" and urging that no copy
of it be made.[56] One reason for Berkeley's caution regarding copies was that his "prophecy" regarding America was
not yet a finished product. When he finally published the
poem a quarter of a century later (in his *Miscellany*, 1752),
he had in the intervening years made several changes. In its
final and more familiar form, Berkeley's philosophy of
history and of America reached its poetic expression in
these lines:

Verses by the Author
on the prospect of Planting Arts and Learning in America

The Muse, disgusted at an Age and Clime
    Barren of every glorious Theme,
In distant Lands now waits a better Time,
    Producing Subjects worthy Fame:

In happy Climes, where from the genial Sun
    And virgin Earth such Scenes ensue,
The Force of Art by Nature seems outdone,
    And fancied Beauties by the true:

In happy Climes the Seat of Innocence,
    Where Nature guides and Virtue rules,
Where Men shall not impose for Truth and Sense
    The Pedantry of Courts and Schools:

There shall be sung another golden Age,
    The rise of Empire and of Arts,
The Good and Great inspiring epic Rage,
    The wisest Heads and noblest Hearts.

Manuscripts Commission, *Appendix to Seventh Report* (London, 1879), 760-
61.
    56. GB *Works*, 8: 152; letter dated Feb. 10, 1726.

    Not such as *Europe* breeds in her decay;
      Such as she bred when fresh and young,
    When heav'nly Flame did animate her Clay,
      By future Poets shall be sung.

    Westward the Course of Empire takes its Way;
      The four first Acts already past,
    A fifth shall close the Drama with the Day;
      Time's noblest Offspring is the last. [57]

    Breathing a good deal of the spirit of his own age, Berkeley in this poem struggled with images of biological vigor and decay, of solar progress across the skies, of Edenic nature and philosopher-kings, of cosmic drama and the ultimate triumph of civilization. These themes, inherited not invented, could be found in various combinations: some displayed more cynicism than hope, others contented themselves more with description than with prophecy, and still others expressed optimism only in God's time beyond the bounds of human history. In Berkeley's special combination, a decayed or decaying Europe, no longer "fresh and young," would now be forced by historical necessity to give way to "a better Time" in a happier clime. European civilization, indeed even classical civilization, would have a rebirth, but in another mode and in a distant place. The New World—and in 1726 North America was in fact still new, still unexplored, unsettled, and uncontaminated—would be touched by "heav'nly Flame"; then her dust, her clay would take on new life and new shape in a purified community and a resurrected civilization. In Henry Newman's words, America was "how the world look'd at the beginning of it after the Flood."

---

57. Ibid., 7: 373. The 1726 title was "America OR the Muse's Refuge: *A Prophecy*," p. 369. A. A. Luce gives both the original and final versions here. Full lines have been changed in the first, second and final stanzas; in the original, the poem's final line read, "The world's great Effort is the last."

In George Berkeley's words, America could be that enchanted
forest "Where Nature guides and Virtue rules."

Voltaire described four earlier periods of human creativ-
ity and freedom: the ages of Pericles, of Augustan Rome, of
the Medici in Florence, and of Louis XIV's France. And
George Herbert a century earlier had explained (in *The
Church Militant*, 1633) how

> Religion, like a pilgrime, westward bent,
> Knocking at all doores, ever as she went . . .

moved from Egypt to Greece and Rome, to Europe and
England, until now

> Religion stands on tip-toe in our land
> Ready to passe to the *American* strand.[58]

The fifth and final act was not the apocalyptic intervention
of God into history;[59] it was, rather, "another golden age,"
the *progress* of "Arts and Learning in America." It was fulfillment, not catastrophe; an achievement of the "wisest
Heads and noblest Hearts," not a surrender by the base and
the weak. When that fifth act moved onto center stage,
poets would sing and a heavenly chorus echo its "Rejoice!"

Berkeley's versification in 1726 repeatedly found more
prosaic expression in the years following. After seeing Newport, he may have slightly shifted the location of those
"happy Climes," but he did not shift his perspective on
history. Nor did his confidant and friend, Henry Newman,
who wrote to him in 1729 that "some good Men are appre-
hensive that the time is coming when the Gospel that has
left the Eastern parts of the world to reside in the Western

58. Both Voltaire and Herbert quoted in Rexmond G. Cochrane, "Bishop
Berkeley and the Progress of Arts and Learning . . . ," *Huntington Library
Quarterly* 17, no. 3 (May, 1954): 244, 239–40.

59. See Ernest L. Tuveson, *Redeemer Nation: The Idea of America's
Millennial Role* (Chicago, 1968), pp. 92–94.

parts of it for some Centuries past is now, by the just judgment of God, taking leave of us, to be receiv'd in America."[60] Berkeley responded the following March, indicating that now that he had actually seen the New World, he believed more strongly in its ultimate destiny.

> What you observe of the growth of Atheism and Irreligion hath a fatal aspect upon England but it is no more than hath been carrying on for many years past by a set of men who under the notion of liberty are for introducing License and a general contempt of all laws Divine or Humane. Political societies have their diseases as well as natural bodies and this seems that which will be the death of Great Britain. God governs the world and knows his own times and seasons.[61]

History favored the West, it favored America, perhaps it favored even Newport. But after more than a year in Rhode Island, Berkeley could not help but wonder whether history favored him. In that same letter to Newman quoted above, written in March of 1730, Berkeley commented that "The delay that our affair depending in the Treasury hath met with is no small discouragement."[62] The "affair" concerned, of course, the £20,000, and the "delay" now amounted to a year and a half from the time Berkeley had left England's shores. To further aggravate the situation, it became apparent that more than mere bureaucratic bumbling was involved.

Hardly had Berkeley settled in Rhode Island before some Americans, like the English and Irish before them, began taking shots at the whole lofty conception enunciated in the *Proposal* and now, perhaps, on the brink of execution. Berkeley's first stop in the New World, a ten-day pause in Virginia, gave him an opportunity to replenish the ship's

60. SPCK New England Letters, vol. 3; letter dated Sept. 17, 1729.
61. GB *Works*, 8: 207; letter dated March 29, 1730.
62. Ibid., p. 206.

exhausted supplies and to enjoy the governor's hospitality. Unfortunately, it also gave Virginians an opportunity to hear firsthand of the Bermuda scheme and an occasion for raising their objections. Objections expressed to the dean of Derry did no great harm, but criticism made to the bishop of London, or to other seats of power at London, had a more damaging effect. Especially was this the case when they were voiced with the sharpened wit of William Byrd (1674–1744). Influential planter, sometime politician, and trenchant writer, Byrd chose to direct his remarks to Berkeley's most faithful London supporter, Sir John Percival. When Byrd had first heard rumors of the plan from Percival, he immediately dubbed it "a very romantic one." That was his mildest reaction. The more he thought about the scheme, the madder and wilder it became. "[T]he Dean is as much a Don Quixote in zeal, as that renowned knight was in chivalry." The inhabitants in Bermuda healthy? Well yes, since food is so scarce that they have no choice except to be temperate. The air of Bermuda pure? Well yes, since "it is made so by a perpetual succession of storms and hurricanes." The Indians to be "dragoon[ed] . . . into Christianity"? Well yes, it makes perfect sense for a "wild scheme" to "have wild measures to carry it on." I would be happy, Byrd concluded, to have such men as Dean Berkeley as conversation partners, but "they should be the last I would employ in any affairs that require action and knowledge of the world."[63] To Byrd's damning indictment, Percival could only lamely reply: "I will not undertake to dispute with you the feasibleness of the execution, nor what success it may have. I am sure the intention deserves the utmost."[64]

Fellow Virginians, Governor William Gooch (1681–1751) and Commissary James Blair (1655–1743), shared many of

63. Rand, *B & P*, 243–45; letter dated June 10, 1729.
64. Ibid., p. 259; reply dated Dec. 3, 1729.

Byrd's reservations, though neither expressed himself with Byrd's wit or bite. Blair, already burdened with ecclesiastical duties throughout Virginia and with administrative duties at the College of William and Mary, discovered in 1729—to his utter dismay—that Bermuda had suddenly been added to his responsibilities. That island, he complained to Bishop Gibson, is "at least 300 Leagues from this Country, and as far as I can learn not above two or three ministers upon it." If it really needs a Commissary, I am glad to nominate George Berkeley and hope "upon second thoughts your [Lordship] will think him much fitter for that Employment."[65] Gooch, also writing to Gibson, informed the bishop of London that Bermuda was a most regrettable choice by the dean of Derry. "Bermuda, my Lord, is a very poor Island, but I can't give your Lordship a juster Idea of it than by saying 'tis as if fifty Islands were jumbled together, the largest of which is indeed about twenty miles long & half a mile broad, but the rest very small." Looking ahead, Virginia's governor paved the way for his own colony to play a more central role in this affair. "As the Dean's Charter for this Island is not irrevocable," then when Berkeley learns more about it, he will surely favor the continent—"much the properest Place for his Purpose." On that great continent, Virginia by happy coincidence "seems to be best suited for it."[66]

Religion on tiptoe ready to pass to an American strand; money collected and money invested, waiting only for that final official support; arts and learning prepared and poised for the planting in the New World. How much longer must one wait, how long, O Lord, how long? On March 9, 1730, Berkeley wrote that "My design continues to wait the event." And three weeks later: "I wait here with all the

65. Fulham Papers, 12: 142–43; letter dated Sept. 8, 1729.
66. Ibid., pp. 136–37; letter dated June 29, 1729.

anxiety that attends suspense."[67] It was no doubt true
that "God governs the world and knows his own times
and seasons." But was it possible that politically minded,
calculating men had the power to impede that governance
and delay those times?

---

67. GB *Works*, 8: 203 and 205; letters to Prior and Percival.

4 Charity and Humanity

> Charity and Humanity is the Motive that hath united
> them [the Georgia Trustees], and their End is the reliev-
> ing the want of their Fellow Creatures both in Mind and
> Body; therefore, from their very Institution they are
> obliged to be Assistant to your design since your Motives
> and ends are the same.
>
> James Ogelthorpe to George Berkeley, 1731.

In the eighteenth century a prodigious philanthropy and a
humanitarian spirit expressed themselves in a wide variety
of concerns: the care and cure of criminals, the treatment
accorded servants and slaves, the alleviation of poverty, the
education of the deaf and dumb, the rescue of the shipwrecked, the abolition of duelling, the temperate use of
alcohol, the protection of orphans, and the evangelization
of all. To that age, doing good to mankind inevitably also
meant bringing the gospel (in Ogelthorpe's words) "to
Numberless Nations who never yet heard the glad tidings
of revealed Religion."[1] If charity and Christianity were not
always mentioned in the same breath, they rarely parted
company in individual minds or in institutional goals. Berkeley's years in America, whatever else they accomplished or
failed to achieve, gave witness to his century's better nature,
a nature that looked to "the wants of their Fellow Creatures,"
wants both spiritual and material.

Berkeley's own benevolence expressed itself most

---

1. On the "humanitarian spirit" in England, see chapter 6 in Michael Kraus's
The Atlantic Civilization (Ithaca, N.Y., 1949); and Part 1 in David E. Owen,
English Philanthropy 1660-1960 (Cambridge, Mass., 1964). Ogelthorpe's long
letter to Berkeley, dated May, 1731, may be found in BM, Add. Ms. 47033; it
is also printed (with some errors) in Rand, *B & P*, 275-79.

conspicuously in education and, within that domain, most
visibly in books. Something of Berkeley's bibliomania can
be discerned from a letter written about a year before his
voyage to Newport. In preparing for that event, he shipped
from Dublin to London "fifty eight boxes, whereof fifty
five contain only books."[2] And before he had been in Newport very many months, he urged Henry Newman to send
him even more books—though these were clearly to be
gifts: Richard Hooker's *Ecclesiastical Polity* (eight copies
at 17s each), and the *Works* of William Chillingworth (twelve
copies at 12s 6d each). After these books arrived, Berkeley
inquired of Samuel Johnson, "Pray let me know whether
they would admit the writings of Hooker and Chillingworth
into the library of the College in Newhaven."[3] The dean
soon learned that Yale, still in its adolescent years, was
eager to lay its hands on as many good books as possible.

So was Samuel Johnson. On his own behalf, on the behalf
of his friends and his alma mater, Johnson sought books.
He of course had already received from Berkeley his own
three major philosophical works: *Essay towards a New
Theory of Vision, Treatise concerning the Principles of
Human Knowledge,* and the *Three Dialogues.*[4] Berkeley
also sent along his small Latin essay on motion, *De Motu,*
which had been published in London in 1721.[5] When Johnson and Berkeley got together in Whitehall or at Trinity
Church (where Johnson on occasion was invited to preach),

2. GB *Works,* 8: 187; letter, dated June 7, 1728, to Bryan Fairfax.

3. Ibid., 2: 294; letter dated March 24, 1730. Jessop's note thereon is in
error, for the books in question were already in Berkeley's hand: Newman to
Berkeley, September 17, 1729 (SPCK New England Letters, vol. 3); and Berkeley to Newman, March 29, 1730 (GB *Works,* 8: 206).

4. See above, p. 60.

5. GB *Works,* 2: 280; letter dated Nov. 25, 1729. *De Motu* had been submitted in a contest to the Royal Academy of Sciences at Paris, but the prizes
went elsewhere. For the Latin text (with English translation by A. A. Luce),
see GB *Works,* 4: 1–52.

their conversation inevitably turned to books: their contents, and not infrequently their disposition. When later on Berkeley prepared to return home, he wrote to Johnson:

> I have left a box of books with Mr. [Nathaniel] Kay, to be given away by you—the small English books where they may be most serviceable among the people, the others as we agreed together. The Greek and Latin books I would have given to such lads as you think will make the best use of them in the College, or to the School at Newhaven.[6]

Johnson shared Berkeley's fondness for books as well as for philosophical reflection; he also opened the door for the dean's major benevolence to Yale. Recognizing that Johnson, though now an Anglican, "have still an influence there," Berkeley reached the conclusion that Yale—especially with Johnson standing by in Stratford—offered much promise for religion and learning "in this uncultivated part of the world."[7] He need not have believed that Yale was about to become Anglican, only that the college was unlikely to fall victim to sectarian narrowness or dogmatic rigidity. Convinced of this catholicity by Johnson and others, as well as by his own investigation, Berkeley in July, 1732, conveyed to Yale his home as well as the ninety-six acres of farm, orchard, "arable pasture & meadow & woodland" for the token "sum of five shillings of lawfull money of Great Britain."[8]

Berkeley's intention, spelled out in the deed of conveyance and (at Yale's suggestion) somewhat modified the

6. Ibid., 8: 213; letter dated Sept. 7, 1731.
7. Ibid.
8. Luce, *Life*, appendix 3, 236–38. *The Rhode Island Gazette* reported in its issue of Oct. 25, 1732: "We hear that the Rev. Mr. George Berkeley, Dean of London-Derry, has given his Farm on this island, worth about £3000, to Yale College in Connecticut."

following year, was that the income from this gift be used
to support two or three students "toward their mainten-
ance and subsistance dureing [*sic*] the time between their
first and second degree." Eligible students, after being
examined in Greek and Latin, were to be chosen each year
(May 6) by Yale's president and "the senior episcopal missionary" in Connecticut—namely, Samuel Johnson. To
Johnson, Berkeley explained his reasons for wishing the
money to be used in this fashion: "It is my opinion that as
human learning and improvements of Reason are of no
small use in religion, so it would very much forward those
ends, if some of your students were enabled to subsist
longer at their studies, and if by a public tryal and pre-
mium an emulation were inspired into all."[9] Ever the educator at heart, Berkeley hoped to achieve at Yale something
of what, it appeared, would never come to pass in Bermuda.

These graduate fellowships, the first offered in America,
exercised a remarkable influence in eighteenth-century
colonial education. The initial recipients, Eleazar Wheelock
(later president of Dartmouth) and Benjamin Pomeroy
(later Congregational minister in Hebron, Connecticut),
divided between them the £32 which Yale received in rent
from the Middletown farm. Succeeding "Berkeley Scholars"
included young men later to serve as presidents of Yale,
Columbia, Princeton, Middlebury, Hamilton, and the University of Vermont.[10] To secure this income for these
"Scholars of the House," Yale at first granted short-term
leases of Whitehall and the surrounding ninety-six acres.
Frequent changes of tenancy, however, proved burdensome
to Yale and harmful to the property, which was allowed to

9. GB *Works*, 8: 213–14; letter dated July 25, 1732.
10. Henry M. Fuller, "Bishop Berkeley as a Benefactor of Yale," *Yale
University Library Gazette* 28, no. 1 (July, 1953): 15–16. Ezra Stiles noted in
his diary that not until 1782 did a Berkeley Scholar fail to be appointed;
ibid., p. 16.

deteriorate. Later in the century, therefore, Yale's trustees decided to grant a lease for 999 years, which lease expires on March 26, 2761.[11] At that far distant time, the status of Berkeley Scholars and even of Berkeley's course of empire will no doubt be reassessed.

The gift of house and land, which had been purchased for £2,500 in 1729, did not represent a wholly personal charity, though about £600 of Berkeley's own money was involved in the original purchase.[12] While emphasizing that he acted only as the steward of others' liberality, Berkeley's interest in Yale was personal and decisive. As he hurriedly wrote to Samuel Johnson just before leaving New England: "My endeavours shall not be wanting, some way or other, to be useful; and I should be very glad to be so in particular to the College at Newhaven."[13] The "some way or other" turned out once more to be books.

Again, and by this time predictably, Samuel Johnson served as intermediary and counsellor. "Being desirous so far as in me lies," Berkeley wrote him in 1733, "to promote sound learning and true religion in your part of the world, I judged that the purchasing a good collection of books for the library at Yale College might be a proper application of the liberality of certain publick spirited persons who left it to my disposal." With the aid, also predictably, of the indispensable Henry Newman—who pressed four London

11. In 1900, Whitehall itself came under the care of the Society of Colonial Dames of Rhode Island, who maintain it as a museum and memorial open to visitors every summer. In 1972, the Colonial Dames received full title from Yale to the house, not the farm, until the year 2761.

12. GB *Works*, 8: 201; letter to Percival dated Aug. 30, 1729: "I have got credit for 600 pounds at the legal interest, which Mr. Prior is to pay out of the Deanery. This enables me to perfect the purchase of my land and house in this Island, which purchase in case the College should not go on will be much to my loss." When Berkeley later disposed of the farm, however, he informed Samuel Johnson that it was "without any great loss to myself"; ibid., p. 213 (letter dated July 25, 1732).

13. Ibid., p. 213.

booksellers into frantic service—Berkeley amassed a remarkable collection of about one thousand volumes. This thinking man's library (reckoned in 1742 to be one-third of Yale's total holdings) explicitly reflected Berkeley's own breadth as well as the scope of the cultural riches which England was prepared, when conditions were right, to bestow upon the New World.

The collection displayed a noteworthy balance: from handbooks on agriculture and "vegetable staticks" to the works of Plato and Hippocrates; from Ptolemy's and Strabo's geographies to Sir Walter Raleigh's *Historie of the World*; from Newton's *Opticks* to Edward Wells's *Young Gentleman's Astronomy, Chronology, and Dialling*; from Ovid and Demosthenes to Milton and Pope (Berkeley even slipped in his favorite architect, Palladio). While the dean included much in religion, the historical perspective was impressive (Josephus, Eusebius, Socrates, Plotinus et al.) and the academic bias overwhelming (Novum Testamentum graecum, Biblia sacra hebraea, Lexicon heptaglotten, Biblia sacra polyglotta, and the works of Justin Martyr, Irenaeus, Tertullian, Hippolytus, Origen, Cyprian, Athanasius, Ambrose, Jerome, Augustine, John Chrysostom et al.). No simplified catechetical instruction here! Of his own work, Berkeley included only the recently published *Alciphron* (1732), presuming no doubt that Samuel Johnson shared with Yale his copies of the earlier publications. Valued at about £400, the Berkeley gift (still proudly displayed in Yale's Beinecke Library) deserved the tribute paid it by Yale's President Thomas Clap: "the finest Collection of Books that ever came together at one time into America."[14]

14. Andrew Keogh, "Bishop Berkeley's Gift of Books in 1733," *Yale University Library Gazette* 8, no. 1 (July 1933); Clap quotation on p. 4, listing of the books, pp. 9–26. President of the College from 1739 to 1766, Clap himself organized the library in 1742, giving a special prominence to the Berkeley collection.

In the same year and even in the same ship (the *Dolphin*), Berkeley dispatched a lesser gift to Harvard, with Henry Newman again assisting in all the details from purchasing to crating.[15] If Samuel Johnson served as conduit for Berkeleyan benevolence to Yale, Newman, now more than mere buyer and shipper, filled a similar role with respect to Harvard. Having graduated from the Massachusetts institution in 1687, Newman willingly acted as "Harvard's man in London" when special representations needed to be made or services rendered. Harvard was "our college."[16] Even before

---

Just a generation later, in 1771, Thomas Jefferson was asked to recommend (not donate) an ideal library of more modest cost—around £100 "if bound quite plain." Jefferson's list of 148 titles (379 volumes) duplicated Berkeley's in many instances, though the American statesman, now a generation deeper into the Enlightenment milieu, leaned even more toward literature and the fine arts and away from religion, or at least Christianity (Xenophon, Epictetus, Seneca, Cicero, Hume, and Locke he included under "Religion," while the Bible he placed under "Antient History"). In keeping with the Enlightenment spirit, Jefferson dropped Plato from his list as well as all the Church Fathers. In naming historians, Jefferson went quickly from Livy, Tacitus, and Plutarch to Bayle, Bossuet, and Hume. Berkeley agreed on the first three, but not on the last—though Hume's history came too late for the dean's collection. With respect to literary figures, the two men largely coincided: Milton, Pope, Swift, Shakespeare, Steele, Spenser, Fenelon, Rowe, Otway, Gay, and even *The Spectator, The Guardian,* and *The Tatler.* See Julian Boyd, ed., *The Papers of Thomas Jefferson* (Princeton, N.J., 1950), 1: 74–81.

15. See Newman's letter to Samuel Johnson, May 31 and June 1, 1733: to Benjamin Wadsworth, June 1, 1733; to Timothy Cutler, June 1, 1733; to Elisha Williams, August 31, 1733; and to Samuel Mather, Sept. 15, 1733. Also see Berkeley's letters to Williams and Wadsworth, both dated May 31, 1733; all of the above in SPCK New England Letters, vol. 4.

16. See, for example, Newman's response to Benjamin Colman, who had sought some royal recognition for Harvard. Newman had tried, but observed that Harvard's address to His Majesty had some awkwardness about it, such as a reference to its founders as the "old Puritans": "if the King shd ask who the old Puritans were, some waggish Person near him might be apt to say they were they that took King Ch. the 1st head off." (Letter dated March 30, 1728; SPCK New England Letters, vol. 3.)

In 1740, an incredibly insensitive letter came from Edward Hutchinson, treasurer at Harvard, to Newman asking him to give an accounting for £20 sent him in 1730 and another £20 in 1733. Injured and amazed, Newman replied

Newman's intercession with Berkeley on behalf of his alma mater (obtaining as much "as I could with decency ask"), the dean had from his own library in Newport given Harvard "ancient Greek Authors which I found they wanted."[17] This gift came in September of 1731, coinciding with Berkeley's one visit to the school prior to his setting sail from Boston.

The 1733 gift sent from London emphasized the Latin classics: "all the Latin Classick Authors in quarto being of the fairest Editions and the best Comments," as Berkeley explained in a letter to Harvard's president, Benjamin Wadsworth.[18] Whereas Yale received eight large cases of books, Harvard received only one, presumably about 125 volumes. This wide discrepancy, Newman explained to Wadsworth, resulted from Berkeley's recognition that Yale "was much more in want of Theological books &c." than was the more established Harvard. To Samuel Johnson, Newman commented somewhat more tactfully that Yale received the greater share because its library "was in its infancy State."[19] But Harvard felt no injury, formally voting their thanks to the dean for having "lately procured a valuable collection

---

(Sept. 29, 1740): "I own I was not a little surpriz'd at the expectations you signify the Corporation have of my Accounting to them." Newman, nevertheless, did give "account," telling of his unflagging efforts in Harvard's behalf. Then specifically of the Berkeley gift in 1733, he wrote: "tho' it did not go all to our College, I obtain'd as much as I could with decency ask, and thought his favour confer'd on a Sister or Daughter of Harvard Col. was in a manner given to us." Two years later, Harvard's president, Edward Holyoke, made amends for the earlier gaffe by expressing the appreciation of both corporation and college to Newman. Now calmed and pleased, Newman responded (Aug. 6, 1742) that he only wished he could give "more effectual Proofs of my Zeal in so good a Cause"; SPCK New England Letters, vol. 5.

17. GB *Works*, 8: 298; letter dated July 8(?), 1747.

18. Ibid., p. 220; letter dated May 31, 1733 (also SPCK New England Letters, vol. 4).

19. See note 15, above.

of Books."[20] Furthermore, Harvard had enjoyed the satisfaction of a personal visit, an honor which Yale never managed to win.

As late as 1747, Berkeley continued to have Harvard on his mind as the final remnant of funds (£200) left from the Bermuda project was turned over to the SPG, with the suggestion that £50 thereof "might be usefully employ'd in purchasing" books for Harvard. This time the collection was not of Latin classics, but of "the most approved writings of the Church of England."[21] And that might create a problem in the minds or bosoms of Massachusetts Congregationalists. Philip Bearcroft, secretary of the SPG, wrote to Berkeley volunteering to correspond with Governor William Shirley, happily an Anglican, "to consult him about the matter, as to what books are in his opinion the most proper, and how far he will undertake for their being received."[22] But Berkeley thought all that unnecessary: what do politicians know about books? Besides, in his own experience, Berkeley had found Harvard, like Yale, always ready for more books.

A nervous Bearcroft wrote the Massachusetts governor nonetheless, stressing that while the £50-worth of books did contain "the true Doctrines of our Holy Religion both as to faith and practice," they also "tend to promote the Gospel of Christ, endeavouring to keep the unity of the spirit in the bond of Peace."[23] In conveying its thanks to the SPG and to "the Bishop of Cloyne," Harvard seized upon the opening Bearcroft had provided. These books, Edward Holyoke wrote on behalf of the college, did "very

20. Quoted in Henry J. Cadbury, "Bishop Berkeley's Gifts to the Harvard Library," *Harvard Library Bulletin* 7 (1953): 75.

21. GB *Works*, 8: 297; letter dated before April 10, 1747.

22. Cadbury, "Bishop Berkeley's Gifts," p. 198.

23. Ibid., p. 200.

much tend (as you express it) to promote the Gospel of
Christ, & the Interest of Religion, both in Faith & Practice."[24] Since many of the books were antipapist (and on
that point Anglican and Puritan could agree) or broadly
apologetic in the tradition of the Boyle Lectures, Bearcroft need not have been so concerned. Berkeley was right:
Harvard wanted books. In the burning of Harvard Hall in
1764, much of the Berkeley gift was lost.[25] By then, Berkeley had passed from this earth; otherwise, he almost certainly would have once more resumed his "poor endeavors"
on behalf of books, which is to say on behalf of religion
and learning in America.[26]

Berkeley's "poor endeavors" on behalf of Indians and
blacks constitute a story more complex and in the end less
satisfactory. In the original 1724 *Proposal*, the uncivilized
and unChristianized state of the Indian loomed large in its
author's mind. In that first edition, "Savage Americans"
even won a place on the title page itself. A second edition
which enlarged the sections on the Indians now for the
first time included explicit comment on the blacks. "To
the Infamy of England, and Scandal of the World," Berkeley wrote in 1725, blacks "continue Heathen under Christian Masters, and in Christian countries." Plantation owners
(and Berkeley had the West Indies chiefly in mind here)
must be "rightly instructed and made sensible" that they
have a Christian duty to see that their own slaves are

24. Ibid., p. 201.
25. Henry Cadbury determined that a fair number of the Berkeley books,
being checked out of the library at the time of the fire, did indeed survive. Of
the earlier gifts of Greek and Latin classics, Cadbury concluded that a dozen
books lived through the fire, and of the latter gift "about a score." In the
category of religion, Berkeley's 1747 gift to Harvard bore a strong resemblance
to his 1733 gift to Yale. See all of Cadbury's two articles, pp. 73–87 and
pp. 196–207, both in vol. 7 of the *Harvard Library Bulletin*.
26. See his letter to Thomas Clap, dated July 25, 1751; GB *Works*,
8: 306.

baptized. Moreover, he explained and would explain repeatedly, "Gospel Liberty consists with temporal Servitude."[27]

While to a later age it may seem no great service to blacks to argue that they could lawfully be both Christians and slaves at the same time, the case is otherwise. For if Christianity were a genuine option, then neither blackness on the one hand nor slavery on the other meant a spiritual inferiority or separation. At an irreducible minimum, this meant that black slaves, too, had souls. That Christianity did not eliminate attitudes of racial inferiority and physical degradation is a circumstance too familiar and depressing to require elaboration. But history, like nature, knows no sudden jumps. Berkeley took a step, however tentative and tiny, when he argued for greater intensity and responsibility in trying to Christianize blacks. He even appealed to His Majesty's attorney and solicitor general for a formal opinion on the eligibility of slaves for baptism. When that opinion (holding that being baptized in no way altered the civil status of slaves) reached Berkeley in Newport, he believed that one small obstacle, at least, had been cleared from the missionary's path. "This Opinion they charitably send over," Berkeley commented later, "which was accordingly printed in Rhode-Island, and dispersed throughout the Plantations." In this as in his general evangelizing concern, Berkeley labored to eradicate "an irrational Contempt of the Blacks, as Creatures of another Species, who have no Right to be instructed or admitted to the Sacraments." This virulent racism, as Berkeley along with officials of the SPG and many others all too clearly recognized, had "proved a main Obstacle to the Conversion of these poor people."[28]

27. GB *Works*, 7: 346.
28. GB *Works*, p. 122; in Berkeley's sermon before the SPG, preached February 18, 1732, in St. Mary-le-Bow Church, London. Though Berkeley clearly states that the attorney general's opinion was printed in Rhode Island and elsewhere, I have not been able to locate it.

While Berkeley was awaiting the legal judgment regarding Christianity and slavery, the lord bishop of London, Edmund Gibson, rendered a moral and ecclesiastical one. Explaining that in religious matters, "the Care of Plantations abroad" was very much in his charge, Gibson in 1727 addressed one letter to plantation "Masters and Mistresses," a second and briefer letter to the missionaries. Though he recognized the difficulties in bringing slaves, especially adults, into Christianity, Gibson voiced dismay that attempts to evangelize had actually "been by too many industriously discouraged and hindered." Masters must see themselves as *Christian* masters, which among other things meant not putting profits above lives and not profaning the Lord's Day by requiring slaves to work then, or putting "them under a kind of Necessity of labouring on that Day, to provide themselves with the Conveniences of Life." Like his good friend George Berkeley, Bishop Gibson patiently explained that the act of slaves becoming Christians "does not make the least Alteration in Civil Property, or in any of the Duties which belong to Civil Relations." The laws of humanity as well as of Christianity did, of course, require "Kindness, Gentleness, and Compassion towards all Mankind, of what Nation or Condition soever they be." Just as he would have masters think of themselves as *Christian* masters, so would he have slaves regarded as *human* beings, nothing less.

> [L]et me beseech you to consider Them, not barely as Slaves, and upon the same level with labouring Beasts, but as Men-Slaves and Women-Slaves, who have the same Frame and Faculties with your selves, and have Souls capable of being made eternally happy, and Reason and Understanding to receive Instruction in order to it [*sic*].[29]

29. Letter dated May 19, 1727, in David Humphreys, *An Historical Account of the Incorporated Society for the Propagation of the Gospel* . . . (London,

These sentiments, along with those earlier expressed by Berkeley, provoked a sharp retort from one of those West Indies plantation owners, now much aggrieved. In an anonymous letter to Gibson, the author declared in effect that the lord bishop of London, the scholarly dean of Derry, and the intrusive SPG did not know what they were talking about.[30] Slave masters (of whom he acknowledged that he was one) received all too much unjustified denunciation and abuse; moreover, it was either assumed or stated that it was their "avarice, atheism and ungodliness" which chiefly prevented the conversion of the blacks. What nonsense! But even if it were true, worthy divines should remember that plantation owners did not go to the Caribbean islands "to teach the slaves the Christian Faith and Worship." Their motivation was clearly of another sort. Furthermore, the issue of baptism affecting the civil status of the slave was no issue at all. Did anybody ever really believe that? If there were but "one Example of their Manumission upon Baptism" or even a serious push in that direction, the bottom would drop out of the whole slave market. Then, my learned gentlemen, "what would become of the Nation's Trade to Guinea and the Sugar Colonies?"[31]

Taking specific aim at Berkeley, the author made no great effort to conceal his scorn. One could readily see that neither the dean of Derry nor anyone who thought as he did "was ever upon the Spot." Anyone who took the time to investigate the actual situation—be he "a Doctor of Divinity or a Bishop"—would give up this ridiculous effort to convert the Negro "as impracticable to any Tolerable Degree."

1730; reprint New York, 1969), p. 269; other quotations from pp. 257, 258, and 262. For historical perspective regarding Berkeley's and Gibson's pleas, it is important to recall that abolitionism as a movement of any real significance was still many decades away.

30. *A Letter to the Right Reverend, the Lord Bishop of London, From An Inhabitant of His Majesty's Leeward-Caribee* [sic] *Islands. . . .* (London, 1730).

31. Ibid., pp. 17, 34.

But perhaps practicality was too much to expect from a
cleric who, if the rumors could be believed, was "a Whimsical Man, and one that talks at Randon." One other small
point this hardheaded realist would make to those soft-
hearted idealists who had never been "on the Spot": a good
many of the slave owners hereabouts were Jews, especially
on Barbados and Jamaica. Now there was a problem for
whimsical men to reflect on: did they really expect to convince these Jews of their "Christian duty"?[32] As Gibson
had already conceded, missionary efforts faced enormous
odds, especially "where there is not a good Heart to go
about them."[33]

The bishop's second brief letter of 1727, addressed to
the missionaries, urged those who themselves held Negroes
to set an example, being scrupulous in the discharge of
their own duty to instruct and baptize. One could hardly
expect the laity to take seriously their obligation in this
regard "if they see it wholly neglected, or but coldly pursued, in the Families of the Clergy."[34] Though Berkeley
scarcely needed this specific directive, he faithfully executed it during his Newport stay. In October, 1730, he purchased three slaves; in the following winter at Whitehall he
carefully instructed them, and on June 11, 1731, "Dean
Berkeley baptized three of his negroes, 'Philip, Anthony
and Agnes Berkeley'."[35] At least in Newport that much
of Gibson's intention was met. But the ordinary parish,
whether in Barbados or in Boston, found the way hard.

32. Ibid., pp. 56–57, 59, 84, 102.
33. Humphreys, *An Historical Account,* p. 261.
34. Ibid., pp. 273–74.
35. George C. Mason, *Annals of Trinity Church, 1698–1821,* p. 51. A bill of
sale in the British Museum (Ms. 39316) describes "a Negro man named Philip
aged Fourteen Years or thereabout" sold by Simon Pease (Oct. 4, 1730) to
George Berkeley for £80, and "a Negro man named Edward [Anthony?] aged
Twenty Years or thereabouts" sold by William Coddington (Oct. 7, 1730) for
£86. Agnes does not appear in this record.

Timothy Cutler in Christ Church, Boston, reported in 1727
to the SPG:

> Negro & Indian Slaves belonging to my Parish are about
> 32, their Education & Instruction is according to the
> Houses they belong to. I have baptized but 2. But I
> know of some Masters of some others, who are dis-
> posed to this important good of their Slaves, & prepar-
> ing them for it; however here is too great a remissness.[36]

True to his time, George Berkeley found the image of
savage Americans somehow more fascinating than the reality
of enslaved ones. For all of Europe, the Indian was a genuine exotic, though misnamed at the beginning and mis-
understood from that point on. How much of the *Proposal's*
initial appeal rested on this romance surrounding the Indian
is impossible to say, but that facet of the Bermuda scheme
probably fired more imaginations and loosened more purse
strings than the other more prosaic purpose: namely, that
"the youth of our English plantations might be themselves
fitted for the ministry."[37] Christianizing the Indian, however, appealed more to Englishmen than to Indians. However difficult or unprofitable it might be to convert a servant
or a slave, it was far more difficult and impractical to preach
to the enemy—former, potential, or actual. In 1730, SPG
secretary David Humphreys explained some of the barriers
and frustrations, beyond what seemed to be the Indians'
natural "Aversion" to Christianity. Many of the North
American Indians, for example, had been misled by the
"Artifices of the French Jesuits" who were forever trying
"to seduce them from their Fidelity to the Crown of England."

36. W. S. Perry, *Historical Collections Relating to the American Colonial
Church* (Hartford, 1873; reprint New York, 1969), 3: 230 (hereafter *Hist.
Coll.*); letter dated Oct. 10, 1727.
37. *A Proposal* (1724 ed.), 5.

Besides, the Indians bordering on New-England are the
most cruel and barbarous of all the Savage Nations,
and have destroyed all their innocent Neighbours. They
are always unfixed, either rambling for several Months
together, or hunting, or upon Warlike Expeditions; and
at their return to the Villages, have generally unlearned
all their former Instructions; and it is impossible for
any Minister to accompany them in their Ramble of 3
or 400 Leagues at a Time.[38]

Even the SPG's optimism quailed before the apparently
insuperable problems in attempting to convert the Indians.
Until they were civilized, and many difficulties stood in
the way of that, the Society concluded that its mission to
the Indians was "fruitless."[39]

For Berkeley, too, the case, if not beyond all hope, was
nearly so. The English either exploited the Indian or stood
entirely aloof from him. In a tone clearly commendatory,
Berkeley remarked that "Both French and Spaniards have
intermarried with Indians, to the great Strength, Security
and Increase of their Colonies." Not only had the English
failed to take a similarly positive step, they had taken several negative ones. In Rhode Island, for example, the English had "contributed more to destroy their Bodies by the
use of strong Liquors, than by any means to improve their
Minds or save their Souls. This slow Poison, jointly operat-
ing with the Small-Pox, and their Wars . . . hath consumed
the Indians."[40] If the prospect for rescuing and elevating

38. Humphreys, *An Historical Account,* pp. 291–92.

39. Ibid., p. 306.

40. GB *Works*, 7: 121–22 (sermon before the SPG). Berkeley's direct contact was chiefly with the Narragansett Indians, especially when he crossed the
Bay to visit the parish of James McSparran on the mainland (what Anne Berkeley, with slight exaggeration, referred to as the "inner recesses" of America).
On one such visit, John Smibert, when he saw his first American Indian,
inquired what "Tartars" were doing here. Having painted some Mongolians

the Indian seemed hopeful in 1724, Berkeley a decade later
found such optimism difficult to sustain.

Yet, Berkeley's humanitarian hopes on behalf of both
Indian and black came closer to realization than is generally
recognized. And in that "near miss" of history the names
of Percival, Bray, and Ogelthorpe appear, along with a new
name: Abel Tassin, Sieur D'Allone. Private secretary to
King William III (1689–1702), D'Allone upon his death in
1723 left a major legacy for the conversion of the Negroes
in Britain's plantations. The £900 seemed naturally to fall
within Thomas Bray's domain, since he had been cultivat-
ing D'Allone (and receiving small contributions from him)
for over twenty years.[41] The SPG, however, already engaged
in works among the blacks in the colonies, thought that
the bequest might more properly be theirs. Bray, now no
longer directly involved in the operation of the SPG, responded (February 24, 1725) that "M^r D'Allone had never
given the least Intimation or Hint, by Letter or otherwise,"
of any intent to have the Society "Consulted or Concerned
in that Affair." On the contrary, Bray had full discretion
to use the funds as he saw fit "in forwarding so good a
Work"; moreover, he believed himself to "be at full Liberty
to Associate whom he pleased together . . . to manage that
Trust."[42] With some embarrassment and haste, the Society
backed away from pressing any further claim.[43]

Competition from another quarter, however, appeared
almost immediately upon the scene. That very same year,
1724, the dean of Derry had publicly announced his good

---

during his earlier Italian travels, he was struck by the strong resemblance. See
Wilkins Updike, *History of the Episcopal Church in Narragansett, Rhode-
Island* . . . (New York, 1847), 523 n.; *The Medical Repository* 2 (1811): 176.

41. H. P. Thompson, *Thomas Bray*, 98–99.

42. SPG Archives, Letter Books Series C/am, vol. 15: item 25.

43. See David Humphreys's letter of swift "retreat" to Percival, March 23,
1725; BM, Add Ms. 47030.

intentions and noble design with respect to Britain's plantations. True, conversion of the Negro had not been specifically mentioned in the first edition of the *Proposal*, but that oversight could be and was quickly rectified. Behind the scenes, two of Berkeley's strongest supporters, John Percival and his cousin in Dublin, Daniel Dering, tried to promote Berkeley and Bermuda as the most logical recipients of that £900. They persuaded Lord Palmerston, executor of the D'Allone bequest, "that the Intention of the Testator cannot be so effectively answer'd any way as by giving the Revenue of . . . it to Bermuda."[44] Only a few days later, Berkeley added his excited endorsement to the idea. "Lord Palmerston is desirous," he wrote Percival in 1726, "that nine hundred and odd pounds in his hands should be disposed of to this our college [St. Paul's] for breeding up young negroes according to Mr. Delon's will."[45]

Percival, as was so often the case with this astute man of affairs, occupied a strategic position. Early supporter of Berkeley's dream, he had also been invited by Bray to become one of those "Associates" charged with carrying out D'Allone's wishes. Only four such Associates had in fact been named. "The majority of these," Berkeley reported "are of Lord Palmerston's mind, and your Lordship's concurrence hath been applied for."[46] Even before Berkeley's letter reached Percival, he had heard what was afoot from his Dublin cousin. Responding to Dering, Percival wrote: "I did not intend to concern myself with Mr. Dalones Legacy, and accordingly gave Dr. Bray a positive

44. Daniel Dering to Percival, Jan. 31, 1726; BM, Add. Ms. 47031. On Lord Palmerston, see *Dictionary of National Biography*, "Henry Temple" (1673?–1757).

45. GB *Works*, 8: 152; Berkeley to Percival, Feb. 10, 1726.

46. Ibid. Besides Percival, the remaining three Associates were Robert Hales, his brother Stephen Hales, and William Belitha. Palmerston, who served as executor of D'Allone's English estate, and of course Bray himself, wielded great influence over the four Associates.

Refusal, but since there is a disposition in the other Associates to give the money to Dean Berkeley's Colledge I will on that Condition Act." His astuteness evident once more, however, he recognized that Thomas Bray himself was crucial to the success or failure of this maneuver. "But I think it would be proper Dr Bray should be informed of our Design and his approbation given it in writing." On the other side of the coin, it was also necessary that the dean "oblige himself to instruct a certain number of Negroe Children that shall be offer'd him, that it may appear we come as near answering the Intent of the Donor as we possibly can."[47]

In Dublin, both George Berkeley and Daniel Dering considered these sober cautions but found in them no obstacle. The four Associates had all come around, with even the lord bishop of London agreed that this was "the most effectual way of answering the Intention of the Testator." Berkeley expressed his willingness "to enter into any obligation to maintain and Educate such Blacks" as Percival would decide, being loyal to the spirit of both the *Proposal* and the bequest. That left only Thomas Bray. "As for Dr. Bray," Dering wrote his cousin two weeks later, "the Dean is perfectly unacquainted with him, besides he is Superannuated and dying."[48] This proved a fatal miscalculation.

Superannuated perhaps (he was sixty-eight years old), but not dying—though in fact Bray had been seriously ill. It was his illness which had prompted Lord Palmerston to urge Bray to gather together those "Associates" just in case the worst did come to pass. But Thomas Bray had four years of life left, long enough to see that Berkeley and his friends came no closer to touching that £900 than the SPG had succeeded in doing. Bray's confidence in Berkeley's

47. Percival to Daniel Dering, Feb. 12, 1726; BM, Add. Ms. 47031.
48. Ibid., Dering to Percival, Feb. 28, 1726.

plan, as discussed above,[49] fell even lower than his confidence in the current management of the SPG. If Bray managed to keep the Society at arm's length, he would try to hold Berkeley as far from the funds as Bermuda was from England. To "Dr. Bray's Associates" and to them alone would belong the duty of determining how best to promote Christianity among the colonies' blacks. Not only did the D'Allone money never reach Berkeley, but other monies initially designated for Bermuda ultimately merged with that from D'Allone to support a project quite removed from the dean's design—an irony that even a philosopher found it hard to appreciate.

Thomas Bray did die, on the fifteenth of February in 1730. By that time, Berkeley had been waiting for more than a year in Newport; also by that time, the original group of four Associates had grown in number to twenty-nine. One member of that larger group, James E. Ogelthorpe, had come to Bray's attention as a man much interested in prison reform. When Bray sank low in his final days, no one stood at the helm and nothing much seemed to be happening—not with the money, not with the blacks, not with the causes of charity and humanity anywhere. Ogelthorpe appealed to Percival as a mover of men and promoter of projects to somehow get the Associates off dead center. If they were not prepared to execute Mr. D'Allone's purposes, Ogelthorpe had a few of his own.

Just two days before Bray's death, Ogelthorpe first met with Percival, where he heard of the latter's hope "to assist Dean Berkeley's Bermuda scheme, by erecting a Fellowship in his college for instructing negroes; that in so doing the charity would be rendered perpetual, whereas to dribble it away in sums of five or ten pounds to missioners in the plantations, the money would be lost without any effect."

49. See above, pp. 42–47.

Ogelthorpe, on the other hand, ventured to suggest "that religion will not be propagated in the Indies by colleges." The better plan, he argued, would be to encourage clergy already in the colonies to do more for the blacks but "without any reward," using the modest income from the legacy to send over religious books specifically for the Negro.[50]

Ogelthorpe's interests, however, extended beyond the blacks, and his resources extended, eventually, well beyond D'Allone's £900. He mentioned to Percival that "a very considerable charity" (£15,000) might be deliverable to the Associates. Given that awesome possibility, Ogelthorpe suggested that a separate trusteeship be established to oversee his bold new plan, already discussed with appropriate officials in government. "The scheme is to procure a quantity of acres either from the Government or by gift or purchase in the West Indies, and to plant thereon a hundred miserable wretches who being let out of gaol by the last year's Act, are now starving about the town for want of employment."[51] To Percival, it must have sounded like a play he had seen before: another scheme only half thought out, wholly idealistic and "whimsical," dependent upon good will expressed and promises implied, and to be located off somewhere in the West Indies (Ogelthorpe failed only to name the name "Bermuda"). The differences between Berkeley's design and what soon became the colony of Georgia were, of course, many. In 1730 and 1731, however, the similarity was such as to suggest that Georgia was simply dying Bermuda brought back to life.

50. Historical Manuscripts Commission, *Diary of the First Earl of Egmont* (Viscount Percival), 3 vols. (London, 1920, 1923), 1: 44–45; hereafter, Percival, *Diary.*

51. Ibid. The act referred to, in all probability, was one made final in 1732 relating to "the charitable corporation for relief of the industrious poor"; see George Knight, *A History of the English Poor Law* (rev. ed. New York, 1898), 2: 23.

In May, 1731, Ogelthorpe wrote to Berkeley in Newport,
explaining that he had learned "of the many difficulties
and Obstacles you had met in that Glorious Design." It did
not surprise him, he consoled the philosopher in residence,
that Parliament had not delivered on its promise of £20,000
for Bermuda. For in passing such a bill "no private Views
was [sic] to be gratified, no Relation served, nor Pander
prefer'd, nor no depraved Opposition indulged." (Ogelthorpe presumably regarded the letter as totally private!)
But the main reason for writing, James Ogelthorpe continued, was to tell Berkeley about a new group of men "(of
whom I have the honour to be one) associated together for
the carrying on some good designs." A few of Berkeley's
friends in London "thought that we might be of some
Service here toward effecting your truly Christian undertaking." In other words, as graciously and gently as possible,
Ogelthorpe hinted that where Berkeley alone had failed,
perhaps Berkeley and Ogelthorpe together could succeed.
Our "Motives and ends are the same."

Ogelthorpe then explicated his scheme directed at allevi-
ating the miseries of the poor, especially those in debtors'
prisons. Merely to obtain their release from jail was only to
grant them "the privilege of starving at large." With some
excitement, he informed Berkeley that all had gone well in
the royal councils, chambers, and committees; and, oh yes,
the West Indies were no longer judged an appropriate site.

> The Society have obtained the Kings Order for a Grant
> of all the Lands in South Carolina lying between the
> Rivers Savannah and Alatamaha and Licences for Col-
> lecting all Charitys, and receiving all the Legacys and
> Donations as shall be given to them.[52]

In language that Berkeley must have found disquietingly
familiar, Ogelthorpe spoke of preventing luxury, idleness,

---

52. Ogelthorpe to Berkeley, "May 1731"; BM, Add. Ms. 47033.

and vice; of keeping intoxicants away from the Indians; and, of the great benefits that would accrue to the Christian religion. "From the very beginning," moreover, all men "are to be established as freemen and not as servants." Slavery and slave-owning was to be dealt with in the simplest manner conceivable: prohibiting its introduction.

The question, of course, was whether such vision could fare any better in 1731 than it seemed to do in 1728 or 1729 or 1730. Berkeley might well be excused for finding little reason to think it would. Percival, on the other hand, as he broke the Georgia news to Berkeley some months earlier, saw the central difference between the two designs. Ogelthorpe's plan served more than the interests of religion and learning. His venture, unlike that of Bermuda, would extend the outposts of empire, serve as a bulwark against Spanish and Indian incursions from either south or west, and in general work "to the great advantage of England." Because the plan is "entirely calculated for a secular interest," it will pass, Percival predicted, and it will be funded. Even the merchants "commend the design"—a statement no one could ever make about the Bermuda scheme. And the poor? Well, even if the mulberry trees do not grow and no silk is produced, at least "London will be eased of maintaining a number of families which being let out of gaol have at present no visible way to subsist."[53]

When at last Berkeley returned to London, neither his pride nor his disappointment prevented his meeting with Ogelthorpe to advise and assist in what Percival now called "our Carolina project."[54] And that project became the fashionable charity for Britain's philanthropists in the 1730s as Berkeley's now doomed scheme had been seven or eight years earlier. In March of 1732, Percival even went so far as to invite the dean to join in the philanthropy. "I

---

53. Rand, *B & P*, 270–71; letter dated Dec. 23, 1730.
54. Percival, *Diary*, 1: 214; entry for Jan. 12, 1732.

asked him if . . . he would care to turn over to our Carolina
Settlement some part of the subscriptions that were made
to his scheme."[55] Yale, Berkeley explained, came first. The
final irony appeared with the sale of those lands on St.
Christopher's Island, for from that sale the—did Berkeley
now think mythical?—£20,000 was to have come. In 1733,
the lands brought in £90,000, £80,000 of which went as a
dowry for the marriage of George II's daughter to the
prince of Orange. Of the remaining £10,000 Percival preserved this note:

> Wednesday, 16 [May, 1733]. — Went to town to
> attend the Grand Committee upon money to be given
> for Georgia. Colonel Bladen made the motion in our
> favour, which was to give the sum of 10,000 l. out of
> the money lying in the Exchequer . . . for carrying on a
> settlement in the Province of Georgia. Nobody spoke
> against it, but one or two Noes were heard.[56]

So the last of America's colonies, named after so generous
a king, came into being to serve the poor and the persecuted,
the Indian and the black, the state and the church. The
Georgia design shared one final similarity with the Bermuda
plan: subsequent realities mocked earlier dreams.

When in 1730 Percival had first informed Berkeley of
Georgia's rising fortunes and Bermuda's falling ones, he
tried to cushion the blow. With respect to your plans and
hopes, he wrote, it "seems too great and good to be accomplished in an age where men love darkness better than light,
and nothing is considered but with a political view." But
while the project could hardly succeed in its original conception, "who knows what sparks of fire may yet remain
among the ashes."[57]

55. Ibid., p. 236; entry for March 14, 1732.
56. Ibid., p. 375; entry for May 16, 1733.
57. Rand, *B & P*, 269–70.

5 The Church and the Word

By the Last Ships from London we had some pleasant
Intimations of Two Bishops being appointed for America, which have in a manner given New Life to our people and it would be of a Sad Consideration to have their
Expectations frustrated.

James Honeyman to Bishop Edmund Gibson,
November 14, 1725

George Berkeley arrived in Newport, Rhode Island by
choice, not by accident. And one of the reasons dictating
that choice, as has been noted above, was the solid position of Anglicanism there. Since 1704 James Honeyman
had labored for the SPG in Newport with increasing effec-
tiveness and visible results. Even more, this "considerable
place" had become a gathering ground where New England's Anglican clergy could consider joint actions and
share mutual counsel. By the time of Berkeley's protracted
visit, Rhode Island had shown itself more hospitable to the
Church of England than either of its near neighbors, Connecticut and Massachusetts.

True, Boston had services according to the Book of Common Prayer as early as 1685, but only as a result of a direct
political intrusion from England. Not until the very end of
1723 did Boston have an Anglican church appear in a less
authoritarian, less obtrusive manner. The newly ordained
rector of that second church, Timothy Cutler, reported to
the SPG that on the final Sunday of the year (December
29, 1723) the congregation celebrated "the first time of
our assembling" in a just-completed building. Cutler added:
"I can't yet say what numbers will frequent our worship

in this New Church but it is thought we shall have upwards
of 50 Families besides the share we expect of seafaring
persons."[1] Earlier, a struggle within the Congregational
church at Newbury resulted in 1709 in the withdrawal of a
faction determined to build "at their own charge . . . a
church for the worship of God after the mode used in the
Church of England."[2] And in 1715 St. Michael's parish
was organized in Marblehead, with David Mossom and
George Pigot serving as early missionaries resident there.

   Connecticut's first Church of England opened on Christ-
mas Day, 1723, when Samuel Johnson led divine services
in Stratford. Earlier missionaries had preached there, but
now the town had its own building set apart for Anglican
worship. Johnson, like George Pigot before him, also conducted divine services with some regularity in nearby Fairfield, until in 1727 the SPG appointed Henry Caner, a young
Yale graduate whom Johnson had groomed specifically for
the Fairfield parish. Fairfield soon outdistanced Stratford
in both membership and financial strength. Tiny Rhode
Island, meanwhile, had four parishes of some stability by
the end of the 1720s: besides Newport, these were located
in Narragansett (with James McSparran as missionary and
rector since 1721), Bristol (guided by John Usher, a Harvard graduate), and Providence (where the near-ubiquitous
George Pigot resided from 1723 to 1727).[3] By the end of
the decade, Newport's prominence as an Anglican center
was further enhanced by the death of Samuel Myles
(King's Chapel, Boston), making James Honeyman the
senior Church of England Clergyman in all of New England. Who could more logically serve as George Berkeley's

   1. W. S. Perry, *Hist. Coll.,* 3: 142–43.
   2. Ibid., p. 109.
   3. For brief biographical sketches of Caner, McSparran, Usher, and Pigot,
see William B. Sprague, *Annals of the American Pulpit* (New York, 1861;
reprint New York, 1969), 5: 61–62, 44–45, 48–49, and 50n.

host than Honeyman? Where more logically could the dean
of Derry reside than in Newport?

At the time of his arrival in January of 1729, some but
not all of the excitement of the 1722 defection of Johnson, Cutler, and Brown had worn off. That "grand revolution," as Honeyman had called it, erupting on Yale's
campus on Commencement Day (September 12), still
charmed New England's Anglicans as sure harbinger of a
better day. Likewise, it still infuriated the "old Puritans"
and their heirs, who saw in it a most cavalier and callous
dismissal of all that was meant by "New England." "The
axe is hereby laid to the root of our civil and sacred enjoy-
ments," a correspondent wrote Cotton Mather,[4] while his
father, Increase, turned to prayer where he "much bewail'd
the Connecticut Apostacie."[5] Two Yale trustees, having
every reason to feel particularly injured, lamented, "How
is the gold become dim! and the silver dross. and the wine
mixt with water!"[6]

As soon as Yale's trustees recovered from their shock,
dismissing Cutler, Johnson, and Brown, the wounded college began to build anew. For the apostates themselves,
even more wounds needed to be healed and more rebuild-
ing of lives begun. Far more than a quiet academic debate
over valid ordination and what Cotton Mather called "that

4. Quoted in Joseph Ellis, *The New England Mind in Transition: Samuel
Johnson of Connecticut, 1696–1772* (New Haven, 1973), p. 78; see all of
chapter 4 therein.

5. Quoted in Richard Warch, *School of the Prophets: Yale College,
1701–1740* (New Haven, 1973), p. 110.

6. Ibid. Yale's willingness a mere decade later to accept Berkeley's gift of
books is noteworthy, for books (those gathered earlier by Jeremiah Dummer)
received much of the blame for the Great Apostacy. Dummer explained that
while Anglican authors were to be found in Yale's library, so also were the
ablest of all dissenting scholars represented there. Remarkably, Yale's library
suffered no purge even after the defection, though the faculty was now
obliged to subscribe to the Saybrook Platform's Confession of Faith;
Warch, p. 114.

vile, senseless, wretched whimsey of an uninterrupted succession,"[7] the bitter break caused severe disquiet of mind
and soul. In his notes recorded just after that fateful commencement day, Samuel Johnson revealed the personal
angst involved.

> Being at length brought to such scruples concerning
> the validity of my ordination . . . I have now at length
> . . . this commencement made a public declaration of
> my scruples and uneasiness. . . . It is with great sor-
> row of heart that I am forced thus, by the uneasiness
> of my conscience to be an occasion for so much un-
> easiness to my dear friends, my poor people, and
> indeed to the whole colony. Oh God, I beseech thee,
> grant that I may not . . . be a stumbling block or
> occasion of fall to any soul. Let not our thus appear-
> ing for thy Church be any ways accessary, though
> accidentally, to the hurt of religion in general or any
> person in particular. Have mercy. Oh Lord, have
> mercy.[8]

Part of the difficulty and dread which the apostates
faced concerned the logistics of ordination itself. If valid
orders were the real sticking point (and church polity
more than theology lay at the root of the hard decision),
then clearly the earlier Puritan ordination no longer served.
And an episcopal ordination which clung to that "vile"
apostolic succession was nowhere to be had in all America.
On November 5, 1722, therefore, Cutler, Johnson, and
Brown sailed for England, an England that received them
virtually as conquering heroes.[9] Conquest was precisely
what the new converts had in mind. After ordination,
Brown planned to go to Rhode Island (either Bristol or

7. Quoted in Warch, p. 111.
8. Johnson, *Writings*, 1: 62.
9. Ellis, *New England Mind*, p. 81.

Providence), Johnson to Connecticut, and Cutler—the only Harvard graduate among them—to Massachusetts Bay. By this encirclement, the loving bands of Anglicanism could be more tightly drawn around all New England.

The plan was shaken, though not destroyed, when Brown contracted smallpox and died. Cutler and Johnson, however, survived the honors, the rites, and even the voyages, to return safely to New England in late September, 1723.[10] And however much Congregationalism dreaded their return with all that it might augur, the Church of England folk applauded and rejoiced and elevated their expectations. If now all the lords of Canterbury and London would see that the momentum did not slow, then we shall (said the Trinity Church vestry in Newport) "Shake the Foundations of Schism in these Countreys."[11] Expectations and emotions did stay high. At Newport, as already noted, a beautiful new church went up in 1724. In Stratford, Samuel Johnson found progress most encouraging, despite his being surrounded by "generally rigid Independents" of "uncharitable and therefore unchristian spirit."[12] And in Boston, Timothy Cutler in 1724 gave thanks that "there are many serious persons belonging to us both young and old, devout in the Church & consciencious in their conversations & maintaining as unblemished characters for all moral virtues as any of the Dissenters with us."[13] Two

10. SPG Committee Book 3 (1718–34), Minutes for Jan. 21, 1722: "Cutler be appointed the Society's Missionary at the New Church now building in Boston" at an annual salary of £60. Johnson (as soon as he was "in priests order") was to take Pigot's place at Stratford, with Pigot being transferred to Providence, Rhode Island, at his own request. Brown (this being four months before his death) was named to Bristol in the same colony.

11. Fulham Papers, 8: 133–34; Honeyman and his vestrymen in a letter to Bishop John Robinson, October 29, 1722.

12. Johnson, *Writings*, 3: 217; Johnson to Bishop Edmund Gibson, Jan. 18, 1724.

13. W. S. Perry, *Hist. Coll.*, 3: 163; report to the secretary of the SPG, July 31, 1724.

years later, he was even more ebullient: "My own Church is so numerous that it is the envy rather than the scorn of Dissenters."[14]

Sometimes, however, all of this euphoria was hard for London authorities to translate into precise terms of pounds and shillings, communicants and salaries, church houses and schools. The answers to Bishop Edmund Gibson's "Queries," as these drifted back into England in 1724, clarified the picture somewhat.[15] Some of the questions, such as "What extent is your parish?" and "Have you a House and Glebe?", were ill-suited to the New England scene, but others elicited responses which indicated a steady progress in the instruction of youth, the regularity of worship, and the conversion of "Infidels." Most New England missionaries preferred simply to ignore the question, "Is due Care taken to preserve your House in good Repair?", but George Pigot in Providence could not restrain himself: "The People here use neither Care nor Expense on a Minister's Acc^t, especially whilst their Church is building."[16]

Though complaints about inadequate housing and marginal salaries were most common, the Anglican clergy in Massachusetts and Connecticut expressed even greater dismay over their being victims of harassment and of legal discrimination. Repeatedly, these clergymen sought relief from taxes levied to support the Congregational establishment, appealing to the "Venerable Society," or to the bishop of London, or to the Privy Council, or to anyone else who might conceivably assist.[17] As Samuel Johnson

14. Ibid., p. 668; to Zachary Gray, May 7, 1726.
15. Summaries of the responses as well as the questionnaire itself (17 "queries" in all) may be found in William W. Manross, *The Fulham Papers in the Lambeth Palace Library* (Oxford, 1965).
16. Fulham Papers, 8: 190.
17. See, for example, Calendar of State Papers, Colonial Series, *America*

explained to Bishop Gibson in 1726, it is difficult to believe that the king's own church should not, in the king's own dominions, "be at least upon a level with the Dissenters and free from any oppressions from them."[18] To his further dismay, Johnson found that those "rigid Independents" in New Haven even refused to sell him any land on which to build a church. Some day a church would be erected there, he promised, though Anglicans must for a while longer "labour under great Opposition & Discouragement."[19]

In 1727 five ministers collectively complained to the SPG secretary about the "insults and ill treatment, the frowns & the resentments," the legal impediments and threats that blocked the church at every turn. As long as the laws of Connecticut and Massachusetts stood unrepealed and as long as Anglican church members were obliged "to support Dissenting Teachers & the dreadful schism," so long will the Church of England and its flock suffer "both in honor & estate, powerful arguments in a world guided by sense. As for Rhode Island, that fertile soil of Heresy & Schism," it was true that the church fared better from a purely legal standpoint, but on the other hand what, really, can one expect "from the commander in chief, an Anabaptist, & his Deputy, a Quaker"?[20]

---

and the West Indies, 1726-7 (London, 1936), Document #638 (July 14, 1727); this is a detailed petition from Timothy Cutler, Samuel Johnson, Samuel Myles, James McSparran, George Pigot, and Matthias Plant—all asking to be excused from paying "rates to the Independent teachers."

18. Johnson, *Writings*, 3: 223; letter dated Sept. 26, 1726.

19. Fulham Papers, 1: 235; letter to Bishop Gibson, dated Sept. 21, 1728.

20. W. S. Perry, *Hist. Coll.*, 3: 224-27 (July 20, 1727). See a letter of the same date addressed to Bishop Gibson, complaining particularly about the exclusion of Anglican clergy from Harvard's Board of Overseers: Fulham Papers, 4: 21-22; and, Perry, *Hist. Coll.*, 3: 210-19 et passim.

The "Anabaptist" governor alluded to was Joseph Jenckes (1656-1740), and the Quaker, Jonathan Nichols (1681-1727).

These and other difficulties brought frustration to the
Anglican minority, discord and division to the missionaries, and irritation to all those attempting to worship
"after the mode used in the Church of England." To set
this upside-down world aright, however, the simple solution was at hand: send a bishop. From the New England
clergy, the prayer was plaintive, repetitive, and unanimous:
"the fountain of all our misery is the want of a bishop,"
Johnson wrote in 1724; dramatic conversions such as those
at Yale would multiply many times over if only they could
have a bishop.[21] "We humbly conceive," the clergy
declared in 1725, that "nothing can more effectually
redress these grievance and protect us from the insults of
our adversaries than an Orthodox and Loyal Bishop residing with us."[22] In 1726, Honeyman explained: "Many are
the Arguments that plead for the Necessity of our having a
Bishop in these parts"; he then proceeded to detail a few
of the "Severest Cases and Doubts"—for example, whether
it is permissible to baptize by immersion when one is
requested to do so—that arose concerning which the clergy
had nowhere to turn.[23] Once more in 1727, the gathered
clergy noted that in the very nature of things it was impossible for them "to observe our Rubrick or obey our Can-
ons without a Bishop to whom we may have immediate
recourse."[24] Personal feuds could be settled, legal complexities adjudicated, children confirmed, young men
promptly ordained, and enemies put to rout.

So much was a bishop wished for, so searchingly were
the horizons scanned for signs of his coming, that Honeyman heard of not one but *two* actually on their way to

21. Johnson, *Writings,* 3: 218.
22. W. S. Perry, *Hist. Coll.,* 3: 178.
23. Fulham Papers, 8: 203.
24. W. S. Perry, *Hist. Coll.,* 3: 226.

America.[25] When Johnson first heard of Berkeley's Bermuda plan, he wrote:

> I cannot see what could move the good Dean . . . to
> think of settling himself on so obscure an island as
> Bermuda. Much more good methinks might be done
> here on the continent. And I wish seeing he is so
> piously disposed as to come abroad, he might be the
> gentlemen who might be our bishop. God grant we
> may have such a blessing![26]

And fear as well as wish could father the thought. When the Baptist Thomas Hollis in London learned of Berkeley's "enthusiastick undertaking," he wrote to Boston's Benjamin Colman that this was quite possibly a scheme on the part of the bishop of London "to promote the Church and bring all you Sectuaries over to it [and] appoint him a Suffragan Bishop."[27]

If, however, all the rumors, the fears and hopes, fell short of reality, then perhaps the dean of Derry could at least be persuaded to act as a bishop. That seemed almost the minimum to ask for in order to forestall that "Sad Consideration" of frustrating the people's fully aroused expectations. Berkeley would soon be put to the test. Within weeks of his arrival, he received an urgent appeal from Gabriel Bernon, a Huguenot refugee and lay member of the Providence church. That church, St. John's, had been thrown into turmoil following the departures of

25. Fulham Papers, 8: 199 (November 14, 1725).

26. Johnson, *Writings*, 3: 222; letter to J. Berriman, Aug. 12, 1725. Forty years later, Henry Caner, still (!) pleading for a bishop, noted: "I remember when Dean Berkeley . . . was in the Country, the people of all persuasions were so charmed with him, that they universally shed Tears at his Departure from us." K. W. Cameron, ed., *Letter-Book of the Rev. Henry Caner . . .* (Hartford, 1972), p. 125.

27. Harvard College Records, in *Publications of the Colonial Society of Massachusetts,* 50: 594; Hollis to Colman, Jan. 9, 1727.

the worthy George Pigot and the unworthy Joseph
O'Hara.

But the dean of Derry knew he was not a bishop, certainly not a bishop appointed to New England, even if
some of his over-eager contemporaries thought he was or
soon would be. Politely, he declined the invitation to intervene, informing M. Bernon that he, Berkeley, was a simple
sojourner in this country, quite without authority or jurisdiction "sur les Eglises de cette colonie." Since my own
jurisdiction is many thousand miles away, he added, I must
refer you to "Monseigner l'Evêque de Londres & l'honorable
Societé."[28] Despite Berkeley's refusal to intervene, one
must note that the very next year, 1730, Providence had as
its rector one Arthur Browne, a Trinity College man![29]
And when Browne discovered that O'Hara had stolen all
the parish library, he appealed to Berkeley. Bishop or no,
George Berkeley never turned down a request for books,
supplying Browne (the latter reported) "with such books
as I wanted, otherwise I would have been at a loss."[30]

Few other such personal appeals or responses survive,
though the dean's presence obviously proved tempting to
those who wanted either to treat him as a bishop or to
demonstrate how desperately they needed one. When in
1725 the clergy prayed for the "benign Influences of Episcopal Power" to be bestowed upon their tender but "thriving

28. GB *Works*, 8: 192; letter dated April 9, 1729. In referring Bernon to the
bishop of London, Berkeley of course acted with total propriety and probably
with the knowledge that Gibson was desperately trying to place his authority
over the colonies on a more solid legal base. See Norman Sykes, *Edmund
Gibson, Bishop of London* (Oxford, 1926), 334–39; A. L. Cross, *Anglican
Episcopate,* chapter 1; and, Calendar of State Papers, Colonial Series, *America
and the West Indies, 1730* (London, 1937), Documents #20, #55, and #208.

29. Browne, who received his M.A. in 1729, came to Newport in September of the same year. After about one year there, he removed to Providence
for six years, then on to Portsmouth, New Hampshire; Sprague, *Annals of the
American Pulpit,* 5: 76–77.

30. Fulham Papers, 8: 266; letter to Bishop Gibson, Aug. 31, 1730.

Nurseries," the petitioners included Timothy Cutler, Samuel Johnson, James McSparran, Matthias Plant, George Pigot, and, of course, James Honeyman. But two of their number, Henry Harris of Boston and David Mossom of Marblehead, were absent without leave. At the bottom of their boycott of the Newport meeting was a personal dispute of volcanic intensity between Harris and Cutler. Though the vituperation had risen to levels probably beyond anyone's power to lower, Berkeley was spared the inevitable appeal for arbitration only by the death of Harris soon after the dean's arrival.[31]

Rejecting the temptation to assume the role of bishop, Berkeley did act as gracious host and rapt observer. When he and his family moved into Whitehall, he opened that home to gatherings both formal and informal, and to individual visitors for "conversations" of several days' duration. Anne Berkeley later recalled that "the Missionaries for 70 Miles Around agreed to meet at his house twice a Year & receive his instructions."[32] Though a full-scale assembling of all Anglican clergy in New England appears to have been neither as frequent nor as patriarchal as this later memory suggests,[33] neighboring clergy—dissenters as well as Anglicans

31. Ibid., p. 195 (July 21, 1725); and, SPG Archives, Letter Books, Series A, 19: 234–37. Harris apparently got the feud going by charging Cutler with holding popish views and with being an improper and ineffective rector. Since Cutler had not long been on the Boston scene when all this began, some speculated that Harris was miffed at not being named rector of the "New Church." In 1724, Harris wrote Gibson: "my present opinion of him is that his behavior is so imprudent his notions so wild & extravagant & his principles so uncharitable that I may venture to affirm that the Church will never flourish under his care." Cutler gave his side of the story to the SPG in that same month, July of 1724; a year later, in a private letter, he observed that his difficulties all arose from "the covetous and malicious spirit of a clergyman in this town, who, in lying and villainy, is a perfect overmatch for any Dissenter that I know"; W. S. Perry, *Hist. Coll.*, 3:156–57, 162–63, and 663.

32. Anne Berkeley, in Stock's *Account of the Life of George Berkeley*; quotation may be found opposite page 21.

33. Cutler, as late as May 9, 1730 (fifteen months after Berkeley's resi-

—who did seek Berkeley out found both warm hospitality and friendly counsel awaiting them. Not really "a recluse in Rhode Island,"[34] Berkeley also watched with fascination the religious variety and activity going on all around him. "The inhabitants are of a mixed kind," he wrote Thomas Prior early in his stay, "consisting of many sects and sub-division of sects." The Baptists alone accounted for four separate categories; then, there were "Presbyterians, Quakers, Independents [i.e., Congregationalists] and many of no profession at all."[35]

But in this "strange medley of different persuasions," with their doctrinal peculiarities and liturgical eccentricities, all Rhode Islanders seem able to "agree in one point, viz., that the Church of England is second best."[36] George Berkeley's good-humored tolerance of dissent only rarely failed him, but occasionally the "spirit of delusion and enthusiasm" proved too much to bear—quietly.[37] In general, he not only followed a moderate path himself, but urged his fellow clergymen to "conciliate Men of different Sects unto themselves," to avoid being provoked by "trifles of the Moment," and to refrain from giving offense by "walking about in Pudding Sleeve Gowns—wch they detested."[38] Apparently satisfied that this advice as well as his own example was being followed, Berkeley in 1732

---

dence began), has still not met the dean; "I have yet wanted the happiness of paying my respects to him"; W. S. Perry, *Hist. Coll.*, 3: 671.

34. A. C. Fraser, *Life and Letters of George Berkeley, D. D.* (Oxford, 1871), title of chapter 5.

35. GB *Works*, 8: 196; letter dated April 24, 1729.

36. In a letter to Percival, March 28, 1729; ibid., pp. 191–92. Also see his letter to Martin Benson, April 11, 1729; *ibid.*, 193–94.

37. Ibid., p. 202; letter to Percival, Aug. 30, 1729.

38. Anne Berkeley, in Stock's *Account of the Life of George Berkeley*; quotation may be found opposite p. 21. A "pudding sleeve," according to the *Oxford English Dictionary*, is "a large bulging sleeve drawn in at the wrist or above." See Berkeley's own comment on his simple dress in GB *Works*, 8: 202.

reported to the SPG that their New England missionaries had

> by their Sobriety of Manners, discreet Behaviour, and
> a competent Degree of useful knowledge, shewn them-
> selves worthy the Choice of those who sent them; and
> particularly in living on a more friendly Foot with
> their Brethren of the Separation; who, on their Part,
> were also very much come off from that Narrowness
> of Spirit, which formerly kept them at such an unamic-
> able Distance from us.[39]

Initially impressed by the ability of so many sects to
live together "peaceably with their neighbors, of whatever
profession," Berkeley later came to view much of that good
will as only a cloak for casual indifference to all religion.[40]
Even the ameliorated attitude toward the Church of England might not be all gain; if one were honest with oneself,
the prospect loomed that too many of Rhode Island's
inhabitants had "worn off a serious Sense of all Religion."[41]
If that truly were the case, one had to move beyond charity
and tolerance to advocacy. And to promote religion meant,
for Berkeley, to advance the claims and cause of Anglicanism. He no doubt joined with other "well-dispos'd Gentlemen at Boston, Newport and Marblehead" in assisting some

39. GB *Works*, 7: 122. The SPCK policy toward dissent closely matched
that pursued by Berkeley in Rhode Island. According to Newman, "The
Society have purposely declin'd . . . to concern themselves with the Contro-
versie between the Establish'd Church & Dissenters . . . the common result of
disputes among Protestants being rather a lessening of Charity than conviction
of Truth.

"The Dissenters of all sorts generally increase by all resemblances of persecution but dwindle when left to cool reflection, and to see themselves outliv'd
in respect of good morals by those of the Established Church." Henry Newman to "the Rev. Mr. Paley at Leeds," May 27, 1727; SPCK Society Letters,
vol. 18.

40. GB *Works*, 8: 196; letter to Prior, April 24, 1729.

41. Ibid., 7: 121; SPG sermon, Feb. 18, 1732.

citizens of nearby Warwick, Rhode Island, "to build a decent and commodious Church." Those citizens then appealed to the SPG for a missionary, since for four hundred families the only other options were a Baptist church and a Quaker meeting, "the latter very seldom frequented."[42]

Berkeley's churchmanship in America was evident, however, chiefly in his role as minister and preacher. He officiated at baptisms and weddings,[43] and perhaps at funerals, though no record of that has survived. He encouraged young Americans contemplating holy orders to pursue their goals and, later, was even in a position personally to ordain them.[44] But above all else he preached—regularly and effectively, in Newport and beyond. Anne Berkeley indicated that "he preached every Sunday either in the Church of New Port in Rhode Island, or on the Continent," the "Continent" in this instance being anything beyond Aquidneck Island itself. "And Numbers came whenever he preached," she added; "he spoke freely & clearly & without Books." Like Saint Paul, he "became all things unto all men that he might gain some—he drew them by the Cord of Love & Esteem."[45]

Berkeley himself stated that "many Quakers and other

42. Fulham Papers, 8: 267; petition dated Oct. 1, 1731.

43. On May 27, 1729, Berkeley performed the marriage between Honeyman's only daughter, Elizabeth, and William Mumford. In addition to baptizing his three slaves (as noted above, p. 94), Berkeley baptized his son Henry, Sept. 21, 1729; Mason, *Annals of Trinity Church*, pp. 47, 48.

44. See GB *Works*, 8: 241; letter to Samuel Johnson, June 11, 1735, postscript.

45. Anne Berkeley, in Stock's *Account*; quotations opposite pp. 21 and 25. In a letter written at the time, the dean related that he preached "every Sunday" while in Newport (i.e., while living in town with the Honeymans), but that "now in the country," (i.e., Whitehall) he preached "occasionally, sometimes in Newport, sometimes in the adjacent parts of the continent"; GB *Works*, 8: 202. In a letter to the SPG (Sept. 9, 1731), Honeyman also confirms Berkeley's sermonic activity; SPG Archives, Letter Books, Series A, 23: 259.

sectaries heard my sermons,"[46] evoking from Percival a
delighted response to the news that Quakers "come to our
Church to hear you. . . . Should you be able to do no more
than bring them over, it were a service to religion worthy
your voyage."[47] Newman heard (possibly wrongly) that
Berkeley even attended some Quaker meetings in Newport;
it was further rumored (probably rightly) that the dean for
the sake of dissenters did "dispense with the Surplice and
some other observances here as would disgust weak people."
"I believe," Newman concluded "that St. Paul would have
done the same if he had been in that place."[48] Part of his
popularity as a preacher stemmed from Berkeley's tendency
to concentrate on "those general truths agreed to by all
Christians."[49] Neither abstruse nor exotic, his sermons were
designed to be clear, honest, straightforward. They were not
thinly disguised academic essays; neither were they philosophical treatises in capsule. Though a classicist of considerable
sophistication, Berkeley made no effort to embroider his sermons with erudite illustrations from antiquity. His choice of
texts was almost commonplace, his use of Scripture, traditional and deferential. His sermons were catholic and evangelical,
biblical and rational, exegetical and hortatory.

If Berkeley spoke "without Books," as his wife reported,
he fortunately did not speak without notes; for these notes
which enabled him to preach the same sermon over again
also enable later generations to assess and appreciate George
Berkeley as a preacher. Notes survive for fourteen of his
Newport sermons, with now and then a complete sentence
tucked away in the outline. Most of these sermons are dated;
but since they represent no discernible theological develop-

46. GB *Works*, 8: 202; Berkeley to Percival, Aug. 30, 1729.
47. Rand, *B & P*, p. 248; Percival to Berkeley, June 12, 1729.
48. SPCK, New England Letters, vol. 3; Newman to Berkeley, Sept. 17,
1729.
49. GB *Works*, 8: 202; Berkeley to Percival, August 30, 1729.

ment, they may be more helpfully considered by broad
categories. Three groupings emerge: sermons that deliberately emphasized "those general points agreed to by all
Christians"; the more controversial sermons that addressed
themselves to and possibly aggravated the "strange medley
of different persuasions"; and, those sermons that tell us
more about the preacher himself.

In a colony that boasted of religious liberty and contained
such undeniable variety, it made excellent sense to concentrate on the unities, the verities, the "fundamental truths."
This the dean of Derry did most explicitly in a sermon
based on this text: "Thou shalt love the Lord thy God with
all thy heart & with all thy soul and with all thy mind.
This is the first & great commandment" (Matthew 22:37,
38).[50] In all factions and divisions of men, the Preacher
pointed out, one found "a chief tenet or principle." So it
is with religions generally and surely with Christianity
specifically: the chief principle there was love. Love, of
course, had its gradations and degrees, from our attachment
to "sensible objects," to our affections toward inferiors,
then equals, then superiors, and then to our love of virtue
and excellence. But the highest love is of God, a love that
expresses itself in our keeping of "His commandments, I
John 5:3." As members of his flock, we are called to charity, temperance, resignation, and a true spiritual worship—
not "lip worship" but "inward & Evangelical." Upon learning to love God with heart, soul, and mind rest the happiness and the virtue of all mankind.

50. All of the Newport outlines are printed in GB *Works*, 7: 53–84. I have
also consulted the manuscript copies in BM, Add. Ms. 39306 and Add. Ms.
46689. None of the Newport sermons bears a title. Biblical texts are quoted
just as Berkeley wrote them out, but scripture citations are given in accordance with modern usage. It has been necessary to provide a few punctuation
marks for clarity, since these outlines were never intended to serve as "fair
copy" for the printer. For the first sermon under discussion (delivered in
August, 1730), see GB *Works*, 7: 71–72.

If this sermon, even in barest outline, represented the
theoretical foundation on which all Christians could agree,
two other sermons elaborated the practical fundamentals,
the essence of the Christian ethic. "For the Kingdom of
God is not meat & drink," declared Saint Paul in his letter
to the Romans (5:17), "but righteousness and peace and
joy in the Holy Ghost." [51] Again, the Preacher would have
his hearers distinguish between the "essentials & circum-
stantials in Religion." Righteousness, which must be found
in our deeds no less than in our words and thoughts, was at
the heart of Christ's golden or "summary rule." Christian
peace meant first an inner harmony, then an "outward
peace: i.e., charity & union with other men." And joy
God calls all of us to, not sourness, sullenness, or morose-
ness "but rejoicing." Righteousness, peace, joy: here was
the common ground, the brotherhood, the bond. "Since
we have so great things in view, let us overlook petty differences, let us look up to God our Common Father, let us
bear one another's infirmities . . . let us practice those things
wherein we agree." [52]

Not every sermon, however, displayed such conciliation.
Writing to Percival in August, 1729, Berkeley acknowledged
that on the previous Whitsunday "(the occasion being so
proper) I could not omit speaking against that spirit of
delusion and enthusiasm which misleads those people: and
though I did it in the softest manner and with the greatest
caution, yet I found it gave some offence, so bigoted are
they to their prejudices." [53] Almost certainly the sermon
in question took its text either from James, "Speak not evil
one of another" (4:11); or from the Psalms, "Lord who
shall abide in thy tabernacle? who shall dwell in Thy holy

51. Ibid., 7: 58–60; the sermon was delivered during July, 1729.
52. A similar emphasis may be found in Berkeley's sermon preached in
March 1729, with Philippians 4:8 as his text; GB *Works*, 7: 81–82.
53. GB *Works*, 8: 202; letter dated August 30, 1729.

hill? He that backbiteth not with his tongue, nor doth evil
to his neighbour nor taketh up a reproach against his neighbour" (15:1, 3).[54]

Every country had its peculiar vice, Berkeley observed:
for example, "intemperate lust in Italy, drinking in Ger-
many." Rhode Island's particular vice appeared to be the
backbiting tongue: "they who have no relish for wine have
itching ears for scandal." To speak evil of others is contrary
both to charity and to justice. The one speaking injures himself, revealing a lack of merit and "a malignant nature"; he
also injures those whom he slanders. Recall the words from
the Book of Proverbs (10:18), "He that uttereth slander is
a fool"; and the words from Titus (3:2), "Speak evil of no
man." We are, Berkeley concluded, "all criminals at the
same bar." In using terms such as *fools*, *Pharisees*, and
criminals, Berkeley may have thought he was speaking in
the "softest manner" possible, but sectarians in the congregation might well have come to a different conclusion. On
the other hand, the dean's deliberate and extensive use of
the Bible, literally citing chapter and verse, may have been
a bid for support among those who rested all upon biblical
foundations, or it may have been a desire to prove to the
"bigoted" that an Anglican dignitary actually knew the
Scriptures. But in taking his harsh words from the Bible,
he turned familiar phrases suddenly into sharp chastisers.

Treading on other sensitive toes, the Preacher also
addressed himself to the questions of baptism and the
Eucharist, liturgical arenas of great controversy throughout
Christian history—and certainly so in Rhode Island.[55]

54. Ibid., 7: 66–67, 78. Though listed as two separate sermons by Luce
(#6 and #11), they are actually one in content. Neither is dated, but the
probability that their content represented the remarks for 1729's Whitsunday
is high.

55. Quakers dismissed the sacraments as external, potentially idolatrous
snares to a truly spiritual faith. For Baptists, the sacraments were not "sacra-

Berkeley's Eucharist sermon, taking its text from 1 Corinthians 11:26, developed the several purposes of the sacred meal.[56] In the course of that explication, the dean encouraged Christians to imitate the practice of the early church—"than whom none wiser or better now." But, of course, the critical question remained: what was the apostolic practice? Rejecting the "errors" found either to the left or to the right of Anglicanism's via media, Berkeley took Catholics to task for understanding the notion of sacrifice too literally, "not considering [that] circumcision is called the covenant, lamb the passover, cup ye new testament." "Enthusiasts," on the other hand, rejected the Lord's Supper "as not spiritual; but why pray, why preach? why build houses of worship? because these are signs or means of grace [of] things spiritual."

If this homily hit Catholics and Quakers directly, Berkeley's sermon on baptism (text from Acts 2:38) was clearly aimed at the Baptists. The Bible states that you must believe in order to be baptized, the Baptists argue, and that infants therefore should not be baptized. All right, responded the Preacher, the Bible also states that those who will not work should not eat: are infants "hereby excluded from eating?" Another objection to infant baptism was "that no mention is made of infants being baptized in Scripture; but neither is mention made there of women receiving the eucharist." But if Berkeley stood against Baptists on the subject and mode of baptism, he sounded like the most evangelical among them when he called on any unbaptized listeners to attend to that rite. After expounding all the wrong and foolish reasons men and women give for postponing or

ments at all: that is, they were not divinely ordained channels of God's saving grace. They were "ordinances" or commands; one observed them as a sign of discipleship and obedience. But precisely how and when these were to be observed led to Baptist schisms and "subdivisions of sects."

56. GB *Works*, 7: 75–76.

avoiding baptism, Berkeley virtually turned Trinity Church into a revivalist's tent. How do you know that you have not waited too long already, too long delayed, neglected, and denied? "Who assured you that you shall live to be old, that you shall not die suddenly, that you shall not die to-morrow, or even this very day?" "All things are ready," declared the Preacher; "God now calls."[57]

From these sermon notes, a fascinating portrait begins to emerge: the irenic man of charity standing above the sectarian fray and proclaiming the essential unities of Christian faith and practice, but also the dedicated churchman quite prepared to enter into that fray on behalf of the special genius of England's and Ireland's National Church. From still other notes (and full texts of sermons outside of Newport), something of Berkeley's own deepest convictions and dearest truths enriches the detail of the portrait. Judging from all of his surviving sermons, this preacher's favorite text was drawn from 1 Timothy: "Without controversy, great is the mystery of godliness" (3:16).[58] Again and again, Berkeley returned to the theme of "mystery," not because he was troubled by it, but because he warmly embraced it. The greatest error, the greatest arrogance, of his generation was the supposition that man could comprehend all, that the universe was wholly within his grasp. In that prideful, Promethean grasp, all humanity fails, all humanity falls. Not only deists and free thinkers but these days even Christian theologians can be found who act and write as though reason were all and revelation, nothing.

57. In this same sermon, Berkeley also attacked those who would deny baptism to their slaves, offering as their excuse the specious argument that "baptism makes slaves worse." What made slaves worse was the unchristian example of the masters and their "neglect of instruction."

58. Preached at Newport Aug. 3, 1729; and, in King's Chapel, Boston, Sept. 12, 1731. Manuscript copies of two other sermons based on the same text have survived, though the dates of their composition or delivery are not known. See GB *Works*, 7: 61-63, 83-84, 85-92, 93-104.

Religion, however, "is not in the head or mouth but in the heart." In matters religious, we grievously err if we think that the highest truths are the most sophisticated, erudite, and elusive. No, in nature the "best things for life & nourishment [are] the most common & easiest to get: e.g., the elements, corn, milk." So is it in religion: "the necessary saving truths are so clear that he who runs may read."[59]

And the simple, saving truth—a companion text to 1 Timothy 3:16—was that "The Word was made flesh & dwelt among us" (John 1:14). This most glorious mystery, while "not repugnant to natural reason," can never be comprehensible to natural reason alone. Faith, therefore, has its true place. One must simply believe, one must simply trust in that "most adorable instance of the divine goodness . . . the deep and mysterious counsel of God for our redemption." By means of the Incarnation and by that means alone, it is given to Christians to know the mysteries of heaven (Matthew 13:11). Those to whom these mysteries are revealed "form a peculiar people who are styled the church . . . new creatures . . . renewed in their minds . . . regenerate or born again." Holy Scripture described this set-apart Christian society in many ways: "a chosen generation, a royal priesthood, an holy nation . . . a building aptly fitted together whereof Christ is the foundation." But whatever emblems or signs or words may be used, they all agree in this: "they set forth the Messiah as a Prince and ruler of a great people, a people holy and chosen, wch from sinners he has made pure, from slaves he has made free, from dead he has made alive."[60] Thus saith the Newport Preacher.

Far away from Newport, George Berkeley continued, of course, to function as churchman and preacher, spending much more of his professional life in these roles than in those of philosopher and academician. And in those long

59. Ibid., p. 84.
60. Ibid., pp. 61, 84, 85–86, 89–90.

continuing capacities, his commitment to the church in
America did not flag. He maintained his close ties with
Henry Newman and the SPCK; he strengthened his association with the SPG, joining its ranks in 1732 when it was
managing to maintain some thirty-eight missionaries in the
colonies.[61] At Honeyman's request, he interceded with the
Society to urge the appointment of David Scott as schoolmaster in Newport, Berkeley testifying that he was "satisfied of his Merits, both as a Scholar, a Man of good Morals,
and a diligent Schoolmaster."[62] In a somewhat more delicate matter, Berkeley also urged the Society to increase the
Reverend Mr. Honeyman's salary (Honeyman hoped the
raise might be as much as £20 per year) "as he is the oldest
missionary in America, as he hath done long and excellent
Service in that Station, and is a person of good qualifica-
tions for life and learning." The venerable Society, however,
decided not "to enlarge Mr. Honeymans Salary, he having
as large a Salary as any Missionary, and having a rich congregation." To mitigate that denial, the SPG did agree to
provide him with Scott as a schoolmaster.[63]

The clearest indication of Berkeley's continuing interest
in church matters generally and those of Trinity Church
specifically came in the form of an outright gift. This time,
however, the gift was not books: it was an organ. And
before that complex transaction was concluded, George
Berkeley, to say nothing of Henry Newman, must have

61. SPG Archives, *Reports, 1733*, p. 47. The thirty-eight missionaries were
distributed as follows: New England, 12; New York, 7; New Jersey, 3; Pennsylvania, 6; and the Carolinas, 10.
62. SPG *Journal*, vol. 6; entry for Feb. 16, 1733 (N.S.). Also see SPG Committee Book 3; entry for Jan. 15, 1733 (N.S.). For Berkeley's letter, see SPG
Archives, Letter Books, C/Am, 9: 32 (Feb. 10, 1733).
63. Honeyman continued to pursue the matter of a salary increase, though
in vain, in a series of letters to Bishop Edmund Gibson: April 26, 1732; Sept.
20, 1732; May 2, 1734; and Oct. 29, 1735. See Fulham Papers, 8: 274–75,
276, 277–78, 281–82.

decided that books were far simpler. For not only did a builder have to be found and the instrument paid for; the organ then had to be played in a sort of trial run, then disassembled, packed, shipped, insured, unloaded, uncrated, and reassembled in a New England which had never seen such an object before. Then, of course, a search must be launched to find someone, somewhere, who could play it. Books indeed were simpler.

In the spring of 1733, Berkeley negotiated for an organ "not exceeding 120 Guineas" to be painted "of a plain Walnut Colour with Gilt coverings & moldings."[64] By July, Newman was able to inform Timothy Cutler that this handsome new instrument was "now finish'd." If all went well on this venture, Newman dared to add, "I don't know but upon application from you, [Berkeley] would make the like present to yr Church."[65] At the end of August, Newman dropped a quick note to Berkeley: "I hope to send the Organ by Cap.t Cary but have not been able to see him yet to treat with him about it."[66] But when Captain Cary proved unable or unwilling to bear so heavy a responsibility, Newman hired a Newport captain and ship (Captain Draper and the *Godfrey*) to do the job. Since Draper's ship would first stop at Lisbon and possibly Cadiz "for a Loading of Salt," that "Double navigation" did increase the "Risque." With the dean's permission, therefore, Newman insured the rare package for £150.[67] By the middle of October, the magnificent instrument of 508 pipes was ready to go. "It has been touch'd and approv'd by some of the most Eminent Masters in London but not by so many as I intended being Oblig'd to take it to Pieces as Soon as it was finish'd

64. SPCK Abstract Letter Book, vol. 17; March 26, and April 2, 1733.

65. SPCK New England Letters, vol 4; July 28, 1733. One organ, however, proved to be quite enough both for Berkeley and for Newman.

66. Ibid.; August 28, 1733.

67. Ibid.; in a second letter to Timothy Cutler, Oct. 19, 1733.

for fear of Losing the opportunity of Sending it in so good
a Ship as the Godfrey." Papers accompanying the organ,
Newman assured Honeyman, "will fully instruct anybody
that has Ever Seen the inside of an Organ how to put it
together." Newman hoped to hear of its safe arrival, he
informed the Trinity Church rector, "in Jany. or February
next if not before" and "I hope it may be long us'd to the
Glory of God in celebrating his Praises by the Harmony
and Fervour it may add to the Devotions of those who
attend Your Congregation."[68]

The organ did safely reach Newport. In March, 1734,
Trinity's churchwardens wrote to thank Newman for his
countless efforts on their behalf. They promised, moreover,
to find "the most capable persons the Country can furnish
them with"—which did not say much—to reassemble those
508 pipes. When it came to finding an organist, the churchwardens were less certain that even the whole country could
help. It might be necessary to "apply to their Friends in
London to send an ingenious Master of Musick who wou'd
make a handsome living" in Newport.[69] "Their friends"
would seem to mean Newman once again, but in fact there
was another "friend in Cheapside" who procured and dispatched one Mr. John Owen Jacobi—"a person like to please
you," Newman quickly reported to Honeyman. Wrapping
up the final details of this major logistical operation, Newman informed Berkeley late in 1734 that all was well with
Trinity Church and its music program. "I hear they have
settled 200. L. per an. of Rhode Island money on an Organist
to perform on yoͬ generous present to the Church there."[70]

68. Ibid.; two letters from Newman to Honeyman, Oct. 19 and 24, 1733.
69. SPCK Abstract Letter Book, vol. 18; March 8, 1734. The church paid
£100 to Mr. Charles T. Parchival "for his services, &c., in setting up the organ
in the Church." Mason, *Annals of Trinity Church*, p. 63. Parchival also served
temporarily as organist.
70. SPCK New England Letters, vol. 5; Newman to Honeyman, Aug. 12,

At last the deed was done; the generosity was noteworthy
and the gratitude fully commensurate.[71]

While in Newport for thirty-three months, George Berkeley counseled with and supported the Anglican missionaries
throughout New England; he regularly delivered sermons
both in town and "on the Continent"; he served his church
and proclaimed the Word. While in Newport for thirty-three
months, George Berkeley also waited. He waited on Walpole, waited on the king, waited on the inching tides of
history. In all candor, however, one must acknowledge that
Berkeley himself contributed to the delay and confounded
an already complex political situation. Or to put it in gentler
terms, Berkeley gave his opponents and the foot-draggers
the opportunity and excuse they hoped for.

A mere two weeks after his debarkation in Newport,
Berkeley hastily wrote Percival: "I should not demur one
moment about situating our College here."[72] Two months
later he explained to a fellow churchman, Bishop Martin
Benson of Gloucester, that nothing could better secure His
Majesty's political interests in New England than "planting
an Episcopal Seminary in Rhode Island." Then he added
fatefully, "You will know the proper use to be made of
this hint."[73] If letters could be called back, obliterated in
mid-ocean, overtaken by a cable saying "please ignore,"
Berkeley might well have done one or all of the above. For

1736 (also see Newman to Jacobi, Sept. 1, 1736); SPCK Society Letters, vol.
31; Newman to Berkeley, Oct. 24, 1734. The *Annals of Trinity Church,* p. 65,
list the salary offer to the organist as £20, not £200, the former being a far
more realistic figure.

71. Trinity Church still displays on the front of its balcony a large gilt
inscription just ahead of the organ pipes which reads: "The Gift of D[r] George
Berkeley late Lord Bishop of Cloyne." The original keyboard is preserved in
the Newport Historical Society.

72. GB *Works*, 8: 190; letter dated Feb. 7, 1729.

73. Ibid., p. 195; letter dated April 11, 1729.

soon after the letter was dispatched, he knew that he had committed a serious tactical error. The charter said Bermuda, not Rhode Island; the charter, moreover, could not be amended without giving every royal adviser, every self-interested bureaucrat, every resentful merchant the chance to strike the whole plan down. If all were to be discussed again, all would be subject once more to "the raillery of European wits." On the other hand, were the charter not amended, then Berkeley would be guilty of bad faith, and the entire design must fall.

By June, the dean, writing in some anxiety to Thomas Prior, indicated that he had heard of rumors circulating in Ireland "that we propose settling here. I must desire you to discountenance any such report." The truth was, Berkeley admitted, that if he had the £20,000 in his hands, he would much rather expend it here than in Bermuda. The truth also was, however, that the £20,000 was not in hand; therefore, if this strange rumor (how could it have ever gotten started?) be not scotched, it might "defeat all our designs." [74] To Newman, Berkeley confessed that he had written "some friends in England to take the proper steps for procuring a translation of the College from Bermuda to Rhode Island as soon as the £20,000 . . . is paid," but on second thought—a tragically late second thought—"I don't think it advisable to make this proposition, or say anything about it before the money is received." [75]

A year later, with rumors still flying and ever more discouraging reports returning to Newport, Berkeley tried desperately to backtrack and start over. "I hold myself in readiness to go to Bermuda," he wrote to Percival; "Bermuda after all is the proper place." [76] But time was quickly

---

74. Ibid., p. 198; letter dated June 12, 1729; on p. 199 of this same volume, see Berkeley's letter to Percival, June 27, 1729.

75. Ibid., p. 200; letter dated June 27, 1729.

76. Ibid., p. 210; letter dated July 20, 1730.

running out and the dean of Derry knew it. Time was also running out on that deanery. His prolonged and indefinite absence could not continue; eighteen months was to have been the limit for keeping his preferment in Bermuda. Now he had already used up that much time in Rhode Island without even coming within sight of Bermuda! Early in 1730 his counselor and adviser, Henry Newman, had written to urge Berkeley to "think of returning to secure y^r Deanery before it can be liable to forfeiture." [77]

At the moment, however, the deanery did not seem so dear as the dream. While continuing to hope for the best, another side of him feared the worst. And in 1731, the worst happened. Trying to come to Berkeley's rescue, the bishop of London had managed to corner Robert Walpole to press him directly on whether the £20,000 would ever be paid or not. Walpole's response, according to Bishop Gibson's biographer, was this: "If you put the question to me as a Minister, I must and I can assure you that the money shall most undoubtedly be paid as soon as suits with public convenience; but if you ask me as a friend whether Dean Berkeley should continue in America, expecting the payment of £20,000, I advise him by all means to return home to Europe." [78] To his ecclesiastical superior and dear friend, a deeply disappointed George Berkeley wrote in March, 1731:

> I beg leave to return my humble thanks to your Lordship for the favour of a letter just come to my hands wherein you have been pleased to send me Sir Robert Walpole's answer which leaves no room to deliberate which I have to do. [79]

And in tones yet more somber he wrote to Percival:

77. SPCK New England Letters, vol. 3; letter dated Jan. 27, 1730.
78. As quoted in Luce, *Life*, p. 142.
79. Fulham Papers, 17: 19–20; letter dated March 15, 1731.

I have received such accounts on all hands both from
England and Ireland that I now give up all hopes of
executing the design which brought me into these
parts. I am fairly given to understand that the money
will never be paid. And this long continued delay . . .
made those persons who engaged with me entirely give
up all thoughts of the College and turn themselves to
other views. So that I am absolutely abandoned by
every one of them.[80]

It was over, the college finished before it began, the
scheme thwarted by those who when they saw a vision
called it whimsy. Many things in fact combined to kill the
plan: Walpole's cynicism, Byrd's sarcasm, Bray's opposition,
Bermuda's ill repute, and Berkeley's own temporizing and
uncertainty. Behind all that, however, lay the spirit of an
age. And in that spirit Berkeley believed he saw the real
enemy.

The spirit of our time, said the dean, expressed itself in
"what they foolishly call free thinking." This pseudo-liber-
ation constituted "the principal root or source not only of
opposition to our College but of most other evils in this
age."[81] That being the case, perhaps the time had come to
set the world straight on this so-called free thinking, to hold
up its wickedness and folly for all men and all nations to see.
Berkeley had tried in one way to save Great Britain from
ruin and Western civilization from its swift descent; he had
failed. Now he would try another way, and perhaps not fail.

80. GB *Works*, 8: 212; letter dated March 2, 1731. Also see Percival, *Diary*,
1: 157; the entry is for March 10, 1731. "Abandoned" may be too strong a
term. Of the potential faculty for St. Paul's College, only John Smibert had
actually made the voyage to America. The young Trinity fellows whose names
appeared on the charter presumably remained in Dublin. It is also a reasonable
presumption that they, without ecclesiastical titles or benefices, found it
necessary during the long wait to take other employment.
81. GB *Works* 8:212.

And if he did not fail, then the two- or three-year interlude in Rhode Island might not, sub specie aeternitatis or even in the long view of history, be counted a total loss.

6 *Apologist in Absentia*

I can't but with concern reflect upon our degeneracy at
home; you would be surpriz'd to see what progress Infidelity has made here in a short time. . . .

Henry Newman to George Berkeley,
September 17, 1729

In the 1730s few people in Newport—for that matter, few
people in all New England—swam freely in Europe's swirl-
ing intellectual currents. George Berkeley did. In the course
of his stay in Rhode Island, however, he began to think
that he was swimming across, if not against, most of those
currents.

The first quarter of the eighteenth century saw Europe
turning away from protracted religious wars, from stubborn
religious intransigence, and from ever narrowing sectarian
dogmatism. Eschewing all that, Europe faced in the direction of greater toleration or indifference (to many, the
terms were synonymous), immersing herself in the "real
world" of politics and commerce, in the marketplace of
the reasonable and the natural, as opposed to the revealed
and the supernatural. With the Glorious Revolution of
1688 and its subsequent Declaration of Toleration, England's own religious strife markedly cooled. Toleration, of
course, did not mean disestablishment of the National
Church nor a repeal of the Test Act nor an end to the wondrous mixing of politics and religion. It did mean, however,
a new posture and perhaps a new defensiveness for the
Church of England. Commercial ends overtook religious
ones in the modern scale of values, while in the intellectual
realm a capitalized Reason and a similarly reified Nature

challenged Christian theology throughout western Europe.
For Henry Newman, "degeneracy" and "infidelity" were
unmistakably on the march, prepared to do battle (in the
open or preferably by guerilla tactics) against the purity of
doctrine, the stability of tradition, the integrity of men
and nations.

In quick succession some of infidelity's heavier artillery
boomed: Charles Blount's *Oracles of Reason* in 1693, John
Toland's *Christianity Not Mysterious* in 1696, Anthony
Collins's *Discourse on Freethinking* in 1713, and Matthew
Tindal's *Christianity as Old as Creation* in 1730.[1] Blount,
like his predecessor, Lord Herbert of Cherbury, moved
tentatively away from revelation (it was always safer to
begin with the Old Testament) toward that all-sufficient,
unaided reason vouchsafed to all men. Such reason yielded
its own religion: one that was natural, self-evident, non-
divisive, and free of all superstition. For Toland, the "mystery of godliness" repelled rather than charmed; the siren
call came from reason. With a mixture of anthropology,
Lockean philosophy, and scientific loyalty, Toland stripped
Christianity of all miracle, wonder, ceremony, symbol—
and power. What was true in Christianity must be so because
it was comprehensible to all, even "the vulgar," because it
satisfied plain common sense, and because it proved to be
"as consistent with our common Notions, as what we know
of Wood or Stone, of Air, of Water, or the like."[2] Collins
pointed out, along with many others, that biblical revelation
was so filled with error, contradiction, and ambiguity that
none could be surprised at the historical result: numerous
sects, schisms, quarrels, and contentions. Collins's heavy-

1. For the full panoply of English thought in this period, see Leslie Stephen's
classic, *History of English Thought in the Eighteenth Century,* 2 vols. (London,
1876; reprinted New York, 1962).
2. Quoted in Basil Willey, *The Eighteenth Century Background* (Boston,
1961), p. 9.

handed attack on all priests and "zealous divines" brought
down upon his head the satirical force of Jonathan Swift in
*Mr. Collins' Discourse on Freethinking put into plain Eng-
lish, by way of abstract, for the use of the Poor* (1713).
Collins, according to Swift, spoke such simple and convincing truths as these:

> The clergy, who are so impudent to teach the People
> the Doctrines of Faith, are all either cunning Knaves
> or mad Fools; for none but artificial designing Men,
> and crackt-brained Enthusiasts, presume to be Guides
> to others in matters of Speculation, which all the Doc-
> trines of Christianity are; and whoever has a mind to
> learn the Christian Religion, naturally chuses such
> Knaves and Fools to teach them.[3]

Finally, Matthew Tindal demonstrated that the God of all
mankind was indistinguishable from the God of Moses and
the noisy theologians; the gospel was only a reissuing of the
law of nature, and obedience to nature was all one knew or
needed to know. For English deism, certainly by 1730, the
thinking man's religion had been reduced to barest outline:
God exists, religion is inseparable from morality, death may
not be the end.

Of orthodoxy's many critics, two require particular attention. Just before Anthony Collins's book appeared, the
third earl of Shaftesbury published in three volumes his
Characteristicks of Men, Manners, Opinions, Times (London, 1711). A collection of essays printed over the previous
dozen years, *Characteristicks* did not deliberately set out to
destroy all that Berkeley would preserve; yet its tone of
mockery as well as its hymns of rhapsody did threaten much
of England's heritage and Christianity's unique position.

---

3. Herbert Davis and Louis Landa, eds., *Prose Works of Jonathan Swift:
Polite Conversation, etc.* (Oxford, 1964), p. 29.

Nature, "All-loving and All-lovely, All-divine," was the only deity required, the only revelation heard.

> O mighty Genius! Sole-animating and inspiring Power!
> Author and Subject of these Thoughts! Thy influence
> is universal: and in all Things, thou are inmost. From
> Thee depend their secret Springs of Action. Thou
> mov'st them with an irresistible unweary'd Force, by
> sacred and inviolable Laws, fram'd for the Good of
> each particular Being; as best may sute with the Per-
> fection, Life and Vigour of the Whole. The vital Prin-
> ciple is widely shar'd, and infinitely vary'd: dispers'd
> throughout; nowhere extinct. All lives; and by Suc-
> cession still revives. . . .[4]

Such elevation of nature left little room for what suddenly seemed a parochial or almost private religion, bound by time and space and petty spirits. This "divine Characterizer of our times," to use Berkeley's appellation, found no merit in revelation and no virtue in a cosmic penal system enforced by the hope of heaven and the fear of hell. On the contrary, virtue rested upon man's obedience to his innate moral sense, upon his faithful following of Nature. In order for Nature's pure and simple morality to shine through, however, one must clear away a good deal of accumulated rubbish: super-stitions, false notions, dogmas, "magick." If Nature is divine, human nature approaches that beatific status; it would come even closer if self-appointed messengers did not talk so much of commandments and prohibitions, of rewards and punish-ments. Let man follow his good tastes, be loyal to his good instincts, and correct in his good manners.[5]

4. From the section of the *Characteristicks* entitled "The Moralists: A Philosophical Rhapsody,"; quotation from pp. 366–67 of volume 2 (Lon-don, 1723 edition).

5. See Stanley Gream, *Shaftesbury's Philosophy of Religion and Ethics* (Athens, Ohio, 1967).

In 1714 Bernard Mandeville first published a far more
scandalous and derisive work, *The Fable of the Bees.* Like
Shaftesbury, Mandeville appeared to undermine almost
everything that Berkeley had boldly announced from a
Newport pulpit. And, like Shaftesbury, Mandeville served
as a target for Berkeley's pointed counterattack. In the
Fable, unlike the *Characteristicks*, human nature does not
tend automatically toward virtue and a clear moral sense;
on the contrary, men and women are driven solely and
powerfully by self-interest. Natural impulses compel all
persons to seek their own benefit. Berkeley argued that,
for the good of society, "human Nature should be extoll'd
as much as possible; I think [wrote Mandeville], the real
Meanness and Deformity of it to be more instructive."[6]
If one knows what truly makes people tick, Mandeville
contended, then one knows how to conduct a life or a
state. In statecraft, one must recognize, for example, that
private vices produce public benefits. Rather than discourage luxury and conspicuous consumption, the perceptive
ruler will promote it; for these vices create more jobs,
·enlarging the demand for both goods and services. With
respect to the poor, they should be sent not to school but
to work, where they can contribute to the economy both
in what they produce and what they consume. The statesman who rids his land of vice rids it also of prosperity, and
the statesman who encourages religion destroys trade—
unless he carefully keeps the first from interfering in any
way with the second.

Mandeville granted that this way may not be the world
we wish for or dream of, but it is the world we have. Nor

6. *Fable of the Bees,* first published in 1714, reached its final form in 1724,
the year of Berkeley's *Proposal.* Modern editions include the authoritative two-
volume study edited by F. B. Kaye (Oxford, 1924) and the convenient abridge-
ment in the Pelican Classics series (1970). The quotation is from Mandeville's
response to Berkeley, *A Letter to Dion* (London, 1732), p. 48.

does it help anything to attack the messenger. My real message, Mandeville declared with mock seriousness, is for everyone to choose virtue rather than vice since to do otherwise leads to eternal damnation—obviously too high a price to pay for earthly prosperity. "The Question is not, which is the readiest way to Riches, but whether the Riches themselves are worth being dam'd for."[7] But Mandeville knew as he wrote, just as Berkeley knew as he read, that for more and more Englishmen in the eighteenth century, the question uppermost in their minds was not how to get to heaven, but what was "the readiest way to Riches."

As early as 1713, in writing for the *Guardian*, George Berkeley had confessed that "nothing raises my indignation more" than this tendency of freethinkers, these instant philosophers, to see themselves as all-wise, too clever, emancipated, enlightened, cosmopolitan, "persons of superior sense, and more enlarged views."[8] But how effective was mere indignation in dealing with the smoothness and good taste of a Shaftesbury or with the cynicism and empirical "reporting" of a Mandeville? How did one answer a sneer or a smirk? The Age of Reason was also the age of ridicule,[9] with Shaftesbury composing "An Essay on the Freedom of Wit and Humour" and with Mandeville writing nearly everything with tongue in cheek and rapier ready.[10] Civilization

7. *Letter to Dion*, p. 34.
8. GB *Works*, 7: 209.
9. See John Redwood, *Reason, Ridicule and Religion: The Age of the Enlightenment in England* (Cambridge, Mass., 1976).
10. In Shaftesbury, *Characteristicks*, 1: 59–150. On Mandeville, see, for example, his "parable of the small beer" from *Fable of the Bees* which he repeated in the *Letter to Dion*, pp. 25–29. Mandeville also advanced his thesis for what might be called, "The Petticoat Principle and the Rise of Capitalism." "The Reformation has scarce been more instrumental in rendring the Kingdoms and States, that have embraced it, flourishing beyond other Nations, than the silly and capricious Invention of Hoop'd and Quilted Petticoats . . . [The Reformation] has from its first Beginning to this Day, not employ'd so many Hands, honest industrious labouring Hands, as the abominable Improvement

must be free to laugh, to rail, to discuss all openly and even flippantly. Ridicule only destroys cant, never substance, the freethinker argued; but Berkeley was less sure. To laugh at all could be to subvert all. Are we so civilized that we are prepared to ridicule civilization into the dust? Can anything be more ridiculous, Berkeley asked, than freethinkers themselves: "advocates for freedom introducing a fatality; patriots trampling on the laws of their country; and pretenders to virtue destroying the motives of it."[11] This seemed more a tragedy than a joke. Besides, what sort of philosopher is it who can argue only by innuendo and a wink?

> How much more delicate and artful is it, to give a hint, to cover one's self with an enigma, to drop a *double entendre*, to keep it in one's power to recover, and slip aside, and leave his antagonist beating the air![12]

In a less satirical vein, Bishop Gibson in 1728 warned his clergy: "When you meet with any book upon the subject of religion, that is written in a ludicrous or unserious manner, take it for granted that it proceeds from a deprav'd mind, and is written with an irreligious design."[13]

All this might be granted, but the question remained: how to answer a laugh, especially when the laughter seemed so widespread and so damaging. One could hardly respond with vulgar raillery and comic retort, for the subject was too serious and the stakes were too high. On the other hand, if one took too high a road, then the rejoinder was never heard where it most needed to be: that is, in the coffee houses and taverns, in the polite circles of high

---

on Female Luxury . . . has done in Few Years. Religion is one Thing, and Trade is another." *Letter to Dion*, pp. 67–68.

11. GB *Works*, 3: 319.

12. Ibid., p. 284.

13. Bishop Gibson in a Pastoral Letter; quoted in Redwood, *Reason, Ridicule and Religion*, p. 26.

fashion and facile conversation. Here, not in divinity school cloisters or next to dusty library shelves, was England's future being shaped. And it was this wider audience that Dean Berkeley, far away in Rhode Island, wanted to reach. When he finished his counterattack, he called it *Alciphron, Or the Minute Philosopher*; and he noted in the "Advertisement" that "the author hath not confined himself to write against books alone." He wrote against a jest, a mood, the spirit of an age; against a trivialization of verities that neither England nor any nation could afford to scorn. To reach the "cultured despisers" that Berkeley wanted to reach called for artful delicacy, nimble style, and a masterful control of both language and thought: it called for *Alciphron*.

Ireland's only philosopher turned out also to be one of Ireland's finest stylists. Berkeley's association with Swift and Addison, with Alexander Pope and Matthew Prior, had left its mark. A master of prose, a composer of "suave glittering sentences" (as another Irishman, William Butler Yeats, observed), Berkeley was a literary craftsman whose "lucidity of style testifies to the lucidity of the thought behind it."[14] Having already proved himself in 1713 an artist with the dialogue form (the *Three Dialogues*, said Yeats, were "the only philosophical arguments since Plotinus that are works of art"),[15] Berkeley in Newport turned once again to that form. Perhaps, in this mode, he could

14. See Bonamy Dobree, "Berkeley As a Man of Letters," *Hermathena* 82 (November, 1953): 49–75. Yeats's words are on p. 59; the final quotation (by Donald Davie) is on p. 72.

15. Ibid., p. 64. Berkeley bibliographer and scholar, T. E. Jessop, also noted in this 1953 issue of *Hermathena* that virtually anything which Berkeley touched "turned to literature. He was an outstanding stylist in an outstanding age; further, in the entire line of those who have handled English well he emerges as one of the sovereigns of our prose; and yet further, in all European literature he comes next to Plato in the easy and lively shaping of philosophical dialogue" (p. 2).

reach an age that "is very indulgent to everything that aims
at profane raillery." All that was necessary for a book or a
tract to be popular, it seemed, was for it to make fun of
religion. No matter how bad the writing or dull the thought,
such inferior products were greedily bought and indulgently
read.

> You may behold the tinsel of a modern author pass
> upon this knowing and learned age for good writing;
> affected strains for wit; pedantry for politeness;
> obscurities for depths; ramblings for flights; the most
> awkward imitation for original humour; and all this
> upon the sole merit of a little artful prophaneness.[16]

In 1729 Berkeley had informed Samuel Johnson that he
had "no inclination to trouble the world with large volumes."[17] But now that Christianity itself seemed threatened,
now that Christian community, having survived the furious
zeal of enthusiasts only to be challenged by the mocking
laughter of infidels, was under fire, a mighty salvo might
be needed. Between Levellers on the one hand and Diests
on the other, was there not a via media broad enough to
embrace both passion and reason, wise enough to encom-
pass both mystery and understanding, and catholic enough
to accept both tradition and revelation? The provocation
and the challenge required a big book; Berkeley produced
his longest.

Alciphron was one of those sparks to arise from the ashes
of Bermuda.[18] "Events are not in our power," Berkeley
conceded on the opening page of volume 1, but it is in our
power "to make a good use even of the worst." If he
wished, he could write in some detail about "the affair
which brought me into this remote corner of the country"

16. GB *Works*, 3: 136.
17. Ibid., 2: 281; letter dated Nov. 25, 1729.
18. See above, p. 104.

and "of its miscarriage," but that was not the pressing task at hand. Other matters required immediate, sustained attention. Happily, Rhode Island, "this distant retreat," granted him the necessary "liberty and leisure" which he would not have found in "that great whirlpool of busines, faction and pleasure which is called *the world.*"[19] The liberty and leisure were sufficient to enable the New World apologist artfully to construct seven dialogues, each taking place on a separate day of unhurried conversations along the beaches or in the meadows near Whitehall.[20] The principal participants are Crito and Euphranor as defenders of religion (and the voice of George Berkeley) and Alciphron along with the younger, brasher Lysicles as the antagonists (and voices of freethinking and fashion). Dion is a mere recorder of the conversations, pledged to see that all is fairly relayed to "the world."[21]

In the first Dialogue, some of the terms of the discussion, as well as courteous rules of the game, are spelled out. These early pages also contained characterization, if not caricature, of the major positions to be attacked or defended. On behalf of England's "better sort," Alciphron pointed out that just as the act of thinking separated man from the beast, so a certain kind of thinking (namely, "free") separated some men from other and lesser breeds. He also explained that "free thinking" meant that which was

19. GB *Works*, 3: 31.
20. Though local mythology identifies the precise ledge where George Berkeley sat to compose *Alciphron*, it was probably written somewhat nearer to one of Whitehall's several fireplaces—at least during the winter of 1730-31. Berkeley's lyrical landscape descriptions, however, certainly owe their inspiration to his immediate environment in Rhode Island.
21. The full title is *Alciphron: Or, the Minute Philosopher. In Seven Dialogues. Containing An Apology for the Christian Religion, against those who are Called Free-Thinkers.* 2 vols. (London, 1732). All quotations are taken from T. E. Jessop's text (following the London edition of 1752), as found in GB *Works*, 3: 21-329.

unburdened by schools and systems, unimpeded by sects
and priests, "those great masters of pedantry and jargon."
Freethinking came from none of these sources, but was
"only to be got by frequenting good company." In such
company, true gentlemen "have spent as much time in
rubbing off the rust and pedantry of a college education as
they had done before in acquiring it." Learning now "is
grown an amusement," with the understandable result that
freethinking has become vastly more popular than "dry
academical" learning ever was. Crito professed amazement
to hear that so much wisdom could be found "Where our
grave ancestors would never have looked for it—in a drawing-room, a coffee-house, a chocolate-house, at the tavern,
or groom-porter's."[22]

Though impressed, Crito, the village parson, and Euphranor, the obscure but intelligent farmer, were unsure whether
freethinking was to be understood as the exact equivalent
of serious inquiry. For the latter, all had agreed, was what
these seven days of conversation were intended to be about.
"To avoid confusion," therefore, Euphranor suggested that
we "call your sect by the same name that Tully . . .
bestowed upon them": minute philosophers. A most appropriate designation, Crito added, since modern freethinkers
"diminish all the most valuable things, the thoughts, views,
and hopes of men." Ideas were reduced to sense experiences, men to animals, and time to this brief shadow. Not
too disturbed either by the name or the characterization,
Alciphron accepted the title because all of their sect neither
exaggerated nor diminished but merely reported faithfully, like a mirror, what life was truly like. Besides, he
could accept the term in the sense of "their considering
things minutely, and not swallowing them in the gross, as
other men are used to do." But whatever the title—deists,

22. Ibid., pp. 36, 48–49.

atheists, skeptics, freethinkers, or minute philosophers—we
know of whom we are speaking, Lysicles volunteered:
namely, "the best bred men of the age, men who know
the world, men of pleasure, men of fashion, and fine gentlemen." Yes, I know the type, Euphranor replied, "but
should never have taken them for philosophers."[23]
   As noted above, the grand word and newly crowned
deity of eighteenth-century enlightened thought was
"Nature." And that word even more than the phrase "free
thinker" cried out for definition. When Alciphron rhapso-
dized about stripping the mind of all prejudice and superstition, thereby "reducing it to its untainted original state
of nature. Oh nature!," Euphranor calmly asked for some
clarification. "By what mark" can one recognize the "natural"? With confidence, Alciphron responded:

> For a thing to be natural . . . to the mind of men, it
> must appear originally therein; it must be universally
> in all men; it must invariably be the same in all nations
> and ages. These limitations of original, universal and
> invariable exclude all those notions found in the
> human mind which are the effect of custom and edu-
> cation.[24]

Stalking that tempting prey with Socratic stealth, Euphranor
led Alciphron to admit step by step that, well, he did not
really mean that something to be natural had to be (1) original, (2) universal, and (3) invariable.

> *Euphranor*: Tell me, Alciphron, if from a young apple-
> tree, after a certain period of time, there should shoot
> forth leaves, blossoms, and apples; would you deny
> these things to be natural, because they did not dis-
> cover and display themselves in the tender bud?

23. Ibid., pp. 46–47
24. Ibid., p. 55.

Alciphron: I would not.

Euphranor: And suppose that in man, after a certain season, the appetite of lust, or the faculty of reason shall shoot forth, open, and display themselves, as leaves and blossoms do in a tree; would you therefore deny them to be natural to him, because they did not appear in his original infancy?

Alciphron: I acknowledge I would not.

Euphranor: It seems, therefore, that the first mark of a thing's being natural to the mind was not warily laid down by you; to wit, that it should appear originally in it.

Alciphron: It seems so.

Euphranor: Again, inform me, Alciphron, whether you do not think it natural for an orange-plant to produce oranges?

Alciphron: I do.

Euphranor: But plant it in the north end of Great Britain, and it shall with care produce, perhaps a good salad; in the southern parts of the same island, it may, with much pains and culture, thrive and produce indifferent fruit; but in Portugal or Naples it will produce much better with little or no pains. Is this true or not?

Alciphron: It is true.

Euphranor: The plant being the same in all places doth not produce the same fruit—sun, soil, and cultivation making a difference.

Alciphron: I grant it.

Euphranor: And since the case is, you say, the same

with respect to all species, why may we not conclude, by a parity of reason, that things may be natural to humankind, and yet neither found in all men, nor invariably the same where they are found? . . .

Answer me, Alciphron, do not men in all times and places, when they arrive at a certain age, express their thoughts by speech?

Alciphron: They do.

Euphranor: Should it not seem, then, that language is natural?

Alciphron: It should.

Euphranor: And yet there is a great variety of languages?

Alciphron: I acknowledge there is.

Euphranor: From all this will it not follow a thing may be natural and yet admit of variety?

Alciphron: I grant it will.

Euphranor: Should it not seem, therefore, to follow that a thing may be natural to mankind, though it have not those marks or conditions assigned; though it be not original, universal, and invariable.

Alciphron: It should.

Euphranor: And that, consequently, religious worship and civil government may be natural to man, notwithstanding they admit of sundry forms and different degrees of perfection?

Alciphron: It seems so.[25]

25. Ibid., pp. 55–57.

Alciphron hereafter moving more warily inquired, "if a man makes a slip, it be utterly irretrievable?" Euphranor assured him that, for his part, he aimed "not at triumph, but at truth."

In the second Dialogue, Berkeley stalked bigger game: namely, Bernard Mandeville and his degrading view of human nature and civil society. Young Lysicles had led off with a facile explanation of how vice in fact did work to public advantage. Consider drunkenness, for example: it is no pernicious vice but a distinct contribution to employment, tax revenue, and a proper balance of trade. So also with gambling and prostitution and many other dearest vices. "Your moralists and divines have for so many ages been corrupting the genuine sense of mankind, and filling their heads with such absurd principles, that it is in the power of few men to contemplate real life." As a result, not many people were able to follow this complex line of reasoning, "to pursue a long train of consequences, relations, and dependences, which must be done in order to form a just and entire notion of the public weal."[26]

Euphranor drew the inevitable conclusion: "Vice then is, it seems, a fine thing with an ugly name." Uneasy with that, however, he, along with Crito, began "to take to pieces what is too big to be received at once." After such dismantling, they dared to suggest that all recorded history demonstrated that encouraging vice was "the likeliest way to ruin and enslave a people." In any event, since this approach was so experimental and untried, surely the minute philosophers would set it to work somewhere else before putting dear England to the test. But no, Lysicles responded, "our own country shall have the honour and advantage of it."[27] Of course, one might still need some

26. Ibid., p. 68.
27. Ibid., pp. 75–76. Later, Lysicles was urged to try his philosophy out first

rules and regulations "to bind weak minds, and keep the vulgar in awe," but true genius "breaks his way to greatness through all the trammels of duty, conscience, religion, law." Appetite and passion alone were to be heeded, and "riches alone are sufficient to make a nation flourishing and happy."[28] Here at last reality can be found, the youthful instant philosopher explained, and not in all the talk of religion and virtue and order and duty which were "of an airy notional nature."

Taking those airy notions as their line of defense, Euphranor and Crito protested that appetite and passion paved the road to slavery, not freedom. Besides, an Englishman wasn't very good at that sort of thing, being "the most unsuccessful rake in the world. . . . He is neither brute enough to enjoy his appetites, nor man enough to govern them." It may be true that men against their better judgment will succumb to their lusts and their emotions, but to deliberately declare in favor of such, to be "wicked from principle," was to move beyond all hope of rescue or reform. "Enthusiasm had its day, its effects were violent and soon over." Now, however, Western civilization was faced with insidious freethinking that "infects more quietly, but spreads widely." One could quell an open rebellion; "a corruption of principles works its ruin more slowly perhaps, but more surely."[29] Berkeley employed no ambiguity or double entendre here. Of one thing he was sure: this cavalier, sophisticated, fashionable praise of folly was the greatest folly of all.

Recognizing himself as the target under assault, Bernard

---

on the Hottentots and Turks; he declined on the ground that "their diet and customs would not agree with our philosophers" (p. 102).

28. Ibid., pp. 78–80.

29. Ibid., pp. 84, 91–92, 99, 103. Martin Van Buren recorded this maxim in a private journal he kept in the 1820s; see Matthew A. Crenson, *The Federal Machine* (Baltimore, 1975), p . 44.

Mandeville responded quickly and hotly with a *Letter to
Dion*. The most charitable judgment I can make, Mandeville informed Dion (i.e., Berkeley), is that you have never
read my book—an insult that Berkeley had himself sometimes suffered at the hands of his critics. "I know very well,
Sir, that I am addressing my self to a Man of Parts, a Master
in Logick, and a subtle Metaphysician," and such a man, if
he had ever read the text, would simply not make the stupid
mistakes which you have made. So, let us be gentlemen
about this matter: if you give me your word that you have
never read *Fable of the Bees*, I'll give you my word never
to hold that dreadful omission against you. Convinced,
however, that you have never read the book, I will take the
liberty to repeat part of it now, but "these Citations will
be as new to you as any other Part of my Letter."[30]

If Berkeley in his second Dialogue parodied Mandeville,
the latter returned the favor with high humor and telling
effect. Of Euphranor's plastic antagonists, Lysicles and
Alciphron, Mandeville shrewdly observed that such "Un-
dauntedness in assaulting, and Alacrity in yielding . . .
never met in the same Individuals before." But tactics of
debate aside, our fundamental difference is that you,
Berkeley, find Christians everywhere in England, while I,
Mandeville, do not. "This is certain, that when once it is
taken for granted, that to be a Christian, it is sufficient to
acquiesce in being call'd so . . . it saves the Clergy a vast
Deal of Trouble." Like Free Masons, you cannot tell a
Christian from anyone else: "Out of their Assemblies, they
live and converse like other Men."[31] Berkeley had no

---

30. *A Letter to Dion, Occasion'd by his Book, call'd Alciphron, Or, the
Minute Philosopher* (London, 1732), pp. 5, 7, 10. In the fashion of the day,
Mandeville's name did not appear on the title page, any more than Berkeley's
did on *Alciphron*. Nonetheless, putting the right names with the right books
was not too strenuous a parlor game.
31. Ibid., 3: 53, 63–64.

opportunity to respond to the response, for Mandeville
died shortly after dispatching his *Letter to Dion*.

In Dialogue 3, on the other hand, Berkeley took on an
opponent incapable of issuing a rejoinder, for Shaftesbury
had died in 1713. The apologist's attack against the earl
occurred on two fronts: first Shaftesbury's effort to make
morality altogether a gift of nature, a "given"; and second,
his embrace of "wit and humour" as a legitimate weapon
against "the Tutorage and Dogmaticalness of the Schools."[32]
The advantage of our philosophical position, Alciphron
explained to his conversation partners, is that we are "not
to be tied down by any principles." This "noble freedom"
permits us not only to disagree with each other "but very
often the same man from himself." Not being "governed
by gross things as sense and custom," each of us follows
"an instinct of nature" or heeds "a certain interior sense"
or acts in accordance with "a delicate and fine taste." With
all of this, religion has nothing whatever to do; one might
even go so far as to say that "the less religious the more
virtuous." Certainly, "there is no need that mankind should
be preached, or reasoned, or frightened into virtue, a thing
so natural and congenial to every human soul." In an effort
to forestall objection, Alciphron explained that this natural
gift to every man, this special faculty, this moral sense,
could not be rudely probed or coldly analyzed; it was
"something so subtle, fine and fugacious, that it will not
bear being handled and inspected, like every gross and common subject."[33]

But handling and inspection were precisely what Euphranor and Crito intended to do. The moral sense having been
compared to another of nature's gifts, a sense of beauty,
the Berkeleyan voices pointed out that reason and judgment

32. *Characteristicks*, 1: 76.
33. GB *Works*, 3: 112, 116-17, 118, 119.

determine beauty, not the eye alone. For one must judge
proportion, symmetry, and purpose in assessing the quality of beauty in, for example, architecture.[34] "It is, therefore, one thing to see an object, and another to discern its
beauty." How then, can one pretend to find beauty in a
moral system that is without "end or design," or beauty
in a brand of virtue based only on "chance, fate, or any
other blind principle?" Perceiving that an attempt was
being made to smuggle religion back into morality, Alciphron resisted, but Crito pressed on. Conceding that there
might be "a certain vital principle of beauty, order, and
harmony, diffused throughout the world," Alciphron
urged that Providence, at any rate, be left out of the whole
question of morality. Crito responded that either this
"principle" was intelligent or not. If not, then we are back
once more to fate or blind chance. And if intelligent, then
willy-nilly Providence returns to the scene, making possible
a genuine moral beauty; for now design, order, symmetry,
and purpose were assured.

> In such a system or society, governed by the wisest
> precepts, enforced by the highest rewards and dis-
> couragements, it is delightful to consider how the
> regulation of laws, the distribution of good and evil,
> the aim of moral agents, do all conspire in due sub-
> ordination to promote the noblest end, to wit, the
> complete happiness or well-being of the whole. In
> contemplating the beauty of such a moral system, we
> may cry out with the Psalmist, "Very excellent things
> are spoken of thee, thou City of God."[35]

Here was moral seriousness, but not moral blackmail.
Shaftesbury was anxious that "Men may be frighted out

34. See p. 71, above.
35. GB *Works*, 3: 124, 128–29.

of their Wits: But I have no apprehension they shou'd be
laugh'd out of 'em. . . . A mannerly Wit can hurt no Cause
or Interest for which I am in the least concern'd."[36] From
his own recent personal history, Berkeley, on the other
hand, knew what harm "profane raillery" could work. And
Alciphron, acknowledging that "our raillery and sarcasms
gall the black tribe," gleefully added, "and that is our comfort." "Our ingenious men make converts by deriding the
principles of religion . . . the most successful and pleasing
method of conviction." So Aristophanes dealt with Socrates, Crito observed, but what did it prove? "Wit without
wisdom, if there be such a thing, is hardly worth finding."[37]
And—much later in the conversation—if the world really
needed something to laugh at, regard the minute philosophers "and then say if anything can be more ridiculous."[38]

If Shaftesbury's effect was to make God redundant and
his existence irrelevant, Berkeley's aim in Dialogue 4 was
to demonstrate God's undeniable reality and indispensable
immediacy. This he accomplished by means of a brilliant
new argument for the existence of God, an argument
dependent upon the dean's youthful *Essay on Vision*, which
he therefore appended to *Alciphron*. In that 1709 seminal
work, Berkeley explained that vision itself is a kind of
divine language, with God himself serving as the connect-
ing link or mediator "between the signs and the things
signified." Distance, for example, is perceived "not immediately, but by mediation of a sign, which hath no likeness to
it, or necessary connexion with it, but only suggests it from
repeated experience, as words do things." Just as time and
experience are necessary to understand the language of the
ears (to make the connection accurately between words
and what they stand for), so for the language of the eyes

36. *Characteristicks*, 1: 96.
37. GB *Works*, 3: 137–38.
38. Ibid., p. 319.

time and experience are likewise necessary. But while language that is heard differs from country to country, language that is seen is everywhere and always the same: "the Author of Nature constantly speaks to the eyes of all mankind."

This line of reasoning failed to impress Alciphron. Do you really think, he asked, "that God Himself speaks every day and in every place to the eyes of all men"? And Euphranor affirmed, "That is really and in truth my opinion . . . you have as much reason to think the Universal Agent or God speaks to your eyes, as you can have for thinking any particular person speaks to your ears." We make our greatest mistake in trying to locate God far away and remote like some absentee landlord, whereas in fact (Euphranor quoting another favorite text of Berkeley's) "In Him we live, and move, and have our being."[39]

It must be a trick; "some fallacy runs throughout this whole ratiocination," Alciphron complained. Lysicles was prepared to admit that this argument may show that some sort of God exists, but nothing about what sort of God or "what sense the word *God* is to be taken in."[40] The most convincing response to that concern comes much later in the book.[41] With the seventh Dialogue, Berkeley's great apologia not only ends, it soars. And there, in order to deal meaningfully with the nature of God, it was necessary once again to treat the nature of words and of language itself.

Alciphron had been persuaded that words were signs or symbols; that being so, "words that suggest no ideas are insignificant." And precisely there lay the difficulty with

39. Ibid., pp. 151, 155, 157, 159. The text cited is taken from the Book of Acts (17:28).

40. Ibid., 3: 157, 163.

41. Dialogue 5 on the usefulness of Christianity and Dialogue 6 on the truth of biblical revelation probably strike the "typical" twentieth-century reader as the most defensive and dated and, to that degree, the least convincing apologetics. In style and literary merit, however, they rank equally with the others.

Christianity and with everything that preachers and theologians talked about. The Christian religion, or for that matter all religion, Alciphron argued, was filled with words, mere noises, that signified absolutely nothing. Faith, by its very nature "impracticable, impossible and absurd," took refuge in discourse without sense or meaning. Too many men and women seemed content to have their minds "rather stored with names than ideas, the husk of science rather than the thing." The ultimate absurdity in religion was that zealots attacked each other, berated each other, persecuted and killed each other—all over words that were without meaning! [42]

Berkeley, who did not insist on giving all the fair speeches to his own spokesman, permitted Alciphron to continue at length—and eloquently. Take, for example, the word *grace*, Alciphron began. This word, which seems to be "the main point in the Christian dispensation," means exactly what?

> Grace taken in the vulgar sense, either for beauty, or favour, I can easily understand. But when it denotes an active, vital, ruling principle, influencing and operating on the mind of man, distinct from every natural power of motive, I profess myself altogether unable to understand it, or frame any distinct idea of it; and therefore I cannot assent to any proposition concerning it, nor consequently have any faith about it. . . . [43]

Whenever I read about "grace" or hear the word used in theological discussion, I stop and look within my own mind, Alciphron confessed, to see what image or idea or significance is there evoked. What I discover is "a perfect vacuity or privation of all ideas." I am honest enough to admit this. If other persons were similarly candid, they

42. GB *Works*, 3: 286–88.
43. Ibid., pp. 289–90.

"would agree with me that there was nothing in it but an empty name." They would see that this is but another one of those deplorable instances where a word "is believed intelligible for no other reason but because it is familiar."[44]

Grace, indeed the centerpiece of Christian theology, the redemptive dimension in all human history—grace nothing but "an empty name"! So sincere and sensible were Alciphron's difficulties with this elusive theological abstraction that Berkeley appears almost to have given way too much. Girding up his loins, however, Euphranor began. The problem lay, he argued, not with "grace" but with the insistence upon considering it only in the abstract. The resulting difficulty has nothing to do with religion or with Christianity, as a few examples far removed from theology would show. Consider "an idea of number in abstract, exclusive of all signs, words and things numbered." Can you, Alciphron, form a clear and distinct idea in your mind of "number"? Or consider another favorite scientific term: namely, "force." "Let us examine what idea we can frame of force abstracted from body, motion, and outward sensible effects." When we thus honestly examine "number" or "force" or "fate" or even personal identity, we learn that none of these—even if you "shut your eyes to assist your meditation"—yields a clear and distinct idea *when considered only in the abstract.*[45]

But, gasped Alciphron, force at least has "sensible effects," whereas grace remains aloof, remote, without contact or effect in the real world. There for all the world to see, replied the apologist, was the capital error of all freethinkers and nonbelievers. Nothing could be more falsely stated concerning grace. For, in fact, grace is the active, moving, effecting, saving side of God. Grace is Divine Love *in action,*

44. Ibid., p. 290.
45. Ibid., pp. 293-94.

just as faith is man's *active* response to that love. Christians, unlike those on the outside looking in, never think of "grace" and "faith" as abstract terms; "the saving faith of Christians is quite of another kind, a vital operative principle, productive of charity and obedience." And Crito, hoping to drive the point home, added: "Faith, I say, is not an indolent perception, but an operative persuasion of mind." When we junk the utterly artificial attempt to treat these living realities as disembodied abstractions, we dispense with and dispose of a very great many difficulties. We also begin to understand that anomaly which free-thinkers regularly bring up; "in proportion as men abound in knowledge, they dwindle in faith." In his longest speech, Euphranor discussed this fatal fascination in eighteenth-century polite circles for vagueness, for high-sounding but utterly unnourishing rhetoric.

> Be the science or subject what it will, whensoever men quit particulars for generalities, things concrete for abstractions, when they forsake practical views, and the useful purposes of knowledge for barren speculation, considering means and instruments as ultimate ends, and labouring to obtain precise ideas which they suppose indiscriminately annexed to all terms, they will be sure to embarrass themselves with difficulties and disputes.[46]

If the present age was distinguished for its infidelity and doubt, it was not because men know so much, but because they talk so much and float too high: "in the present age thinking is more talked of but less practised." Also, it is the unhappy fate of our age, Crito concluded, that "those who have the most influence have the least sense."[47]

46. Ibid., p. 308.
47. Ibid., pp. 323, 329.

Long before Immanuel Kant issued his *Critique of
Practical Reason* (1788), George Berkeley—to many the
symbol of abstraction or skepticism or idle speculation—
called for common sense in religion, for theology to be
applied and Christianity to be practiced. Berkeley the
Christian apologist found knowledge in action, grace in
creative love, and faith in the reach of the human spirit.
Berkeley the Christian pastor warned against those all
around who "pretend to an ocean of light, and then lead
us to an abyss of darkness." With such enemies to be
found in eighteenth-century England in abundance,
Berkeley chose his epigraph for *Alciphron* from the Book
of Jeremiah: "They have forsaken me the Fountain of
living waters, and hewed them out cisterns, broken cisterns
that can hold no water" (2:13).[48]

This remarkable, artful philosophical dialogue, defending
ancient revelation against modern reason, hoary truths
against recent sophistications, stable tradition against
flighty fashion, and God against mammon, made only a
modest splash in England.[49] In the preface to his own
works, Alexander Pope declared, "for it is with a fine

48. Ibid., p. 322; title page, p. 21.
49. Besides Mandeville's *Letter to Dion*, other major English reactions to
Alciphron include Lord John Hervey, *Some Remarks on the Minute Philoso-
pher. In a Letter from a Country Clergyman to his Friend in London* (London, 1732); Peter Browne, *Things Divine and Supernatural conceived by
Analogy, with Things Natural and Human* (London, 1732); and, Andrew
Baxter, *An Enquiry into the Nature of the Human Soul* (London, 1733).
On George Berkeley as a theologian, see I. T. Ramsey, in *Hermathena* 82
(1953): 115–27; Edward A. Sillem, *George Berkeley and the Proofs for the
Existence of God* (London, 1957); and Jonathan Bennett in *Philosophy* 40,
no. 153 (1965): 207–21. T. E. Jessop discussed Berkeley as "religious apologist" in Warren E. Steinkraus, *New Studies in Berkeley's Philosophy* (New
York, 1966), pp. 98–109, where he argued that Berkeley's entire philosophical
system is "a piece of religious apologetics, the outline of a constructive natural
theology, of a theistic metaphysic." For an opposing view, that not even
Alciphron should be regarded as "apologetic," see John Wild, *George Berkeley* (Cambridge, Mass., 1936), chapter 13.

Genius as with a fine fashion: all those are displeas'd at it who are not able to follow it."[50] Since *Alciphron* was directed against just such as were not able, certainly not willing, to follow where its learned author led, it is not surprising that its success was limited—though two editions appeared the first year. And the book was quickly translated into Dutch (1733), French (1734) and German (1737).[51] Nonetheless, Berkeley was, as he feared, rowing across or against those currents which later in the eighteenth century swept crowns and mitres before them. Within the field of Christian apologetics itself, Bishop Joseph Butler's *Analogy of Religion* (1736) soon bestrode the battleground like a colossus, apparently requiring no other champion to take up arms.

In America, where fashion was not so fine, *Alciphron* fared better. Jonathan Edwards named the apology in his catalogue of reading and showed evidence of its influence in his later writing.[52] In his *Nature of True Virtue* (written in 1755 but published posthumously a decade later), Edwards, like Berkeley, found beauty a useful analogue, or more, in attempting to understand the nature of virtue. Indeed, for Edwards, "virtue is the beauty of the qualities and exercises of the heart, or those actions which proceed from them." If ever we can understand beauty in general, we must view it "most perfectly, comprehensively and universally, with regard to all its tendencies, and its connections with every thing to which it stands related."[53] Or,

50. *The Works of Alexander Pope* (London, 1717), p. iv.

51. See Geoffrey Keynes, *A Bibliography of George Berkeley,* pp. 36 ff.

52. Edwards's manuscripts, Catalogue of Reading, Yale University Library. The library's copy of *Alciphron* (1732 edition) bears the signature of Edwards's son Jonathan, dated in 1793. Thomas A. Schafer, in a letter to me (Dec. 3, 1978), states that the *Alciphron* entry was made in Edwards's notebook "within a year or so" of the book's publication in 1732; it is relevant to add that Edwards's idealism continued to develop throughout his life.

53. Jonathan Edwards, *The Nature of True Virtue* (Boston, 1765, under the title *Two Dissertations . . .* ; reprinted Ann Arbor, 1960), pp. 2–3.

as Euphranor explained to Alciphron, "as there is no
beauty without proportion, so proportions are to be
esteemed just and true only as they are relative to some
certain use or end."[54] And, as already noted, this idea of
end or purpose or design led Euphranor—his opponents
protesting all the while—to "a society of rational agents,
acting under the eye of Providence, concurring in one
design."[55] One knows neither beauty nor virtue (in
Berkeley's words) except in "proportioning our esteem to
the value of things,"[56] except (in Edwards's words) in
realizing "that true virtue must chiefly consist in love to
God . . . the foundation and fountain of all being and all
beauty; from whom all is perfectly derived, and on whom
all is most absolutely and perfectly dependent."[57] Against
Shaftesbury, both men agreed that virtue was more than
sentiment or innate sense, more than an accident of taste
or an arbitrariness of manners. Virtue, in short, was built
into the very nature and purpose of the universe.[58]

When Edwards's grandson, Timothy Dwight, prepared
as Yale's president to lead all of New England against novel
and fearful waves of infidelity, he called not on Butler's
Analogy but on Berkeley's *Alciphron*. Persuading a New
Haven printer in 1803 to bring out the first American
edition, Dwight himself provided the preface. *Alciphron,*
he declared, had served Americans "as a store-house,
whence many succeeding writers have drawn their materials,

54. GB *Works*, 3: 128.
55. Ibid., p. 129.
56. Ibid., pp. 178–79.
57. *Nature of True Virtue*, pp. 14–15. In his magisterial "inner biography" of
Jonathan Edwards (New York, 1949), Perry Miller stated: "Actually there is no
evidence whatsoever that Edwards read Berkeley, then or later" (p. 61). I argue
with this assertion, as well as his comment that "Bishop Butler was almost as far
outside New England's ken . . . as John Gay, and Berkeley as little prized as
Matthew Prior" (p. 109).
58. Compare Dialogue 3 of *Alciphron* with chapter 8 of *The Nature of True
Virtue*.

and their arguments." Since Berkeley had never really been
answered, moreover, it was expedient that latter-day
Americans come to know this philosopher-humanitarian,
this churchman-apologist who in time of need defended
Christianity against its fashionable enemies in a "masterly
performance" of "first merit."[59] Marshalling all of
Berkeley's intellectual forces along with his allies nearer
at hand, "Pope" Dwight led the Irish dean into battle, not
against Mandeville, Shaftesbury, Toland and Tindal, but
against Voltaire and Diderot and Paine, against French
Jacobinism and Jeffersonian deism, against all those in
Dwight's new nation who, as in Berkeley's old one, seemed
willing, even eager, to "quit particulars for generalities,"
to forsake the fountain of living waters for broken cisterns.

By the summer of 1731, the Newport manuscript was
finished. So was all hope for St. Paul's College, either in
Bermuda or elsewhere. Another winter approached; another
career choice had to be made. No flickering ray encouraged
Berkeley to linger any longer, away from his deanery,
away from his bishop, away from his faithful supporters,
away from dear and old friends. As soon as his wife and
new daughter Lucia were strong enough to travel, the
family would embark. On September 5, 1731, baby Lucia
died and was buried in Trinity's churchyard. Clearly, the
time had come to go home.

"My poor confused and divided Country," Samuel
Johnson wrote Bishop Gibson the following April; "the
Church has been very unfortunate in the defeat of the
Noble Design of the Rev.d the Dean of London Derry."
Then he added, as a kind of elegy for all the dreams, mon-
ies, and labor that had now collapsed, if only the Berkeley
plan could have been "executed on the Continent," it

---

59. Published by Increase Cooke & Co. in 1803; quotation from p. iii.

"would have been of vast Advantage to the Interest of Religion & Learning in America."[60] In the defeat, much had truly been lost to America, but not all—especially not all for "Religion & Learning."

60. Fulham Papers, 1: 249–50: letter dated April 5, 1732.

7 *America: 1780*

[H]e that hath not much meditated upon God, the human
mind, and the summum bonum, may possibly be a
thriving earthworm, but will most indubitably make a
sorry patriot and a sorry statesman.

George Berkeley, *Siris* (Sect. 350), quoted on title
page of Samuel Johnson's *Elementa Philosophica*,
1752

Mr. [William] Channing returned from Newp^t & bro't
the Congresses Declaration of INDEPENDENCY dated
at Philad^a the fourth day of July Instant. This I read at
Noon, & for the first time reallized Independency. . . .
The thirteen united Colonies now rise into an Independent Republic among the Kingdoms, States & Empires on
Earth. May the Supreme & Omnipotent Lord of the
Monarchical Republic of the immense Universe, shower
down his Blessings upon it, & ever keep it under his holy
Protection!

Ezra Stiles, July 13, 1776

Four days after Lucia's death, the Berkeleys left Newport
for Boston to prepare for their embarkation to Britain.
Though living only about sixty miles from New England's
metropolis (population around 13,000—the largest colonial
town in the 1730s), Berkeley had refrained from earlier
visits to that city. As the "capital" of Congregationalism,
Boston harbored great suspicions of the SPG, the SPCK,
and of Anglican clerics of whatever dignity or stripe. For
his part, George Berkeley thought it best to give no unnecessary offense to anyone while waiting for the cumbersome, capricious machinery of state to grind out its favors.
Those favors having been denied, Berkeley—now on his

way home—posed neither clear nor present danger to the
New England Way. His attitude toward that Way, moreover, had markedly mellowed since that ill-tempered evaluation of Harvard and Yale hastily offered in 1724.

So the Berkeleys spent twelve busy days in Boston,
making ready for another ocean voyage, renewing ties with
John Smibert, and accepting the kindnesses extended by
Puritan and Anglican alike. The family enjoyed the hospitality offered by a fellow Anglican, Colonel Francis Brinley, a Londoner who in 1710 had emigrated to Newport,
then to Boston, then to nearby Roxbury where in 1723
Brinley had built a fine house. On Sunday, September 12
of 1731, Berkeley preached in New England's first Anglican
house of worship, King's Chapel, taking as his text that
favorite (and anti-Toland) theme: "the mystery of godliness." One member of the large congregation gathered for
the occasion reported it "a fine sermon; according to my
opinion I never heard such a one."[1] On Thursday evening,
September 16, President Benjamin Wadsworth of Harvard
College entertained Dean Berkeley "at a Dinner in the
Library by ye Invitation of ye Corporation."[2] And on the
following Tuesday, September 21, husband, wife, and son
sailed for London, with SPG missionary George Pigot
joining them for the trip home. Fortunately, Captain
Carlin proved a worthier seaman than had Captain Cobb
three years earlier; instead of spending nearly one-third of
a year "blundering about the ocean," the Berkeley party
(George, Anne, Henry, and the manuscript of *Alciphron*)
all safely arrived in London in only five weeks.[3]

1. Boston shopkeeper Benjamin Walker, unpublished diary; quoted in Benjamin Rand, *Berkeley's American Sojourn* (Cambridge, Mass., 1932), p. 45.
2. "Benjamin Wadsworth's Book," in *Publications of the Colonial Society
of Massachusetts* 31 (1935): 483.
3. Rand, *Berkeley's American Sojourn*, pp. 51-52, citing the Boston news-
papers as well as Walker's diary. Berkeley and family arrived in London,
October 30, 1731.

Delivering his manuscript to the printer (Jacob Tonson), renting a house in London's Green Street, calling on Percival and other friends, Berkeley at once began to set his professional house in order. When and if the proper forum were presented, however, he also had unfinished business pertinent to America. That forum came the following winter with an invitation from the archbishop of Canterbury for the returning sojourner to preach the anniversary sermon before the SPG. In London's St. Mary-le-Bow parish church, on Friday, February 18, 1732, Berkeley delivered a sermon which, Henry Newman reported, "put the Mission to America in the clearest light that has yet appear'd."[4] All things considered, the SPG itself deemed it an appropriate time to elect this missionary without portfolio or stipend as a full member of its own ranks.[5]

The Society's newest member provided that organization with a firsthand report on its missionaries and its mission across the sea, offering along the way some of his own views on disestablishment, dissent, and the evangelical enterprise. Since he knew Rhode Island best, Berkeley concentrated on developments there; nonetheless, the sermon broadened to include all America and, once again, all Western civilization now threatened by the plague of infidelity and freethinking. Nothing that he personally observed in Rhode Island encouraged Berkeley to recommend to his countrymen a headlong plunge into the untested waters of religious liberty. John Clarke's "livelie experiment" was, so far as this preacher was concerned, an experiment whose results were not yet in. It was true that Rhode Islanders "have worn off part of that Prejudice,

4. Henry Newman to Lewis Thomas, Feb. 29, 1732; SPCK Society Letters, vol. 24.

5. SPG Journal, vol. 6; pp. 1, 16. Berkeley was proposed for membership on Feb. 18, 1732, and that membership was confirmed the following April 21. His election to the Society may have been eased by the death of Thomas Bray two years earlier.

which they inherited from their Ancestors, against that national Church of this Land." It was also true, however, that in wearing off that prejudice "too many of them have worn off a serious Sense of all Religion." The majority of the inhabitants managed to survive without the sacraments and without much attention to the essentials of Christian faith and practice. "And as for their Morals, I apprehend there is nothing to be found in them that should tempt others to make an Experiment of their Principles, either in Religion or Government."[6] In other words, England's monarchy and England's church still deserved the support of all right-thinking men and women.

On behalf of the SPG missionaries he left behind, Berkeley publicly commended them as having proved "themselves worthy the Choice of those who sent them." Salaries should be augmented for some, and the recruiting of new clergy, even from "the dissenting Seminaries of the Country," would be encouraged "if Provision were made to defray their Charges in coming hither to receive Holy Orders."[7] But since he was preaching a sermon, not giving a mere traveler's report, Berkeley made his major homiletic point: "After all, it is hardly to be expected, that so long as Infidelity prevails at home, the Christian religion should thrive and flourish in our Colonies abroad." We must do all that we can about "domestic Infidels, if we would convert or prevent foreign ones."[8] Believing this message worthy of the widest circulation, the SPG voted to print 2,500 copies of the sermon, a decision that Newman found especially commendatory since Berkeley, being ill at the time he spoke, was "heard by very few."[9]

6. GB *Works*, 7: 121.
7. Ibid., p. 123.
8. Ibid., pp. 123, 126.
9. SPG Committee Book 3; the vote on publication was taken on March 13, 1732. Also see SPCK Society Letters, vol. 24.

Meanwhile the dean, who in Newport had grown accustomed to waiting, found himself in London waiting once more. He waited to learn what ecclesiastical preferment might be settled upon him: in Ireland? in England? or none at all? As though George Berkeley had not suffered enough over the ill-fated Bermuda plan, it now appeared that this "noble Design" could wreck his entire future. In the years that he had been away, "Bermuda" had become a byword and a joke, standing for folly, failure, and fanaticism; Berkeley himself had become a madman, a dreamer, a disappointed solicitor now "disaffected to the Government." Highly placed churchmen in Ireland seemed determined to thwart any opportunity for Berkeley to acquire a new position. If this fanatic had not deigned to function as dean of Londonderry, if he had even refused his bishop's urging to come home, what claim now did he have, why should further aspirations be gratified? Why now, for example, should the deanery of Down (just south of Belfast) be given to him in preference to a man who "had spent 1,400 1. in defending the king's right to a presentation"?[10] To the archbishop of Dublin, John Hoadly, the answer was quite clear: no reason at all to prefer George Berkeley over Richard Daniel. To John Percival, however, all reasons weighed the other way, since Daniel was "one of the meanest in every respect" in Great Britain, while Berkeley by contrast was "the worthiest, the learnedest, the wisest, and most virtuous divine of the three kingdoms [who] is by an unparalleled wickedness made to give way."[11] Ever the loyal friend, Percival seized the chance to beard the lion, or at least the brother of the lion, in church one

10. Perceival, *Diary*, 1: 230; entry for February 27, 1732 (quoting Bishop Benjamin Hoadly of Salisbury).

11. Ibid., p. 224; entry for February 22, 1732. Also see the long excerpt from Lord Wilmington's letter to the duke of Dorset, in John Wild, *George Berkeley*, pp. 371-72.

Sunday in February, 1732. During services, Percival carried on a whispered conversation with Benjamin Hoadly, bishop of Salisbury and brother of John, Dublin's archbishop and Berkeley's nemesis. Percival complained bitterly not so much that Berkeley was passed over, as that it was done in so malicious a spirit: "taking away Dean Berkely's [sic] reputation was wicked and unpardonable." The bishop of Salisbury, however, thought that little reputation remained to be taken away. "Dean Berkley [sic] had done himself a great deal of hurt," he told Percival, "by undertaking that ridiculous project of converting the Indians, and leaving his deanery, where there was business enough for him to convert the Papists." When Percival responded sharply that not everyone thought the project so ridiculous, the bishop retorted that "he knew not one wise man approved it." Not one? What of the whole House of Commons, asked Percival, the ministry, "and both the late king and the present" who granted a charter and authorized the payment of monies? Well, the bishop calmly replied, "all that was done out of regard to the man, not the design."[12]

Neither Percival nor Berkeley (if he knew of it) could have found that conversation encouraging concerning prospects of preferment in Ireland. But if Ireland held little promise, England held less. Bishop Gibson explained to Percival that to make an English bishop out of this Irishman "would revolt all the clergy of England; besides the nobility, who have friends to promote, would effectually oppose it." About the only way that Berkeley might acquire even a deanery in England would be for some sort of exchange to be worked out. That is, Berkeley could assume a deanery in England if a current English dean would accept an appointment in Ireland. But, the perceptive bishop added, "no clergyman who has interest or pretensions to

12. Percival, *Diary*, 1: 230.

be advanced in England, will go to an honourable banishment in Ireland." Besides, Gibson inquired, why should
Berkeley aspire to be a bishop in England? He has no
desire to be a bishop in Ireland or in England, Percival
responded. Berkeley sought the deanery of Down for two
reasons only: one, as a mark of royal favor to remove the
stigma of failure now associated with his name; and two,
to gain the additional income (Down bringing in £200
more than Derry) which would permit him to repair some
of the damage done to his private fortune.[13]

What all of this proved was that the returning prodigal
needed some friends. Happily for Berkeley, Queen Caroline
numbered herself within that group. When it appeared that
all of Ireland's cathedral doors would be closed against
Berkeley, she declared that she was ready to "provide for
him in England." And when *Alciphron* emerged from the
London printer in the winter of 1732, the queen personally
and "publicly commended it at her drawing-room."[14]
Through the continuing intervention and intercession of
such powerful friends at court, preferment did come at
last to Berkeley, and it did come in Ireland. Far from the
deaneries of either Derry or Down, in southernmost Ireland,
the market town of Cloyne (later to be eclipsed by Cork
and even Cobh) was about to receive a new bishop, and
Berkeley was about to receive an "honourable banishment."
Nearly two years had passed since that testy exchange between Percival and Hoadly before Berkeley learned that
"he had the King and Queen's hands for the Bishopric of
Cloyn [sic]." The stipend of £1,300 per year ("effectually"
£1,100, said Percival) was enhanced by the presence of a
"good house" near the modest cathedral.[15] When, in
January of 1734, Berkeley "kissed their Majesty's hands

13. Ibid., p. 237.
14. Ibid., p. 229.
15. Ibid., 2: 9; entry for January 17, 1734.

for the Bishopric of Cloyne," he knew little about the
details of the appointment. In the middle of the month he
wrote to his trusted Dublin friend, Thomas Prior: "Pray
send me as particular an account as you can get of the
country, the situation, the house." And four days later he
impatiently wrote again, "I shall be glad to hear from you
what particulars you can learn about this Bishopric of
Cloyne."[16]

What little Berkeley had already heard suggested that the
office would provide sufficient income and security,
though he questioned "whether the dignity will much contribute" either to his well-being or his cultural interests.
From one "remote corner" of the world, Newport, George
Berkeley was now destined for another "remote corner,"
where he would spend almost all the rest of his life. Archbishop Hoadly, cautious of the queen, may well have concluded that banishing Berkeley to Cloyne was as agreeable
a solution as possible to a prickly puzzle. With some satisfaction, Berkeley observed that "Those who formerly
opposed my being Dean of Downe [*sic*], have thereby
made me a Bishop." He added, in his note to Percival, that
this rank in the church, "how desirable soever it may seem,
I had before absolutely determined to keep out of."[17]

Though appointed in January, Berkeley did not actually
take up his office and residence until May. Bad weather, ill
health, late ships and the complexities of the move (including his "coach and six") were among the factors
responsible for the delay. Berkeley also tactfully wished to
wait until the incumbent, his close friend Edward Synge,
had departed for his new post. Now, as a wiser and more
cautious man, Berkeley also delayed in resigning the

16. GB *Works*, 8: 223-25; letters dated Jan. 15 and Jan. 19, 1734. According
to Wild, *George Berkeley* (p. 399), Cloyne at this time consisted of 44 churches and 14,000 Protestant souls.
17. GB *Works*, 8: 225-26; Jan. 22, 1734.

deancry at Derry until absolutely certain that no remaining legal or parliamentary hitches stood between him and Cloyne. During these several months before the move, other and richer sees fell vacant. When Thomas Prior urged Berkeley to apply for one or more of these, the newly-named bishop of Cloyne declared that he would not "so much as open my mouth to any one friend to make an interest for getting any one of them. To be so very hasty for a removal, even before I had seen Cloyne, would argue for a greater greediness for lucre than I hope I shall ever have." Finally, on May 19, 1734, in St. Paul's in Dublin, George Berkeley received the dignity of the episcopal office. Before the end of June, he and his family were in Cloyne.[18]

The subsequent career of George Berkeley, though never marked by the excitement and vision of either his philosophical or his Rhode Island adventures, was not without its wisdom and its daring. His first year at Cloyne saw the publication of *The Analyst* (1734), an attack upon the obscurity and inexactitude of that clearest and most exact of all the sciences: mathematics. At the same time, the *Analyst* was, like most everything else that Berkeley wrote, a defense of Christianity, whose obscurity and mystery did not exceed that of mathematics ("He who can digest a second or third fluxion . . . need not, methinks, be squeamish about any point in divinity").[19] Provoking sharp con-

18. Luce, *Life*, p. 159. Also see Berkeley's many letters to Thomas Prior during this period from January through April; GB *Works*, 8: 222-39.

19. For the text of *The Analyst*, with introduction by A. A. Luce, see GB *Works*, 4: 53-102; quotation is from the introduction, p. 57. The full title of this brief work (Berkeley perhaps still concerned about those who never got beyond the title page) was as follows: *The Analyst, or, A Discourse Addressed to an Infidel Mathematician. Wherein it is examined whether the object, principles, and inferences of the modern Analysis are more distinctly conceived, or more evidently deduced, than religious Mysteries and points of Faith.* Luce concluded that the "infidel mathematician" whom Berkeley had in mind was Edmund Halley (1656-1742) of comet fame.

troversy, even at his own college, Berkeley felt obliged to respond to his critics the next year with *A Defense of Free-thinking in Mathematics* (1735), arguing therein that mathematicians had no corner on the use of reason and bishops no intrinsic defect that prevented their agility with numbers.[20]

From 1735 to 1737, Berkeley revealed himself very much the Irishman as he unveiled yet another dimension of his restless mind. Ireland's economic woes worsened as England's aloofness or exploitation had earlier called forth Jonathan Swift's bitter satire, *A Modest Proposal* (1729). In a series of rhetorical questions, collectively called *The Querist*, Berkeley argued for a national bank (none came until 1783), for a more favorable treatment of Ireland's exports such as wool, flax, and hemp (England granted none until disconcerted by a revolution in America), and for legislation as well as common sense that would, above all else, stimulate work and discourage luxury and vice. An early critic of mercantilism, Berkeley saw work—not money, not land—as the road to cure of Ireland's ills. And in Cloyne itself, the bishop in his roles as employer, planner, humanitarian, and pastor tried to apply an ethic that made both economic and Christian sense.[21]

In 1741 Cloyne and the surrounding country, having

20. See GB *Works*, 4: 103-41. Also in 1735, Berkeley spoke his last word on these matters in another tract, *Reasons for not replying to Mr. Walton's "Full Answer,"* ibid., pp. 143-56.

In 1736 (Feb. 7), Edmund Gibson commended Berkeley for attending "to your mathematical Infidels . . . [thereby] doing good service to religion." But what bothered Bishop Gibson most were not the "profess'd Infidels" but the "Semi-Infidels, who under the title of X^{ns} are destoying the whole work of our Redemption by Christ, and making Christianity little more than a system of morality." Six months later, in another letter to George Berkeley, Gibson agreed "that ye men of Science (a conceited generation) are the greatest sticklers against reveal'd Religion, and have been very open in their attack upon it." BM 39311; second letter dated July 9, 1735.

21. See GB *Works*, 6: 87-122, the introduction here being by T. E. Jessop.

endured near starvation as a result of the previous year's severe frost, suffered from a plague of smallpox. Berkeley, long concerned with his own health,[22] now sought to alleviate pain and suffering in the wider community. Writing what was to become his most popular work both in Europe and America, Berkeley addressed himself to a most unlikely subject: tar water. Convinced that tar water had a broadly therapeutic efficacy, Berkeley in 1744 issued his last major work: *Siris, A Chain of Philosophical Reflexions and Inquiries Concerning the Virtues of Tar-Water, and divers other Subjects connected together and arising One from Another.* The title page bore this counsel from Galatians: "As we have opportunity, let us do good unto all men" (6:10).

The public's initial attention fastened upon tar water, gliding over the philosophical reflections "and divers other Subjects." And Berkeley too began with tar water, though he ended with a defense of the Trinity (thereby encouraging at least one cleric to preach a sermon on "Tar-rinity").[23] Whatever medical virtues the preparation may have pos-

---

22. Berkeley suffered from "habitual cholic," severe gout, frequent colds, and, for several months after his return from Rhode Island, from "a great disorder in my head." He was ill when he delivered his sermon to the SPG, and so ill afterward that John Wainwright had to explain his inability to make a formal presentation to the king. In the years between his departure from Newport and his settlement at Cloyne, nearly every surviving letter makes some reference to his health which is "mending," or debilitating, or confining, or in danger of further injury. The cumulative impact of these remarks raises a possibility of hypochondria. Indeed, one American contemporary (though clearly an unfriendly one) noted that one of Berkeley's sermons was two and one-half hours long, "which to me is somewhat strange for such an Hypocondriachal Disposition." Thomas Howard of Boston to Edmund Gibson, July 19, 1731; Fulham Papers, 5: 40-43. In his will, Berkeley also revealed a morbid fear of being buried alive.

23. Geoffrey L. Keynes, *A Bibliography of George Berkeley* . . . , pp. 124-25. For the full text of *Siris* (with introduction by T. E. Jessop), see GB *Works*, 5: 1-164.

sessed, tar water had the clear economic virtue of being
plentiful, cheap, and easy to prepare. Berkeley's recipe was
as follows:

> Pour a gallon of cold water on a quart of tar, and stir
> and mix them thoroughly with a ladle or flat stick, for
> the space of three or four minutes, after which the
> vessel must stand eight and forty hours, that the tar
> may have time to subside; when the clear water is to be
> poured off and kept covered for use, no more being
> made from the same tar, which may still serve for com-
> mon purposes.[24]

One passing comment of Berkeley's, that "the cold infusion
of tar hath been used in some of our colonies as a preserva-
tive or prescription against the small pox," led to the conclusion—almost certainly wrong—that Berkeley learned of
tar water from the Indians while he lived in Rhode Island.
On the contrary, the first therapeutic use of tar water
appears not to have occurred until 1739, and then not in
Rhode Island but in South Carolina; Berkeley learned of it,
moreover, not through direct observation but from the
pages of a learned journal.[25] Yet America was involved,
and America quickly joined the craze.[26] In 1745 Cadwallader Colden (1688-1776), leading New York scientist,
philosopher, and office-holder, published *An Abstract*

24. GB *Works*, 5: 32.
25. Much of the mythology surrounding the origins of tar water as a cure-
all is laid to rest in Ian Tipton, "Two Questions on Bishop Berkeley's Panacea,"
Journal of the History of Ideas 30, no. 2 (April–June, 1969): 203-24.
26. Both England and France succumbed to the allure of this universal
remedy, the degree of zealous attachment being suggested by Horace Walpole's
oft-repeated anecdote. When Walpole asked a London apothecary in 1744
whether he sold tar water, the response was, "Why, I sell nothing else!" GB
Works, 5: viii.

from Dr. Berkeley's Treatise on Tar-Water,[27] in which he separated the "mere historical Part" from the "argumentative Parts" in order to assist the reader of "common Capacities and vulgar knowledge." Thus introduced to tar without Trinity, ordinary sufferers up and down the American coast turned hopefully, even desperately, to that which might alleviate not only smallpox but ulcers, syphilis, pleurisy, indigestion, dropsy, scurvy, and difficulties of teeth, larynx, and lungs. When French troops in America required a guide to American cures for American ailments, Newport in 1780 published a *Compendium Pharmaceuticum* that included tar water among its recommended remedies.[28]

One other publication of Berkeley's found a quick reception in America: *A Word to the Wise: Or, An Exhortation to the Roman Catholic Clergy of Ireland*. Published in Dublin in 1749, this alone of Berkeley's works had an American edition (courtesy of S. Kneeland of Boston) within the year; for colonial Americans, in the mid-eighteenth century still in the grip of great anxieties over "popery," saw in Berkeley's analysis of Irish Catholicism

27. First appearing anonymously as a series in the *New-York Weekly Post-Boy* (Feb. 18 to March 25, 1745), then published separately as an 18-page pamphlet, issued in New York in 1745. On the question of authorship, see Saul Jarcho, "The Therapeutic Use of Resin and of Tar Water by Bishop George Berkeley and Cadwallader Colden," *New York Medical Journal* 55 (1955): 834-40.

28. Jarcho, p. 840. The popularity of the tar water "epidemical madness" (as one medical critic of the time called it) must be understood in the light of (1) the primitive medical knowledge of the time; (2) the human eagerness for universal cures, especially if supported by a metaphysic showing how all the universe is interrelated, body and soul, chemistry and theology; and, (3) the geniune therapeutic value of this aqueous extract, of "the cup that cheers, but not inebriates" (the expression originated with Berkeley). On the last point, modern analysis shows tar water to be effective as a gastrointestinal disinfectant, as an expectorant, and as a deodorant; see James Bell, "Bishop Berkeley on the Tar-Water," *Irish Journal of Medical Science* 6 (1933): 633.

another evil which no pioneering people could tolerate: sloth. If tar water was deemed the cure for all physical maladies, work was regarded as the panacea for all social ills. The theme was sounded over and over: "the sin and folly of sloth," the rectitude and necessity of work. "In vain is the earth fertile, and the climate benign, if human labor be wanting." The spirit of industry—the work ethic as later generations would call it—was, wrote Berkeley, "a sound Catholic doctrine, not limited to Protestants but extending to all, and admitted by all." Calling on Saint Paul for support, the bishop of Cloyne noted that those unwilling to provide for their own were worse than infidels (1 Timothy 5:8). The time was now, the place was here, Reverend Sirs, to awaken "your wretched countrymen from their sweet dream of sloth." Even if we as Protestants and Catholics take different routes to heaven, can we not take "the same steps on earth?"[29] And though Berkeley would not live to see it, even an anti-Catholic colonial America later found it possible to invite a clearly Catholic France to join with her in taking some of "the same steps on earth."

As *A Word to the Wise* was being reprinted in Boston, Berkeley's career in Cloyne was drawing to a close. In that remote corner of the world, he had written, preached, entertained, and grown old. The family had expanded to include three sons (Henry, born in Newport; George, born in London; and William, born in Cloyne) and one daughter (Julia, born in Cloyne). In addition to Lucia, buried in Newport, two other children had died in their first year: John in 1735, and Sarah in 1740. In 1751, William, only fourteen years of age and his father's special "little friend"

29. GB *Works*, 6: 231-49; quotations are from pp. 235-36 and 246-47. On Berkeley's doctrinal differences with Roman Catholicism, see his long letter tŏ his traveling companion aboard the *Lucy*, John James; letter dated June 7, 1741, and written in Cloyne. GB *Works*, 7: 139-55.

also died ("Not content to be fond of him, I was vain of him. I had set my heart too much upon him").[30] Like the bishop's other children, William had been educated in the manse-house "always under mine own eye"; Berkeley had found his St. Paul's at last, not in Bermuda, but in Cloyne.

In October of the same year when William died, Berkeley's closest friend, Thomas Prior, also left a grieving Berkeley behind (Percival had died three years earlier). In 1752 George Berkeley began to put his literary estate in order by bringing out a third edition of *Alciphron* and a collection of scattered pieces, some of which had never before appeared in print (including the poem on America), called *A Miscellany*. That same year Samuel Johnson sent Berkeley a copy of *Elementa Philosophica*, with its indebtedness to the bishop made explicit. And in the summer of 1752, Berkeley and his family left Cloyne for a prolonged visit to Oxford, where the father could oversee the education of his son George, enrolled at Christ Church.

For Berkeley, who had visited the city in his late twenties, Oxford held the pleasantest of memories; describing it then as "the most delightful place I have ever seen," he left it a month later with real regret.[31] And after eighteen years of the "gloom of Cloyne,"[32] he was ready to trade that cultural bypath for Oxford's intellectual stimulation and vitality. But time was running out. Within six months, his fragile health failed and, in January of 1753, George Berkeley was buried in Christ Church Cathedral. Thomas Secker, formerly bishop in Oxford (then dean of St. Paul's), wrote to the widow that "God . . . has taken to Himself, in Wisdom and Mercy no doubt, that excellently good &

---

30. Ibid., 8: 304; this, the most poignant of all Berkeley's surviving letters, was written to Martin Benson on March 8, 1751.
31. Ibid., pp. 68, 71; letters to Percival, July 19 and Aug. 27, 1713.
32. Ibid., p. 310; letter to Isaac Gervais, April 6, 1752.

very great man."[33] And in far away New Haven, Ezra
Stiles addressed Yale's faculty and students at the next
commencement.

> You may perhaps judge me to be too full of wonder,
> my listeners, that I delight so greatly in this man. But
> to admit the truth . . . I cannot help but admire and
> indeed adore the amiable character of his example.
> For it adumbrates such great resemblance to the kind
> Father of the universe and the loving image of his
> benevolence that I am filled with admiration and
> seized with sweetest love. The thought therefore of his
> death, if we look at our lot, should I believe be accom-
> panied with grief and lamentations; yet, if we look at
> him, with reverence and joy:—surely who lived right
> cannot pass away with an unhappy heart since he
> leaves behind many testimonies and memories of his
> virtue. . . .
>
> He is alive, therefore, . . . my listeners: Is he really
> alive? Yes indeed! He lives, without doubt: he lives in
> his literary works; he lives in his good deeds which are
> spreading knowledge; he lives, finally, through the ex-
> ample of those virtues in which he distinguished him-
> self, which from his grave speak to us, and he exhorts
> and urges us to continue in the lauded arts. Moreover,
> his memory will flourish as long as these monuments
> do exist—[monuments] which have been attested as
> being distinguished and judged to be such excelling
> testimonies of praise that they will last forever. . . .[34]

33. BM 39311, dated January 16, 1753; in 1758 Secker became archbishop
of Canterbury.

34. Ezra Stiles Papers, Beinecke Library, Yale University; used by permission
Translated from the Latin by Dr. Josef Purkart, University of California, River-
side.

In contrast with Stiles's evaluation of Berkeley, William Douglass, in his

Stiles's funeral oration symbolized America's continuing interest in Berkeley long after Newport, just as Berkeley, long after Newport, continued to give himself to America's interests, notably in the realms of religion and learning. His philosophical and educational impact in the eighteenth century is most clearly seen, of course, in Samuel Johnson. While Berkeley in his last years was still corresponding with Johnson, the latter was finishing America's first textbook in philosophy, dedicating it "To the Right Reverend Father in God, George, Lord Bishop of Cloyne, in Ireland." *Elementa Philosophica*, published by Benjamin Franklin in 1752, attempted (as so much of George Berkeley's own writing had done) to reconcile the new science with the old religion and to turn back the tide of arrogant and unbridled rationalism. Moving beyond anything that his mentor had tried to do, Johnson also sought to "provide a short general view of the whole system of learning," demonstrating how each field was related to every other and all "to the general end, viz. our happiness." In the "Advertisement," Johnson further acknowledged his intellectual debt.

> Tho' I would not be too much attached to any one author or system; yet whoever is versed in the writings of Bishop Berkeley, will be sensible that I am in a

---

two-volume history of "the British Settlements in North-America" (Boston, 1747-52), berated the Irish bishop on three scores. First, the Bermuda scheme, which sprang from the brain of "a whimsical man," was ill-considered and impractical (e.g., he paid far too much attention to the question of climate, whereas everybody knows that college students can thrive in any environment: witness Harvard). Second, William Douglass, M.D., scorned the tar-water craze as being every bit as fanciful as Bermuda; and, on behalf of all doctors everywhere, he quoted this from a London newspaper: "The bishop's book annoys the learned tribe: / They threaten hard, 'We'll preach if you prescribe.'" Third, *Alciphron* defended mystery and obscurity, championing "a certain enthusiasm in human nature" from which "all religions do sprout" (London edition, 1744, pp. 149-50n.).

particular manner beholden to that excellent philosopher for several thoughts that occur in the following
tract. And I cannot but recommend it to any one that
would think with exactness on these subjects, to pe-
ruse all the works of that great and good gentleman. . . .[35]

Yet the influence of this early text was probably limited
to Johnson's own King's College and to the College of Philadelphia presided over by another Anglican clergyman,
William Smith.[36]
   King's College itself became a principal avenue of
Berkeleyan influence when Johnson assumed its presidency
in 1754.[37] Even before that time, however, Johnson had
been actively involved in preparing and planning for the
projected Anglican educational center in New York. His
own frustration over Anglicanism's failure to control any
educational institution north of Virginia was further
aggravated when the Presbyterians moved in New Jersey to
establish and control still another dissenting academy in
England's own colonies: the College of New Jersey (1746)
out of which Princeton would grow. A couple of years
after that untoward event, Johnson wrote to the bishop of
Cloyne, seeking his counsel concerning the Anglican school
too long suspended in a conceptual stage. Taking time out
from his busy correspondence "with patients who drink
tar-water," Berkeley responded in late August of 1749.
With the Rhode Island experience never far from his mind
and with the scars never totally healed, Berkeley advised

---

35. Johnson, *Writings*, 2: 360.
   36. Ibid., p. 22; illustration of title page opposite p. 359.
   37. The Anglican effort to make King's College unmistakably *their* college—
a source of supply to their ministry, a possible seat for that colonial bishop
who never arrived, and a mighty fortress against "the torrent of irreligion and
which seems coming on like a flood"—is admirably described in David C.
Humphrey, *From King's College to Columbia 1746-1800* (New York, 1976),
chapter 2.

his friend not to bother with courts, kings, boards, or politicians in seeking a charter for the enterprise. Rather than
waste enormous amounts of time, create huge and unnecessary expenses, and in general "cause great trouble,"
it would be better to proceed "to do the business quietly"
among themselves. Would that someone two decades earlier
had so advised him!

As for faculty in this new institution, they should be
drawn from New England and not from Old; for from the
latter none worth having would come. Whatever money
you have at your disposal, he suggested, spend chiefly on
the faculty and not on the buildings. Provide handsomely
for the president and fellows, since the "chief concern must
be to set out in good method, and introduce from the very
first, a good taste into the Society." I would have good
hopes for the College, Berkeley graciously added, "were
you at the head of it." As in Bermuda, so in New York
or anywhere else, Berkeley believed that if the officers of
instruction were wrong, nothing else could be right. Keep
buildings simple and student rooms spare (10' x 10' is
large enough!). Offer prizes, as Berkeley had himself made
possible at Yale, for these "may prove useful encourage-
ments to the students." With respect to curriculum, "Let
the Greek and Latin classics be well taught." That, along
with a concern for "good life and morals," should be
foremost. Requirements for the degree should be compat-
ible with those at Oxford and Cambridge, for "this would
give credit to the College, and pave the way for admitting
their graduates *ad eundem* in the English universities."[38]

38. GB *Works*, 8: 301-02; letter dated August 23, 1749. Johnson's reply,
in *Writings*, 1: 136-37 (Sept. 10, 1750), indicated that Newport had invited
him to replace James Honeyman, whose death Johnson now reported to
Berkeley. Johnson also thanked Berkeley for his donation to the college, probably once again a gift of books, for Johnson wrote: "I had heard your Lordship was collecting some books for a present to the Library of Cambridge
College" and I thought that "if you knew of an Episcopal College going for-

In his reply, Johnson indicated that the bishop's "wise
and excellent" suggestions were being passed on to Philadelphia—Franklin was the actual recipient—in connection
with collegiate plans afoot there. And though Samuel Johnson had been asked to head that school too,[39] Franklin's
choice later fell upon the Scottish Anglican, William Smith
(1727-1803), a graduate of Aberdeen University and
recent emigrant (1751) to America. In his idealized vision
of a proper education for the New World, Smith shared
George Berkeley's dream of what lay ahead for this western
empire.

Publishing *A General Idea of the College of Mirania* in
New York in 1753, Smith prefaced his educational utopia
with verses that "bid a New-Britannia spring to Light!"
Looking toward golden days and brighter periods of history
in "sublimer Lays," Smith could even see "other Bacons,
Newtons, Lockes appear; / And to the Skies our Laureat-
Honors rear." Other "Popes and Spencers" would also
grace the new continent, and even the American savage
would contribute to this new crest of civilization.

> Lo! the wild Indian, soften'd by their Song,
> Emerging from his Arbors, bounds along
> The green Savannah patient of the Lore
> Of Dove-ey'd Wisdom—and is rude no more.

Also like Berkeley, William Smith saw education as the indispensable ally of virtue, particularly in an "Infant-Coun-
try."

---

ward in these parts, you would perhaps rather turn a benevolent design towards
founding a library for that." Berkeley, moreover, had indicated that a gift of
money was made difficult by the fact that Ireland's schools required much
charity and that New York was "a country in proportion much richer than our
own." GB *Works*, 8: 301.

39. Benjamin Framklin's letter to Johnson asking him to head the school at
Philadelphia is in Johnson, *Writings*, 1: 140-43 (Aug. 9, 1750).

The Practice of ancient States, in this respect, is
truly surprizing and worthy our Regard. In their
Infancy they did not busy themselves so much in
making Laws for the Punishment of Criminals, as for
hindering there being any Criminals among them, by
stopping up the great Inlets of Vice, and training up
Youth to be, as it were, constitutionally Good.[40]

Though *Mirania* ("Wonderland") drew Smith to Franklin's
attention and thereby to the leadership of the college,
Smith's personality, politics, and educational philosophy
soon led to a bitter break between the two men. His diminished influence, together with the disturbing rumbles of
revolution, precluded the powerful sway of another Anglican (or Berkeleyan) vision of an ordered society, of a
people elevated culturally and morally, and of a progressive
ripening of history's finest fruit.

Samuel Johnson tried to extend Berkeley's influence
even farther by making a convert of the only other New
Yorker to meditate seriously upon questions of matter and
spirit: Cadwallader Colden. But Colden found Berkeley
more persuasive or perhaps more interesting on tar water
than on those "diverse other Subjects" discussed in *Siris*.
Colden at first differed politely, wishing neither to offend
Johnson nor to show disrespect for "Bishop Berkeley, whose
merit is very conspicuous, and whom I highly esteem."
Berkeley's refusal to grant any independent status or
property or potency to matter, however, continued to
trouble and finally to antagonize Colden. After Johnson
had, with some hope, sent a copy of *De Motu* to Colden,
the latter dropped all restraint: "I think that the Doctor
has made the greatest collection in this and his other
performances, of indistinct and indigested conceptions

40. In Smith's *Mirania* (reprint New York, 1969), the verses appear on
pp. 5-7, the prose quotation on pp. 75-76.

from the writings of both the ancients, and the moderns
that I ever met with in any man's performances."[41] In
his tutorial relationship with Colden, Johnson was apparently no more successful than he had been years earlier
with his Yale students.[42]

By 1780 most of the brief flash of Berkeleyan enthusiasm
had passed, yielding to a much stronger flow of Scottish
realism. By that year Johnson had been dead for eight
years, the bishop's influence at King's College waning rapid-
ly thereafter. At Princeton the flirtation with immaterialism led by Tutor Joseph Periam and his remarkable
student, Samuel Stanhope Smith, shrank before John
Witherspoon's Common Sense philosophy and his explicit
attack on Berkeleyan thought. In the years of revolution
and nation-building, the metaphysical subtleties of Berkeley
together with the skeptical dead end of David Hume, held
little appeal for serious-minded, strongly challenged Americans. Calling upon conscience, reason, and experience, the
Scottish philosophers struck their colonial listeners as so
much more practical, so much more believable. The world
was real, quite apart from the operation of the mind upon
it; the self *did* have identity and continuity through time,
despite whatever difficulty one has in seeing each link in
the chain; common sense *did* count, notwithstanding
efforts of the erudite to belittle it. By way of Francis

41. Johnson, *Writings*, 2: 293; letter dated Nov. 19, 1746; also see his earlier
letter in the same volume, p. 287 (March 26, 1744). In 1745 Colden (1688-
1776) published his first edition of *An Explication of the First Causes of
Action in Matter*. Almost two decades earlier, he had made an important contribution to Indian and colonial history in his *History of the Five Indian
Nations* (New York, 1727). His later career as public servant and lieutenant-
governor ended amid widespread resentment over his continued loyalty to
Britain.
42. Students at Yale pressured Johnson to resign in 1718, charging him with
ineffectiveness as a teacher; Joseph Ellis, *New England Mind in Transition*,
pp. 50-51.

Hutcheson, Thomas Reid, Dugald Stewart, and others,
Protestant and Anglophobic Scotland rose with the tides
of revolution to carry the day for an entire generation of
new nationals.[43]

Yet, if Berkeley's metaphysics slipped from view, his
philosophy of history could not have been more timely
than it was in the Age of Revolution. Soon after drafting
the Declaration of Independence, Thomas Jefferson and
others were called upon to defend this new Eden against
charges of biological inferiority, of moral degeneracy, of
inevitable deterioration and decline. A rash of Europeans—
Buffon, de Pauw, Kalm, Raynal, et al.—concerned themselves not with the ruin of Great Britain or the corruption
of Europe but with the laughable pretensions of uncultivated Americans. Producing no geniuses, possessing no
great cities, boasting of no art or music or literature worth
a second thought, Americans were, according to them, a
shriveled and genetically defective lot. To resist this offen-
sive attitude of superiority assumed by Europe's intellec-
tuals, a nation in the bud searched for assurance of its full
flowering, for promise that it would rise to Europe's
height and, perchance, even beyond. From such as Berkeley
those of lesser capitals than London or Paris could draw
strength and hope of a destiny staggering to the imagination but stirring to the heart. Coming to Yale's commencement in 1781, poet and patriot Joel Barlow compared
America's rise with the decline of Europe's courts:

> And here, what roving views before them spread!

43. See Douglas Sloan, *The Scottish Enlightenment and the American
College Ideal* (New York, 1971), especially pp. 130, 147, 153; R. J. Petersen,
"Scottish Common Sense in America, 1768-1850; An Evaluation of Its In-
fluence" (Ph.D. diss., American University, 1963); and Sydney E. Ahlstrom,
"The Scottish Philosophy and American Theology," *Church History* 24, no.
3 (Sept., 1955): 257-72.

Where this new empire lifts her daring head!
What wide extent her waving ensigns claim!
Lands yet unknown and streams without a name.
Where the deep gulph unfold Floridia's shore
To where Ontario bids hoarse Laurence roar;
Where Missisippi's waves their sources boast,
Where grove and floods and realms and climes are lost,
To where the mild Atlantic's length'ning tide
Laves numerous towns, and swells their naval pride.
And see! by nature's hand o'er all bestow'd,
The last pure polish of the forming God.[44]

In that Age of Revolution which was also an Age of Enlightenment, Berkeley proved more prescient and apt than
most of Europe's philosophers who had found so much to
ridicule and mock. In the America of 1780, the raillery of
wits, the artful dodging, the clever employment of double
entendre scarcely sufficed. Hardly an Age of Reason at all,
John Adams exploded; call it Age of Frivolity if you
will, or even an "Age of Folly, Vice, Frenzy, Fury, Bru-
tality . . . anything but the Age of Reason." If common
sense was called for, so also were sobriety, vigilance, courage, and even prayer.[45] For some years these virtues were
in demand throughout all the colonies, unmistakably so in
that town which Berkeley knew best, Newport. There, as
early as 1771, men had been pressed concerning what they

44. Joel Barlow, *A Poem Spoken at the Public Commencement* . . . (Hartford, 1781), p. 7. These lines were later incorporated into Barlow's major
opus, *The Vision of Columbus*, first published in 1787. Also see Timothy
Dwight, *America: Or, A Poem on the Settlement of the British Colonies*
. . . (New Haven, 1780).
45. The Enlightenment in America has recently received the attention of
these able scholars: Henry F. May, *The Enlightenment in America* (New York,
1976); Donald H. Meyer, *The Democratic Enlightenment* (New York, 1976);
and, Henry Steele Commager, *The Empire of Reason* (New York, 1977).
The Adams quotation is from Meyer, p. xii.

would do if and when British troops marched through their streets. To the infinite disappointment of the town's Congregational pastor (from 1755 to 1776), Ezra Stiles, the Rhode Island General Assembly at first took no strong stand. Stiles, however, did take one. "This Day [May 4, 1771] the Assembly agreed not to obstruct the coming of the Troops, if they come only as marching Troops & not to make any stay." Then the Whig preacher and future Yale president added: "This Concession seals the Death of American Liberty. May God humble us for those sins which have brot down these heavy Judgments & Calamities upon us."[46]

Liberty was not doomed, however, by Newport's early equivocation. Within a few years, both the tempo of events and the rigor of resolve increased. In and around Boston, in New York, in Virginia, and again in Newport, episodes in 1775 crowded "in such rapid Succession," Stiles noted, "that I cannot record all of them." Newport itself, vulnerable to direct fire from British men of war, grew more anxious in the summer of 1775, as the roar of cannon grew louder, readily heard from the town's very own wharves. Officially the citizens inquired of the Assembly "how to act in the momentous Exigency especially if . . . fired on by the Men o' War"; unofficially, many citizens answered the query by escaping from the town, particularly those known to be sympathetic to the American cause. One-half to two-thirds of Stiles's congregation fled, while Ezra Stiles himself stayed on, dismayed at the Tory sentiment of those lingering in Newport and anxious lest the British blockade the town and, by starving it, bring it to its knees.[47]

46. F. B. Dexter, ed., *The Literary Diary of Ezra Stiles* . . . (New York, 1901), 1: 103. Also see the excellent biography by Edmund S. Morgan, *The Gentle Puritan: A Life of Ezra Stiles 1727-1795* (New Haven, 1962).
47. Stiles, *Diary*, 1: 609-11.

By March of 1776 Stiles at last concluded that he and
his family also must move to safer ground; yet, from nearby Massachusetts he could and did return regularly to minister to the remnant of his congregation. When in July
the grand news of "Independency" reached him, he
followed Newport developments even more closely. On
July 20 the Declaration was read publicly at the Colony
house, then to be swiftly endorsed by the Rhode Island
Assembly meeting in Newport. That same session of the
Assembly decreed that no person "shall under Pretence of
Preaching or praying, or in any Way or manner whatever"
acknowledge George III "to be our rightful Lord &
Sovereign." This stricture hit George Berkeley's own
Trinity Church particularly hard, but Ezra Stiles was man-
ifestly unsympathetic. "[T]he people of the Chh. of England
in Newport cried out of Persecution, went and removed all
their Prayer Books &c. & shut up the Church; and had no
Service in it last Lordsday, tho' M^r [George] Bisset their
Parson was well & walking the Streets."[48]
Soon George Bisset could walk those streets in greater
security than Ezra Stiles was able to do. For within six
months of the Declaration's reading in Newport, the British
arrived in force. On December 9, 1776, Stiles wrote:

48. Ibid., 2: 28. Two years earlier, in June of 1774, the Rhode Island Assembly proclaimed a "Day·of Public Fasting and Prayer" as an appropriate response
to Britain's hostile acts, notably the closing of Boston harbor. Bisset's response
was to preach from the text, "Fast not with the hypocrites." Ezra Stiles (who
took his text from Esther 4:3) deplored Bisset's misplaced sympathies and bad
taste.
   Two other Newport ministers, in those tense days, had their loyalties questioned, according to Stiles: John Maxson, an elderly Seventh-Day Baptist,
whose "honest Mind was not Strong eno' to digest this Revolution"; and a
young Philadelphia Baptist, Erasmus Kelly, who equivocated. Kelly "is the first
Baptist in N. England that ever declared ag^t the Unlawfulness of Arms—and
perhaps is the only Man in the World, that can pray for Success to Arms,
while he believes their Unlawfulness" (ibid., pp. 28–29). All together, Stiles
reported, about ninety Tories in Newport came before the Assembly, either
to swear their loyalty to the Patriot cause or to be sent to less sensitive areas
away from the coast.

> This Afternoon we hear that the Enemy landed yester-
> day about the Middle of the West Side of the Isld,
> about Three Thousand Men: & marched into Newport,
> paraded before the Courthouse & there published the
> Kings Proclamation, & formally took possession of the
> Town & erected the Kings Government & Laws.[49]

As more and more British transports and men of war sailed
into the Bay and into Newport's harbor, as Hessian troops
arrived to be fed and quartered in Newport homes, the
population continued to dwindle—from around ten thousand in 1775 to about one-quarter that number at the end
of 1776.[50] When, three years later, the British evacuated
the town, they left it desolated and in economic ruin. Yet
Newport's role in the Revolution was not over. As a result
of the complex diplomacy of Franklin, John Adams, and
others, America's war-weary troops were at last to receive
critical outside help—especially for a command of the sea.
In July of 1780, Comte de Rochambeau sailed into Newport harbor accompanied by a large portion of France's
naval fleet—with more to follow. "The Bell rang at Newp^t
till after Midnight," Stiles joyfully reported, and the next
night, in celebration of a war that now might end, everyone placed candles in their windows, everyone, that is,
but the Quakers who "did not chuse their Lights shd shine
before men, & their Windows were broken."[51]

Rochambeau repaid the warm welcome by immediately
preparing to defend the town against potential counterattack by the British. French troops deployed throughout
the island dug trenches, raised batteries, and built emer-
gency routes to meet the enemy wherever he might land.
"In twelve days," the French general reported, "the
position was rendered respectable by the labour of all the

49. Ibid., 2: 95.
50. Ibid., p. 105.
51. Ibid., p. 454.

hands, both soldiers and sailors, who were able to work; but the scurvy had made sad havock among our men, and two-thirds had been sent up the country to hospitals which had been established for their reception." Though Newport was blockaded and threatened, Rochambeau by his presence and his preparations forestalled that British landing party throughout the anxious summer of 1780. Agreeing to repair those of Newport's houses damaged by the British "on the condition that we should be allowed to use them for winter-quarters for our soldiers," Rochambeau created such a feeling of amity that "there was not a single duel or quarrel recorded between our soldiers and the Americans."[52] After only one winter in that haven, Rochambeau sailed in the summer of 1781 to join George Washington in New York, thence to march overland toward the war's climactic encounter at Yorktown.

By the terms of a most favorable peace treaty agreed to in 1783, the new nation cast off the mother who had long nurtured and protected her. It was what many Britons had feared would happen. Writing to Berkeley half a century earlier, Percival had told of "a very good Lord" who thought it a mistake to provide the colonists or the Indians with much in the way of education—either at Bermuda or anywhere else. Learning "tended to make the Plantations independent of their Mother Country . . . [in] the ignorance of the Indians and the variety of sects . . . was England's security." Percival, scandalized that a man noted for his own "learning and sobriety" would in this matter re-

---

52. *Memoirs of the Marshall Count de Rochambeau* (Paris, 1838; reprint New York, 1971), pp. 9-10, 22-23, 96. The remarkable paucity of duels and quarrels may relate in part to this observation of Rochambeau's concerning America's manners and customs: "Young women are free till their marriage. The first question addressed to a young woman is whether she be married; if she be, there the conversation rests" (pp. 107-08).

duce "all to policy," concluded that the age must be one
in which "men love darkness better than light."[53]

Henry Newman, already concerned about American independence as early as 1732, found solace in the colonists'
political divisions just as Percival's "very good Lord" took
much comfort in the religious divisions. "They can never
become independent," Newman wrote, "while they remain
crumbled into little Provinces and Governments who have
all their Governors and principal Officers from hence." But
the solace was momentary, for something of deeper import
troubled Newman. If England failed to behave like a "wise
Mother," if England yielded "to a General depravation of
manners, Oppression, Arbitrary Government and the En-
croachments of Popery," then independence for America
could not be stopped and did not deserve to be. Should
that be the direction which history took, then England's
truest patriots would be glad "that there are plantations to
retire to, where they may mend the Faults that has [*sic*]
undone their Mother Country, and unite in the advancem^t
of Religion and Virtue in America, when they can no longer
find protection in Europe."[54]

So Berkeley's friend, Henry Newman, foresaw for
Berkeley's inseparable twins, religion and virtue, a fulfillment in the West that might come only through revolution.
If England failed to heed the lessons of Greece and Rome,
then the course not only of empire but also of Christianity and morality would indeed follow the setting sun.

53. Rand, *B & P*, p. 269; letter dated December 23, 1730.
54. SPCK Society Letter, vol. 25; Newman to Rowland Cotton, Sept. 21,
1732. Not only were religion and virtue possibly on their way out in England,
but John Smibert had even heard that art as well had fallen upon hard times.
In 1743 (July 1), he wrote to Arthur Pond that "if the arts are about to leave
Great Britain I wish they may take their flight into our New World that they
may, at least, remain in some part of the British dominions." Massachusetts
Historical Society, *Proceedings* 49 (1915-16): 29.

The hardship and bloodshed of revolution "will have this
good Effect, at least," John Adams wrote to Abigail; "it
will inspire Us with many Virtues, which We have not,
and correct many Errors, Follies, and Vices, which threaten
to disturb, dishonour, and destroy us."[55] An intimate and
essential alliance obtained, many Americans of the revolutionary era argued, between virtue and enduring community,
between virtue and republican rule, between virtue and the
rise—or fall—of civilization. British oppression succeeded
only in making Americans more industrious, more frugal,
more self-disciplined—in making Americans, in other words,
more capable of and more deserving of being free. Religion
and virtue, working hand in hand, could create an enduring
republic, a Christian Sparta (to use Sam Adams's words),
a nation (to use George Berkeley's words) "Not such as
Europe breeds in her decay; / Such as she bred when fresh
and young." Fifty years before the Declaration signed in
Philadelphia, Berkeley had written of a "better Time"
when men will sing of "another golden Age" in which wisdom and virtue, nobility and faith would prevail.

For the founding fathers and first presidents, building a
nation was a more serious business than tearing one down.
Steeling a people for unknown challenges ahead called more
for Berkeley's religion and virtue than for the freethinker's
cynical or fashionable wit. The commander-in-chief become president began his first term of office by declaring
that "No People can be bound to acknowledge and adore
the invisible hand, which conducts the Affairs of men more
than the People of the United States." George Washington

---

55. Quoted in Gordon S. Wood, *The Creation of the American Republic,
1776-1787* (Chapel Hill, N.C., 1969), p. 117. Much of Wood's excellent
volume is pertinent here, as is the perceptive essay of Edmund S. Morgan,
"The Puritan Ethic and the American Revolution," *William & Mary Quarterly*
24, no. 1 (January, 1967): 3-43.

ended his eight years in office by warning that "reason and experience both forbid us to expect that National morality can prevail in exclusion of religious principle."[56] His successor, John Adams, felt even more strongly that religion was not designed to make us "good riddle solvers or good mystery-mongers, but good men, good magistrates and good subjects." And he asked rhetorically, "Have you ever found in history one single example of a nation thoroughly corrupted, that was afterwards restored to virtue? And without virtue, there can be no political liberty."[57]

Rather surprisingly, this concern for the role of religion in the shaping of a new nation did not lead to a National Church or even to any special patronage for Christianity. It led, rather, to an open competitive market, to bold new experimentation, and to an amazing burst of vitality in the early decades of the nineteenth century. Berkeley's own Anglican church suffered from the Tory sentiments of many of its clergy (notably those employed by the SPG), from the abrupt disestablishment inflicted upon it in several states, and from its long identification with political patronage, imperious bishops, and unresponsive monarchy. In moving to reorganize themselves in 1789 as the "Protestant Episcopal Church," Anglicans in New England had finally acquired that for which they had so long prayed and of which they so often despaired: namely, a bishop. And in achieving that invaluable acquisition, the name of George Berkeley was once more invoked.

In 1784 Connecticut churchmen proposed that one of their own number, Samuel Seabury, proceed to London to receive episcopal ordination. But London still required

56. *The Writings of George Washington* (Washington, D. C., 1931-44), 30: 293; 35: 229.
57. *The Works of John Adams* (Boston, 1856), 10: 386.

that obnoxious oath of allegiance to the much despised,
much maligned George III. If Seabury did not take the
oath, he could not be ordained; if he did take the oath,
he could not be received back home. Questions were raised,
moreover, concerning Seabury's precise status. Did he
come on his own, or with the endorsement of a national
assembly of clergy and laity, or with the endorsement of
the United States Congress, or with the endorsement (at
the very least!) of the Connecticut Assembly? All of these
questions and the assumptions that lay behind them posed
a network of difficulties which Seabury through correspondence, travel, petition, interview, and argument tried desperately to resolve, concluding in the long and tiresome
process that England was "certainly the worst country in
the world to do business in."[58]

Fortunately, another country lay not far from England.
Even more fortunately, other intercessors stood ready to
assist: for example, Newport's George Bisset, now back in
Scotland; and George Berkeley, Jr., temporarily in Scotland.
The son of the now deceased bishop of Cloyne had reason
to resent Seabury's awkward position and to deplore that
America's church was still without a shepherd:

> Had my honored father's scheme for planting an
> Episcopal college, whereof he was to have been presi-
> dent, in the Summer Islands, not been sacrificed by the
> worst minister that Britain ever saw . . . Episcopacy
> would have been established in America by a succes-
> sion from the English Church, unattended by any in-
> vidious temporal rank or power. . . . From the churches
> of England and Ireland, America will not now receive
> the Episcopate. . . .[59]

58. E. E. Beardsley, *Life and Correspondence of The Right Reverend Samuel Seabury* . . . (Boston, 1881), p. 122.

59. Ibid., pp. 126–27. Also see Bruce E. Steiner, *Samuel Seabury, A Study in the High Church Tradition* (Athens, Ohio, 1971), chapter 6. Steiner notes that

If not from England or Ireland, then perhaps, with the
help of George Berkeley, Jr., from the small and impoverished Episcopal community in Scotland. Young Berkeley
wrote several letters to the key figure in Aberdeen, Bishop
John Skinner, urging him not to let slip this signal opportunity to do good for all America. Once, fifty years before,
an opportunity to do good for all America had indeed been
missed. "Can any proper persons be found," he asked,
"who, with the spirit of confessors, would convey the great
blessing of the Protestant Episcopacy from the persecuted
Church of [in?] Scotland to the struggling persecuted
Protestant Episcopalian worshippers in America?" In Aberdeen, on November 14, 1784, an affirmative answer was
given to that fervent question. Seabury had his mitre, and
New England would soon have its first bishop.

Seven months after his consecration, Samuel Seabury
landed in Newport, Rhode Island, there to preach his first
American sermon in his new dignity.[60] In Trinity Church,
he climbed the steps of that three-tiered pulpit where
George Berkeley, Sr., had so often stood. And he took his
text from the opening verses of the twelfth chapter of the
Epistle to the Hebrews:

> Wherefore, seeing we also are compassed about with so
> great a cloud of witnesses, let us lay aside every weight,
> and the sin which doth so easily beset us, and let us
> run with patience the race that is set before us, Look-
> ing unto Jesus the author and finisher of our faith:
> who for the joy that was set before him endured the
> cross, despising the shame, and is set down at the right
> hand of the throne of God.

George Berkeley, Jr., had some years earlier offered himself—with the conni-
vance of Samuel Johnson—as an episcopal prospect for North America (p. 178).
   60. Beardsley, *Life and Correspondence*, p. 206.

8 Epilogue

Man can embody truth but he cannot know it. . . . The
abstract is not life . . . You can refute Hegel but not the
Saint or the Song of Sixpence.

William Butler Yeats, 1939

Two hundred years after America's independence, the name
of Berkeley still survives in his almost chosen land. The
name and the spirit of the man persist at several levels,
from the superficial to the profound.

"Berkeley" has remained a name to be honored or invoked as memory or utility or promise may at any time
or place suggest. Within his ecclesiastical household, New
World Anglicans have forgotten neither the courtesy nor
the commitment which Berkeley's extended visit to these
shores represented. In the middle of the nineteenth century
on the island of Bermuda itself, an Anglican clergyman, W.
C. Dowding, thought that neither Berkeley nor his noble
design should be allowed to fade away unremembered.
Writing in 1852, Dowding explained that Bermuda, whose
population was by then predominantly black, should be
the training ground for all Africans in the Western world—
those still enslaved on the continent, and those freed but
impoverished and uneducated in the Caribbean. The
greatest needs, he explained, were moral and religious
training, and a college. Concerning the latter, he added:
"we shall but follow in the track which Bishop Berkeley
has pointed out; and adopt, in great measure, his own
words. It is the essential peculiarity of the scheme now
proposed, that it is the very own scheme of the Bishop

himself; merely writing the word 'negro' where he wrote
'Indian'."[1] But Dowding's appeal to the archbishop of
Canterbury, the bishop of London, and the bishop of New-
foundland (in whose jurisdiction Bermuda then lay) won
even less political support than had its eighteenth-century
prototype.

A century after the bishop's death, an Episcopal seminary
founded in Connecticut, Berkeley Divinity School, proved
a more substantial revival of the name and tribute to his
churchmanship. Located initially in Middletown, the school
in 1928 moved to New Haven, where it enjoyed a close
association with George Berkeley's "other School." In
1971, the Berkeley Divinity School merged with Yale's
Divinity School, an institutional marriage that could only
have gratified the irenic Irishman. At Yale itself, an organization for Episcopal students, formed in 1869, not un-
naturally adopted as its name the Berkeley Association.
This constituted both a recognition of the bishop of
Cloyne and a declaration of the growing Episcopal presence
on Yale's campus since those tumultuous days of 1722.
By the early 1900s about one-third of the student body
were members of the American branch of Berkeley's own
church:[2] Hooker and Chillingworth had clearly done their
duty!

When, after the Revolution, King's College found its
charter restrictive and its name embarrassingly unpatriotic,
the New York legislature in 1784 took steps to rename and
restructure the school. The name should have been changed,

1. William C. Dowding, *Africa in the West: Its State, Prospects, and Educational Needs: With Reference to Bishop Berkeley's Bermuda College* (Oxford,
1852), p. 16. Also see a three-page flyer or advertisement in the SPG Library
entitled, *The Revival of Bishop Berkeley's Bermuda College* (n.p., n.d.).

2. Nelson R. Burr, *The Story of the Diocese of Connecticut* (Hartford,
1962), p. 334. In that other Middletown, near Berkeley's Rhode Island home,
a Berkeley Memorial Chapel was erected in 1882-83.

declared Moses Coit Tyler, to Berkeley College.[3] But given
the sectarian battles through which the school had come,
together with the Loyalist leanings of its most recent
Anglican leadership, "Columbia" was surely a wiser as well
as unarguably a more popular choice. The name of
Berkeley, therefore, gained its most prominent association
with higher education not by the rivers and ocean of the
East Coast but a continent away by the ocean and bays of
the West.

Congregationalists and Presbyterians joined forces in
nineteenth-century America to civilize, Christianize, and
educate those masses moving out across the vast western
spaces. One product of their common venture, Contra
Costa Academy, opened in Oakland, California, in 1853.
Chartered two years later as the College of California, the
small school bore in its leadership and its faculty the un-
mistakable stamp of Yale. The Reverend Henry Durant
(Yale, 1827), its first president, invited the noted theologian
and Hartford, Connecticut pastor, Horace Bushnell (also
class of 1827), to take over the presidency of the infant
institution. In California at the time for his health, Bushnell
held that decision in abeyance while he undertook an
elaborate and extended walking tour across much of northern California, this protracted hike designed to help the
new school find a superior site for its permanent location.
For many months in 1856, Bushnell occupied himself, he
reported, in

> examing views and prospects, exploring water-courses,
> determining their levels and gauging their quantities
> of water, discovering quarries, finding supplies of
> sand and gravel, testing climates, inquiring and even
> prospecting to form some judgment of the probabili-

3. Moses Coit Tyler, *Three Men of Letters* (New York, 1895), p. 60.

ties of railroads. . . . The site of a university, I have
not forgotten, can be chosen but once. . . .

The ambitious plans for the new school fully matched
the exertions expended in finding the best site. What was
envisioned, Bushnell explained, was "a college that will be
the germ of a proper university, and will not fulfill its idea
till it becomes, on the western shore, what Harvard and
Yale are on the other." While such a day no doubt lay far
in the future, the trustees deliberately measured the
grounds and made their plans "so as to leave room for un-
limited growth and expansion believing that the spot on
which they fix is to become at some future day, a renowned
center of literature and science—a name clothed with associations as profoundly historical as Oxford, or Padua, or
Salamanca or Heidelberg."[4]
When, therefore, five sites were narrowed to three, then
finally to one on the east side of San Francisco Bay, the
question of an appropriate name for such a carefully
chosen, such a grandly conceived campus received serious,
sustained, and self-conscious deliberation. For two years
the "college town" or "college grounds" (laid out in 1864)
remained unnamed. Many possibilities were considered, including the name of Bushnell himself. Frederic Law Olmsted, engaged by the College of California trustees to plan
the landscaping, wrote a long letter in 1865 to The Reverend S. H. Willey, then acting president of the college and
of course yet another Yale graduate of 1827. Olmsted
thought "the best way to form an English name is to find
a word signifying something characteristic of the place to
be named, or the name of a person, event or quality which

4. *Movement for a University in California . . . and An Appeal by Dr.
Bushnell* (San Francisco, 1857), pp. 9, 13.

would be satisfactorily associated with it."[5] Then in 1866,
a Presbyterian lawyer and the college's leading trustee,
Frederick Billings, offered to his fellow trustees a name
that seemed most "satisfactorily associated" with an enterprise aimed at advancing religion and learning in the
empire's West. "Berkeley came to me as a sort of inspiration,
and I knew it was the name, proposed it, and they all saw
the fitness."[6]

Having proposed it and having seen it adopted, Billings
did not let the matter rest there. He tried to make the
"presence" of Berkeley meaningful in the life of the school,
even after the private College of California in 1868 turned
over its much-loved site to the newly created public University of California. To still another Yale man, Daniel
Coit Gilman (class of 1852) who became president in 1872,
Billings volunteered his services to ensure that the University at least had a proper portrait of George Berkeley.
When Gilman expressed a desire for a copy of Smibert's
"Bermuda Group," Billings arranged for Yale's art professor,
John F. Wier, to make such a copy. When it was finished,
Billings hoped that President Gilman would be kind
enough to "present it for me to the University when you

5. Olmsted to S. H. Willey, July 25, 1865; Bancroft Archives, University of
California, Berkeley. Olmsted also suggested that since so many English names
had been appropriated, "it seems to me just and proper to fall back on Spanish
at this time in California." He particularly favored some combination with
"villa": e.g., Villarosa, Villabrecha, Villaverde, Villavega, Villaportilla—and
some seventeen more. Of the many suggestions for a Spanish name offered,
one proved a most serious contender: "Peralta."

6. Billings in a letter to Daniel Coit Gilman, June 25, 1873; Bancroft Archives. Olmsted had heard that the names of both Bushnell and Billings had been
suggested. While he was agreeable to either, the temptation with the Golden
Gate in the background to turn the campus name into Billingsgate might have
proved irresistible to the students (see W. W. Ferrier, *The Story of the Naming
of Berkeley* [Berkeley, 1929], pp. 10-11). Ultimately, Frederick Billings, an
original partner of the Northern Pacific Railroad, did have a town named for
him, but in Montana not California.

take possession of the new Hall at the coming commencement in July [1873]." Billings concluded his letter with
these words:

> The University looks out through the Golden Gate of
> the Pacific to the islands of the sea and the uttermost
> parts of the earth. The portrait there of this Christian
> philosopher, who could find in Plato the revelation of
> the New World and prophesied so truly of the Course
> of Empire should be something more than a portrait.
> It should be alike an invocation and an inspiration of
> the largest, broadest and most earnest spirit of Learning
> and Christianity.
>   So may it be![7]

Yet Yale had by no means relinquished to California all

---

7. Billings to Gilman, June 18, 1873; Bancroft Archives. President Gilman
was most receptive to the notion of keeping more than merely the name of
Berkeley alive at this new state institution of higher learning. In his Inaugural
Address delivered in 1872, Gilman offered the following. "I hail it as a omen
of good, both for religion and learning, that the site of this University bears
the name of Berkeley, the scholar and divine. It is not yet a century and a
half since that romantic voyage which brought him to Newport, in Rhode
Island, an English prelate who would found a college in the Bermudas. . . .
He could not do as he would, he therefore did as he could . . . . His fame has
crossed the continent which then seemed hardly more than a seaboard of the
Atlantic; and now, at the very ends of the earth, near the Golden Gate, the
name of Berkeley is to be a household word. Let us emulate his example. In
the catholic love of learning, if we can not do what we would, let us do what
we can. Let us labor and pray that his well-known vision may be true:

> 'Westward the Course of Empire takes its Way;
>   The four first Acts already past,
> A fifth shall close the Drama with the Day;
>   Time's noblest Offspring is the last.' "

*The Building of the University. An Inaugural Address delivered at Oakland,
Nov. 7, 1872* (San Francisco, 1872), pp. 24-25. See also the three-quarter
leather-bound volume, "The Portrait of Bishop Berkeley," presented in 1900
"To the University of California, Guardian of the fame of Berkeley, from
Daniel C. Gilman"; Bancroft Library Archives, University of California,
Berkeley.

rights to honor the name and the man. On the bicentennial of Berkeley's birth, Yale's President Noah Porter in 1885 delivered a lengthy discourse designed "to keep his memory fresh and fragrant in the minds of studious and thoughtful men and women of the present generation." After a detailed review of the life and thought of America's first major intellectual visitor, Porter concluded:

> In the chapel of our daily worship two windows always meet the eyes of the congregation—one honored with the name of Jonathan Edwards and the other with that of George Berkeley. Each was distinguished for acuteness of intellect, for vigor of logic, for Christian and missionary self-devotion, and for an ardent interest in Christian education. May these names ever be honored and the men who bore them; and as Yale College becomes more emphatically and conspicuously than now the home of Christian science and Christian letters, may these names glow with a still brighter lustre in its annals.[8]

A half-century later, Yale polished that lustre by naming two of its newly constructed residential colleges after its distinguished alumnus and its distinguished benefactor. When the cornerstone for Berkeley College was laid on November 2, 1934, passages from *Siris* were read while the stone itself was anointed with tar water! An undergraduate club, "Nephews of Vanessa," was formed the following

---

8. Noah Porter, *The Two-Hundredth Birthday of George Berkeley. A Discourse Given at Yale College on the 12th of March, 1885* (New York, 1885), pp. v, 70. With perfect aptness, Porter dedicated the book to the bishops of Rhode Island (Thomas March Clark) and of California (William Ingraham Kip), "classmates of the writer at Yale who . . . are one with him in honoring the memory of Berkeley."

year, and on March 12 of successive years "Berkeley birthday celebrations" were regularly held.[9]

On a broader and more politicized scale, the name of
Berkeley was also invoked on behalf of Manifest Destiny.
Of course, far more than Berkeley and his familiar poem
went into that wondrous mix of jingoism, geopolitics,
self-aggrandizement, mission, and millennial expectation.
Berkeley, "no proper millennialist,"[10] contributed the idea
of a cultural apex, of a New World civilization built upon
and even exceeding that of both decaying Europe and long
dead Greece and Rome. Horace Walpole (1717-97),
Robert's "literary" son and letter writer extraordinary,
saw American independence in the 1770s as inevitable, for
that land "is growing too mighty to be kept in subjection
to half a dozen exhausted nations in Europe." "The next
Augustan age," he wrote to Sir Horace Mann in 1774, "will
dawn on the other side of the Atlantic. There will, perhaps,
be a Thucydides at Boston, a Xenophon at New York, and,
in time, a Virgil at Mexico, and a Newton at Peru. At last,
some curious traveler from Lima will visit England and give
a description of the ruins of St. Paul's."[11]

While Walpole and many others may have shared the
sentiments of the bishop of Cloyne, yet it was Berkeley
who actually came to America, Berkeley who actually
made a personal and costly commitment to America, and

9. George W. Pierson, *Yale: The University College 1921-1937* (New Haven,
1955), chapter 19; and Russell G. Pruden, *Berkeley College, Yale University,
1934-1939* (New Haven, 1939), pp. 21, 23-24. The college even included
Berkeleyan detail in its architecture: for example, the arms of the sees of
Derry and Cloyne over the Elm Street gate, and appropriate drawings in the
college library (Pruden, pp. 31, 33).

10. Ernest Lee Tuveson, *Redeemer Nation: The Idea of America's Millennial
Role* (Chicago, 1968), p. 92.

11. Quoted in Rexmond C. Cochrane, "Bishop Berkeley and the Progress
of Arts and Learning," *Huntington Library Quarterly* 17, no. 3 (May, 1954):
245.

Berkeley who thereby proved so adaptable and useful to
America. Daniel Webster, on laying the cornerstone of an
addition to the Capitol on July 4, 1851, praised Berkeley's
poetic prophecy concerning this continent as "one of the
most striking passages in our language"—striking not alone
or even chiefly in style but in the grandeur of its conception. Berkeley's view of history and of this nation's place
in it was "strong, ardent, glowing, embracing all time since
the creation of the world and all regions of which that
world is composed, and judging of the future by just
analogy with the past." Quoting these words of Webster's,
Charles Sumner, no mean orator himself, declared that
Berkeley's verses have been so often invoked "as to become
a commonplace of literature and politics. There is nothing
from any oracle, there is very little from any prophecy,
which can compare with them."[12]

In the twentieth century, as the nation's sense of clear
purpose and destiny wavered, Berkeley's name as well as
Berkeley's lines became less a commonplace and his
confidence less widely shared. Following the western sun
across the skies seemed more like chasing rainbows, and a
New World cultural Golden Age struck a jaded generation
as being as quixotic as a New Athens in the wastelands of
Bermuda. Yet for a century and a half George Berkeley
gave to a new nation the courage to move westward, believing that in so doing it would not fall off the edge of
civilization into moral anarchy and barbaric ignorance; on
the contrary, those who crossed the mountains and the
plains were the advance troops of a cultural renaissance
that "By future Poets shall be sung."

12. Charles Sumner, *Prophetic Vioces concerning America* (Boston, 1874),
pp. 24-25. Deists and freethinkers held to a cyclical view of history; George
Berkeley, on the other hand, in advancing that linear view of history which
has dominated American culture, further enhanced his utility to later generations.

"George Berkeley in America" is, however, more than merely a name, more than a single poetic effort. Of both his thought and his spirit, much remains. In 1871, Charles Sanders Peirce, founder of America's most distinctive philosophical "school," wrote a long review of the newly issued four-volume edition of Berkeley's works.[13] Rereading the Irish philosopher convinced Peirce that the former's writings were "the productions of a most brilliant, original, powerful, but not thoroughly disciplined mind." Hume, more disciplined as well as more skeptical, simply took Berkeley's challenge to the independent reality of matter and applied it to the independent reality of mind.

> The innocent bishop generated Hume; and as no one disputes that Hume gave rise to all modern philosophy of every kind, Berkeley ought to have a far more important place in the history of philosophy than has usually been assigned to him.[14]

But what Peirce's own keen eye gleaned from all four volumes of writings emanating from "the innocent bishop" was the tiny seed of pragmatism. Two things, Peirce observed, distinguished experience from imagination in Berkeley's philosophy: "one is the superior vividness of experience; the other and most important is its connected character." Of experience Peirce concluded with barely concealed excitement, we may then say that "Its parts hang together in the most intimate and intricate conjunction, in consequence of which we can infer the future from the past. . . . Here we seem to have a third new conception of reality." And that new conception concerned predictability; it concerned the potential differing consequences

---

13. The four volumes, which included a life of Berkeley, were edited by A. C. Fraser (Oxford, 1871). Peirce's review is in *North American Review* 113 (October, 1871): 449-72.

14. Ibid., pp. 467, 469.

of ideas, and even of words. (One way to avoid "the de-
ceits of language," Peirce noted, was to ask whether two
things described "fulfill the same function practically?"
If they do, drop one of the terms or concepts or propo-
sitions; the argument is merely one about words.)[15] When
Peirce's benefactor and friend at Harvard, William James,
gave Peirce credit for launching the pragmatic school of
philosophy, the latter responded: "Berkeley on the whole
has more right to be considered the introducer of pragmatism into philosophy than any other one man, though I
was more explicit in enunciating it."[16]

The other major philosophical system which flourished
in America after the Civil War is more readily associated
with George Berkeley: namely, idealism. Though America's
version of this "school" owed more to Hegel than to
Berkeley, nonetheless the bishop provided a point of
departure—and of dispute. Josiah Royce, the leading
exponent of idealism in America, alluding to "the wonder-
ful Berkeley" and the "ever-fascinating Bishop Berkeley,"
commented:

> Men of Berkeley's type are born to see God face to
> face; and when they see him, they do so without fear,

15. Ibid., pp. 465, 469.
16. Quoted in R. H. Popkin, "Berkeley's Influence on American Philosophy,"
Hermathena 82 (1953): 136. James also recognized Berkeley as one of his
masters who assisted him to find philosophical solutions by pressing hard for
the practical consequences, for the "cash value" of an idea; ibid., pp. 139-40.
For his appreciation of Berkeley, William James owed something to his widely-
read, wide-ranging father, Henry James, Senior. The latter complained that
few of Berkeley's readers took "pains to understand him." This surely included
England's Dr. Samuel Johnson, "whose towering dogmatism often needed a
very broad base of stupidity." Johnson "fancied that he refuted Berkeley by
stamping on the ground. Had the Doctor consulted his head instead of his
heels, as would have been merely decorous under the circumstances, he would
have found that Berkeley had no intention to affirm the *sensible* nonentity
of matter, but only its *supersensuous* or logical nonentity." Henry James,
Lectures and Miscellanies (Redfield, N.Y., 1852), p. 334.

without mystical trembling, without being driven to
dark and lofty speech. They take the whole thing as a
matter of course. They tell you of it frankly, gently,
simply, and with a beautiful childlike surprise that
your eyes are not always as open as their own.[17]

If one understood Berkeley aright, Royce explained, one
recognized that interpreting the data which the senses
brought to the perceiver was like learning to read. One
must understand the signs, the symbols, the language of
the world. "What is all my life of experience, my seeing,
feeling, touching, moving about," Royce inquired, except
"from first to last a learning to read the language of things?"
And whose language am I reading? "Whose ideas are these
that experience impresses upon me?" Surely the reader of
Alciphron, or of the *Essay on Vision*, or of *Siris* hardly
required an answer. "Is not all my life a talking with God?"[18]
Berkeley, the epistemological mystic, found tongues in
trees, sermons in stones, and the language of God in
everything.

If God's voice was everywhere, Berkeley's seemed nearly
so, as he has over the past two and a half centuries been
appealed to, argued against, invoked, condemned, re-
examined, and reinterpreted with a vigor that shows little
sign of weakening.[19] "America's first philosophical friend,"

17. John J. McDermott, ed., *The Basic Writings of Josiah Royce* (Chicago,
1969), 1: 275, 283, 287-88.

18. Ibid., 1: 290. Since so much in American philosophy in this period took
its cue from the remarkable department at Harvard, see Bruce Kuklick, *The
Rise of American Philosophy, Cambridge, Massachusetts, 1860-1930* (New
Haven, 1977).

19. As one quick index to the pervading influence of Berkeley in the twentieth century (not limited to America), note C. M. Turbayne and R. Ware's
long bibliographical article in the *Journal of Philosophy* 60, no. 4 (1963):
93-111, which listed 362 publications by or pertaining to Berkeley printed
(or reprinted) between 1933 and 1962. The catholicity of subjects treated is
staggering, while the number of disparate fields somehow touched if not shaped

as Richard Popkin characterized Berkeley, remains a central
figure in the nation's philosophical heritage, one "who
must be re-read, re-studied, and re-digested with each stage
of the intellectual evolution of America."[20] While no
attempt has been made here to trace every line of intellectual descent in the United States, it is clear that Berkeley
survives as thinker no less than as eponym.

Finally, what of the spirit of George Berkeley? With
what precision can it be defined? To what degree has it
survived? William Butler Yeats, Berkeley's countryman and
admirer, provides a clue in the search for definition: a
man's spirit is found embodied, incarnate—not alone in
his thought, not alone in his action, but in the persuasive
and lingering conjunction of the two. As a dedicated
enemy of all abstraction, Berkeley found truth not in prop-
ositions and names but in living spirit. The minute philosophers, Berkeley noted in *Alciphron*, "confound Scho-
lasticism with Christianity" whereas "an ideal abstracted
faith is never thought of by the bulk of Christians." This
"wiredrawing of abstract ideas" was a task never imposed
upon either Christian or Jew. Faith, on the contrary, was
a quite different sort of thing: showing itself "in the will
and actions of a man," it is "a vital operative principle."[21]
It is, in short, a word become flesh. Yeats, attracted to the

------

by Berkeley testifies to his intellectual voracity: metaphysics, ethics, episte-
mology, aesthetics, religion, mathematics, physics, economics, literature, education, linguistics, logical positivism, medicine, and history.

20. R. H. Popkin, "Berkeley's Influence," p. 145. Also see Gerard Hinrich's
article, "The Logical Positivism of Berkeley's *De Motu,*" *Review of Metaphysics* 3 (1949–50): 491-505; Hinrich stated that Berkeley "gives physical
science its charter by pointing out in detail the ineptness or irrelevance of
metaphysical language in science" (p. 491). In *Science and the Modern World*
(New York, 1925; reprinted 1948), Alfred North Whitehead declared that
Berkeley, at the very beginning of the modern scientific age, "made all the
right criticisms, at least in principle" (p. 65).

21. GB *Works*, 3: 299-300.

man no less than to the philosopher, believed that in reading Berkeley's "suave glittering sentences . . . we feel
perhaps for the first time that eternity is always at our
heels or hidden from our eyes by the thickness of door."[22]
And we feel this way in large part because the whole man
reaches out to us, because, as Unamuno said in a passage
marked by Yeats, "it is precisely the inner biography that
explains for us most things."[23] What truths, then, did the
living spirit of George Berkeley manifest?

When he published his poetic prophecy, Berkeley at that
time gave it the title, "Verses by the Author on the prospect of Planting Arts and Learning in America." "Arts
and Learning" proclaimed Berkeley's ardent conviction
that culture mattered, that culture needed to be transmitted, that a new generation—especially one in a New
World—must learn from the old so that civilization might
not fall and life not be impoverished. In the eighteenth
century, deists and freethinkers had little to say about
culture. "Nature" was all, with "culture" becoming only a
code word for corruption, arbitrary authority, or vested
interest. On the other hand, few evangelicals or pietists
took culture very seriously either. For them, the word
suggested that worldliness which one must eschew to become a new creature and to experience a new birth. Not
many advocates remained, therefore, to defend the planting of "Arts and Learning" as a matter of first importance
to a people poised on a wave that could recede toward ruin
or flow on toward an empire of merit.

That "nursery of learning" which Berkeley had envisioned
would teach the arts and sciences in the context—the ever-

22. Yeats's introduction to J. M. Hone and M. M. Rossi, *Bishop Berkeley:
His Life, Writings, and Philosophy* (London, 1931), pp. xx-xxi.
23. Cited in Donald T. Torchiana, *W. B. Yeats and Georgian Ireland* (Evans-
ton, Ill., 1966), p. 226, n. 16; see all of Chapter 6 herein.

assumed context—of religion and virtue. Abstraction was
as inimical to education as it was to all other of life's
endeavors. To be learned was not to be conversant with
vague or general ideas or to be given to empty flights of
rhetoric: it was to be the embodiment of a civilized human
being. Those educated at Bermuda (or Dublin or Oxford
or any "proper university") were to be rescued from
savagery "to a life of civility and religion."[24] "Religion"
itself must of course be no flowery abstraction but a
specific creation: namely, Christianity—a Christianity made
vivid and visible and particular in Jesus Christ. That religion
continued its fleshly reality in "a peculiar people who are
styled the church. . . . This society of regenerate persons
into whom new life is put by the Spirit of Christ residing
and dwelling in them."[25] And virtue, too, pertained not to
coffee-house raillery or cheap commendation. It had to be
embodied; and, if Alexander Pope may be believed, Ireland's
philosopher-bishop managed to do just that.

> Ev'n in a bishop I can spy desert,
> Secker is decent, Rundel has a heart;
> Manners with candour are to Benson giv'n,
> To Berkley [sic] ev'ry virtue under heav'n.[26]

In his *Metaphysics of Morals* Immanuel Kant declared
that "there is nothing either in the world or out of it which
is good without qualification except a good will." Berkeley
exuded good will: toward the native American, the enslaved
black, the impoverished Irish, and even the dissenting sons
of Eli. To say that he best represented his age is not to
argue that he escaped it: its phobia against Catholicism, its
pride in any particular form of sectarianism, its conscious-

24. *A Proposal* (1724 edition), p. 7.
25. GB *Works*, 7: 89.
26. Quoted in Luce, *Life*, p. 60 (Epilogue to the *Satires*).

ness of birth and of class. But insofar as he was able (which
is all that Saint Paul dared to ask), he managed repeatedly
and at no small cost to himself to show good will toward
all men, to be—as he had written in 1723—"the mean instrument of doing good to mankind."[27]

How easy it would have been for Berkeley to retreat
from the acclaim of his early philosophical writing into a
world of unfettered imagination or wild prophecy, to nur-
ture his immaterialism into a perfect excuse for never
entering into the disordered worlds of politics, economics,
and ecclesiastical maneuver. On the face of it, the author
of *A Treatise Concerning the Principles of Human Knowledge* makes a most improbable missionary. Except that
the over-riding "principle" was a loathing for that vagueness,
that imprecision, that fuzzy generality that blocks one's
search for truth, for the kind of truth that (in Yeats's
words) "is always moth-like and fluttering and yet can
terrify."[28] When his own dreams collapsed, Berkeley resisted the temptation to weave an interior romance or build
a barrier against an unperceiving and unfeeling world. His
spirit called for advance, not retreat; for hope, not despair;
for communication, not isolation; for life, not "nice
distinctions."

George Berkeley, in the last analysis, stood for a world
which could not stand by itself. The rock which that other
Samuel Johnson kicked offered no genuine refutation to
the true nature of reality. For Berkeley, Johnson's toe and
the convenient stone were, along with trees, mountains,
oceans, and coffee-houses, ideas ever present in and ever
sustained by the mind of God. It was God that mattered,
not matter; it was God that was known more clearly, more
certainly than one's neighbor: "we need only to open our eyes

27. See above, p. 25.
28. Introduction to Hone and Rossi, *Bishop Berkeley*, p. xix.

to see the Sovereign Lord of all things with a more clear
and full view, than we do any one of our fellow-creatures."[29]
If not a God-intoxicated man, he was, then, at least a
"God-appointed" one (Yeats) who saw neither man nor
matter as the measure of all things, but Him in whom we
live and move and have our being.[30] Berkeley differed from
Bunyan's pilgrim in virtually every way imaginable, but
pilgrim he was throughout his life, moving steadily toward,
concentrating fixedly upon, singing philosophical hymns
of praise to the Celestial City whose ruler and maker is
God.

The Incarnation, Berkeley explained in a Newport sermon, did not make God more present, only more visible.[31]
Berkeley's legacy to America was not that he made truth
more present, only that he made it more visible.

29. GB *Works*, 2: 108.
30. On Yeats's characterization of Berkeley, see Torchiana, *W. B. Yeats
and Georgian Ireland*, p. 235; on Berkeley's quotation from the New Testament, see GB *Works*, 3: 159.
31. GB *Works*, 7: 79; sermon is undated.

A Note on the Sources

The chief repository of Berkeley manuscript material is
the British Museum (Additional Manuscripts 39304-16
and 46689); for a detailed description of these and smaller
deposits in Trinity College and the National Library of
Ireland, see T. E. Jessop, *A Bibliography of George Berkeley*
(Oxford, 1934; reprinted New York, 1968), pp. 79-93.
A. A. Luce, who provided the inventory of manuscript
remains for this volume, also listed the widely scattered
repositories of extant autograph letters, though he gives a
more complete accounting in the nine-volume edition of
Berkeley's works, noted below.

Of the publication of the works of George Berkeley,
only three editions require mention. The first, perhaps
edited by Joseph Stock but certainly including a life of
Berkeley by him, was published in both Dublin and London in 1784: *The Works of George Berkeley* . . . , 2 vols.
In 1871, A. C. Fraser published in four volumes *The Works
of George Berkeley* . . . (Oxford). Volume 4 of the Fraser
edition remained the standard biography of Berkeley until
1949, when A. A. Luce published *The Life of George
Berkeley, Bishop of Cloyne* (London). That biography was
part of Luce's total dedication to an examination and a
preservation of the life, times, and thoughts of George
Berkeley. Luce (of Trinity College, Dublin) together with
T. E. Jessop (of University College of Hull) completed
the following decade the now standard edition, *The Works
of George Berkeley, Bishop of Cloyne*, 9 vols. (London,
1948-57; reprinted 1964). All references in the notes are
to this edition.

   The most valuable unpublished manuscript materials pertaining to Berkeley in America are found in the archives of
the Society for the Propagation of the Gospel (15 Tufton
St., London) and the Society for Promoting Christian
Knowledge (Holy Trinity Church, Marylebone Road, London). Some of the SPG material was published in the last
century by W. S. Perry in his monumental four-volume
work, *Historical Collections Relating to the American
Colonial Church* (Hartford, 1870-78; reprinted New York,
1969), but great quantities remain unpublished. The SPG
Journals and the SPG Letter Books (Series A, B, and C)
constitute an invaluable source concerning the mind-
set of Berkeley's contemporaries in New England as well
as in London. The above are now all available on microfilm; the less valuable SPG Committee Reports, also uti-
lized in this book, have not been microfilmed. The SPCK
archives are tiny but precisely relevant to George Berkeley's
American career. The Society Letters and the New
England Letters, now also microfilmed, contain the most
valuable source material, with the Abstract Letter Books
rendering assistance when a fuller text was not available.
Some of the more important letters were reprinted in W.
O. B. Allen and Edmund McClure, *Two Hundred Years:
The History of the Society for Promoting Christian Knowledge* (London, 1898; reprinted New York, 1970).
   Other manuscript collections bear directly though less
fully upon the subject of this book. The Egmont Papers in
the British Museum contain the illuminating correspondence between Sir John Percival, first earl of Egmont, and
George Berkeley; this exchange over a period of many
years may be found in Benjamin Rand, *Berkeley and
Percival* (Cambridge, England, 1914). Percival's diary has
been published under the direction of the Historical Manuscripts Commission, *Diary of the First Earl of Egmont,*

3 vols. (London, 1920–23). The Fulham Papers, consisting chiefly of correspondence between the colonial clergy
and the bishop of London, have been made vastly more
accessible through the calendar and indexes compiled by
W. W. Manross, *The Fulham Papers in the Lambeth Palace
Library* (Oxford, 1965). The papers themselves are now
available on microfilm. Relevant material from the Public
Record Office in London has been printed in the *Calendar
of State Papers, Colonial Series.* An excellent example of
what not to do with manuscript sources is provided by the
disposition of the Edmund Gibson Papers, formerly in St.
Paul's Library. Upon insistence by the family, "77 volumes
were handed over to Mr. C. Dalton by resolution of the
Dean and the Chapter, on Wednesday April 1, 1896." The
subsequent fate of these important papers of the bishop of
London and close friend of Berkeley is unknown.

No important manuscript collection of Berkeley materials exists in the United States, although autograph letters
are to be found in the Rhode Island Historical Society,
Newport's Athenaeum Library, Yale, Columbia, and the
Historical Society of Pennsylvania. The Newport Historical
Society is, of course, the most significant and useful repository for that town's history in the eighteenth century.
Yale's Beinecke Library contains important material relating to Berkeley as well as the latter's gift of books, described in Chapter 4.

Three previous works have concentrated upon "George
Berkeley in America." The earliest of these, essentially a
long article by Moses Coit Tyler, may be found in his
Three Men of Letters (New York, 1895) or as an "illustra-
tive monograph" in W. S. Perry, *The History of the American Episcopal Church, 1587–1883* (Boston, 1885), 1:
519–40. The second is Benjamin Rand's short (79 pages)
Berkeley's American Sojourn (Cambridge, Mass., 1932); on

Berkeley's final few days in Boston before embarking
once more for England, Rand conducted his own independent and useful research. His monograph is otherwise
marred by a dependence upon unreliable sources and a
number of egregious errors. Finally, in 1954 one of Newport's more colorful citizens, Alice Brayton, published
George Berkeley in Newport. Casual and often irreverent,
this chatty account dispels some local myths and perpetu-
ates others. Though generously illustrated, the book is
without documentation.

   In addition to the Jessop bibliography noted above (and
issued in a revised form by Martinus Nijhoff in 1973), one
may profitably consult the more recent work of Geoffrey
L. Keynes, *A Bibliography of George Berkeley, Bishop
of Cloyne: His Works and His Critics in the Eighteenth Century* (Oxford, 1976). Keynes provides detailed notes,
useful indices, and facsimile title pages, as well as locations
for the early editions of Berkeley's writings. As his title
indicates, he also helpfully identifies the publications of
George Berkeley's chief contemporary critics.

Index

(Note: George Berkeley is abbreviated as GB throughout; his writings are indexed under his name.)

Berkeley, George (GB) *(continued)*
  and James Honeyman, 15, 126,
  128–29; at Whitehall, 15–16, 115–
  16; admitted freeman, 17; and
  Indians, 17, 25–26, 32, 95–97;
  and blacks, 17, 34, 90–95, 98–
  100; slaves of, 17, 94, 94*n*; as
  preacher, 17, 118–25, 212; contacts with Harvard and Yale, 32,
  82, 83–90, 164; relations with
  SPG and SPCK, 37, 47, 89–90,
  126, 165, 165*n*; and Thomas
  Bray, 44–47, 97–100; philosophical views, 56–77, 126–29, 132; as
  educator, 65–68, 68*n*; portraits
  of, 71–72, 72*n*; as philanthropist,
  81–90; and James Ogelthorpe,
  100–03; as churchman, 113–14,
  115–17, 118, 125–29; theological
  views, 118–25, 153–58, 158*n*; return to Britain, 129–32, 163–64
—Later life, *1731–53*: sermon before SPG, 164–66; in England, 165–
  71; appointment as bishop of
  Cloyne, 167–71; in Ireland, 170–71;
  health and final days in Oxford,
  173*n*, 177–78; continued associations with America, 180–82
—Posthumous influence: at King's
  College, 180–82, 180*n*, 181*n*; at
  College of Philadelphia, 182–83;
  in Revolutionary era, 185, 192;
  through George Berkeley, Jr., 194–
  95; among New World Anglicans,
  196–97; at College of California,
  199–201; at Yale College, 201–
  03; and Manifest Destiny, 203–04;
  and pragmatism, 205–06, 206*n*;
  and idealism, 206–07; catholicity
  of, 207–08, 207*n*, 208*n*; spirit of,
  208–12
—Published writings: *Advice to the
  Tories,* 22, 22*n*; *Alciphron,* 71, 71*n*,
  86, 141, 142–61, 164, 165, 169,
  177, 179*n*; *Analyst, The,* 171, 171*n*;

Defense of Free-Thinking, 172, 172*n*;
  De Motu, 82, 82*n*, 183–84; in the
  Guardian, 20, 66, 66*n*, 139; *Miscellany,* 177; *New Theory of Vision,*
  19–20, 57–59, 60, 82, 153–54; *Principles of Human Knowledge,* 20,
  57–59, 60, 82; *Proposal, A,* 31–34,
  48–49; *Querist, The,* 172; *Reasons
  for not Replying,* 172*n*; *Ruin of
  Great Britain,* 22–23, 49–50; *Siris,*
  163, 173–75, 183, 202; *Three Dialogues,* 20, 59, 60, 61, 82, 141;
  Verses on America, 74–75, 75*n*,
  177, 201*n*, 209; *Word to the Wise,
  A,* 175–76
—Letters sent: Philip Bearcroft, 89–
  90; Martin Benson, 18, 116, 129,
  177, 177*n*; Gabriel Bernon, 114;
  Thomas Clap, 90*n*; Bryan Fairfax,
  82*n*; Isaac Gervais, 177*n*; Edmund
  Gibson, 131; Samuel Johnson, 61–
  65, 68, 82, 83, 85, 85*n*, 142, 180–
  81; Henry Newman, 82*n*, 130; John
  Percival, 21, 25–27, 37, 65, 79–80,
  85*n*, 98, 116, 129, 130, 132, 170,
  190–91; Thomas Prior, 14, 36, 36*n*,
  39–40, 41, 51, 53*n*, 79, 116, 130,
  170, 171, 171*n*; SPG, 118*n*, 126;
  Benjamin Wadsworth, 87*n*, 88;
  Elisha Williams, 87*n*
—Letters received: Edmund Gibson,
  172*n*; Samuel Johnson, 60–65,
  182; Henry Newman, 82*n*, 119,
  131, 134; James Ogelthorpe, 81,
  102–03; John Percival, 28–29,
  38, 103–04; Thomas Prior, 171,
  171*n*
Berkeley, George, Jr. (son), 176,
  194–95, 195*n*
Berkeley, Henry (son), 14, 118*n*,
  176
Berkeley, John (son), 176
Berkeley, Julia (daughter), 176
Berkeley, Lucia (daughter), 14–15,
  161, 176